Ian POPPLE   Otto WA(

MW01061084

SCUBA DIVE   SNORKEL   SURF
NORTHWEST FLORIDA
G U L F   O F   M E X I C O

Acknowledgments

Reef Smart is indebted to numerous individuals and organizations who contributed their advice, knowledge and support in the production of this guidebook. We would particularly like to thank Alex Fogg, Coastal Resource Manager for Destin-Fort Walton Beach, who provided invaluable help coordinating our mapping trips while in the region as well as assistance in mapping multiple sites. Support was also provided by Panama City Diving, Red Alert Diving, ScubaTech NW Florida, DreadKnot Charters, Waterman Ventures LLC and Kitchen Pass Charters. Grayson Shepard and Dave Fowlkes provided support for mapping the historic wreck of the Empire Mica. Thanks also to Tom Cotton and numerous other recreational divers and dive pros who provided information and their personal observations on the region's dive sites. Special thanks to Lureen Ferretti, David Baily, Virgil Zetterlind, Barry Shively and Bob Cox for allowing us to use some of their incredible images in this book.

Financial support provided by the following:

DESTIN FORT WALTON BEACH FLORIDA

About Reef Smart:

Reef Smart creates detailed guides of the marine environment, particularly coral reefs and shipwrecks, for recreational divers, snorkelers and surfers. Our products are available as printed guidebooks, waterproof cards, wall art, dive briefing charts, weatherproof beach signage and 3D interactive maps, which can be used on websites and as apps. Reef Smart also provides additional services to resorts that are dedicated to offering an environmentally aware experience for their guests; these include marine biology training for dive professionals and resort staff, implementation of coral reef monitoring and restoration programs, and the development of sustainable use practices that reduce the impact of operations on the natural environment.

www.reefsmartguides.com

Table of Contents

How to use this book

Objective

The main objective of this guidebook is to provide a resource for people, particularly divers and snorkelers, who are interested in exploring underwater sites in the Gulf of Mexico along the coast of Northwest Florida. This guide is designed to be used alongside Reef Smart waterproof cards, which can be taken into the water. This book will be most useful for watersports enthusiasts but also includes information that any visitor will find useful.

Mapping

We have attempted to catalog as many of the region's dive sites as we can, starting at the Alabama-Florida border, and working toward the east, ending with Panama City and Mexico Beach, with the inclusion of a few important sites that lie outside this region. We have attempted to catalog all of the dive-focused artificial reefs and shore-accessible sites in this area, with greater detail and focus on 59 sites, with 48 presented using Reef Smart's unique 3D-mapping technology. These maps provide useful information such as depths, currents, waves, suggested routes, potential hazards, unique structures and species information that cannot be found in other guides.

Disclaimer

Reef Smart guides are for recreational use only – they are not navigational charts and should not be used as such. We have attempted to provide accurate and up-to-date information for each site. However, change is inevitable in the marine environment and as such, the information in this guide is accurate only at the time of publication. We have suggested a level (Open Water, Advanced or Tech) based largely on the depth, but also the current and complexity of each

site under ideal conditions. It should be noted that some sites, even those indicated as Open Water level, may include Advanced dive profiles and routes. It is important therefore, to always follow the advice of certified dive professionals on the day you visit these sites and always dive within the parameters of your certification and experience. Suggested routes are optional and the size and location of structures, depths and distances, may vary from the approximations used.

Reef Smart assumes no responsibility for inaccuracies and omissions and assumes no liability for the use of these maps. If you identify information that should be updated, please contact us at: info@reefsmartguides.com.

Information boxes

Additional information for the featured sites is provided in the form of special information boxes, which appear throughout the book:

DID YOU KNOW?

Interesting facts about the site or the surrounding area.

SAFETY TIP

Advice that aims to improve safety.

ECO TIP

Information that will help limit damage to the ecosystem or improve environmental awareness.

RELAX & RECHARGE

Information on where refreshments can be purchased, or where to unwind on land. No compensation was received in exchange for featuring these establishments.

Information of a scientific nature that can help you understand what you see and experience.

Map icons

 SCUBA dive   Surf

 Snorkel   Kiteboard

 Wreck

 Access by boat   Wind surf

 Access by swim

 Access by car   Reef Smart maps

 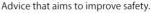

Species identification

The species listed for each location were chosen to represent the most unique or common organisms found at each site, as determined from personal observations, discussions with divers and snorkelers who have experienced these sites, and from scientific studies conducted in these areas. Many of the species described in this publication are mobile or cryptic (or both), and so may not always be found where indicated. However, we have attempted to place key species on each map in the locations where they are most commonly found.

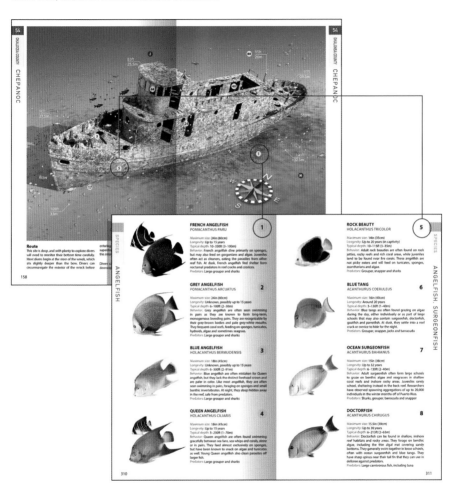

Species description

The species letters and numbers on each map link to descriptions located at the back of the book (on pages 300–332). Reef Smart uses the most frequently cited common name for a species. As common names vary from place to place, we have also provided the scientific name for each species, which remains the same worldwide. Scientific names are usually of Latin or Greek origin and consist of two words: a genus name followed by a species name. By definition, a species is typically a group of organisms that can reproduce together such that it results in fertile offspring; a genus is a group of closely related species.

The descriptions of each species are based on the scientific literature as it existed at the time of publication. Scientific knowledge often advances, however, and the authors welcome any information that helps improve or correct future editions of this guidebook. In-depth species profiles, including images and videos, are available for free on our website – **Reefsmartguides.com**.

7

Our "blue planet"

Oceans

Water covers nearly three-quarters of our planet's surface and approximately 96 percent of this water is contained in the major oceans of the world. The oceans drive our planet's weather, regulate its climate and provide us with breathable air, which ultimately supports every living creature on Earth.

The oceans are also vital to our global economy. They produce the food that billions of people depend on for survival, while being a source of resources, including essential medicines that treat a wide range of ailments and diseases. The oceans also drive local and regional economies through tourism. Every year, millions of travelers are drawn to coastal regions around the world to enjoy activities above and below the water. Considering how important the oceans are to our way of life, it is incredible how little we know about what lies beneath their surfaces.

Coral reefs

The oceans include a wide range of different ecosystems, but perhaps the most frequently visited marine ecosystems of all are coral reefs. Coral reefs are known as the "rainforests of the sea" for good reason – they are one of the most diverse ecosystems on the planet, supporting about a quarter of all known ocean species. This figure is even more astounding when you consider that coral reefs comprise just a fraction of one percent of the ocean floor. They are also particularly vulnerable to degradation, given they are only found in a narrow window of temperature, salinity and depth.

Humans have studied the biology and physiology of corals for decades, but the underwater environment remains largely foreign to many people. Fact is, we have more accurate maps of the surface of Mars than we do of the seafloor. And guides of the marine environment suitable for recreational users are almost non-existent.

Reef Smart aims to change this situation. Our detailed guides seek to educate snorkelers and divers alike. Our goal is to improve safety and enhance the marine experience by allowing users to discover the unique features and species that can be found at each site.

Preserve and protect

Hopefully our guidebooks and handheld waterproof cards will help you get to know the underwater environment in general, and reefs in particular. We believe that the more people can come to appreciate the beauty of the underwater world, the more they will be willing to take steps to protect and preserve it.

The world's oceans are experiencing incredible pressures from all sides. Rising temperatures, increasing acidification and an astonishing volume of plastics that end up both in the water and in marine organisms are negatively impacting these precious ecosystems.

There are some big problems to overcome. But a better, more sustainable future is possible. Each and every one of us can make a difference in the choices we make and the actions we take. Together we can help make sure the coral reefs of this world are still around for future generations of snorkelers and divers to enjoy.

Sincerely, the Reef Smart team

About Northwest Florida

Location and formation

As the name implies, Northwest Florida is in the northwestern part of the state of Florida, which itself is in the southeastern corner of the continental United States of America. This section of Florida is often referred to as the "panhandle," because its shape resembles the handle of a pan attached to the peninsula that forms the rest of the state. It is located on the large body of water known as the Gulf of Mexico, which is an ocean basin in the Atlantic Ocean and is mostly encompassed within North America.

In total, Northwest Florida includes roughly 16 of the state's 67 counties. However, the focus of this guidebook is the five coastal counties that comprise the westernmost reaches of the state, including the counties of Escambia, Santa Rosa, Okaloosa, Walton and Bay. Together these counties include more than 120 miles (200 kilometers) of sandy coastline along the northeastern edge of the Gulf of Mexico. Most of the region's population and development is concentrated along the beaches and barrier islands.

The state of Florida sits on the Florida Plateau, a geological formation dating back 530 million years. The plateau formed through a mix of volcanic activity and marine sedimentation. Many of Florida's features and soils reflect this marine past and Northwest Florida is no exception, although

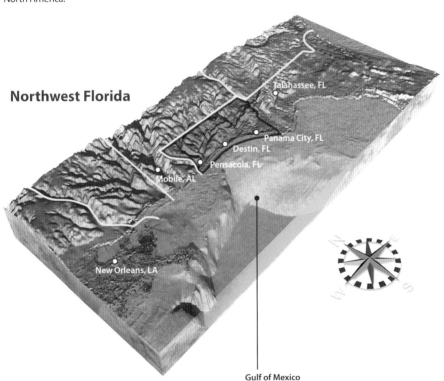

The topography and bathymetry of Northwest Florida and its surroundings.

the panhandle region differs from most of the rest of the state in that it reaches a higher maximum elevation. Near the northern border with the state of Alabama, elevations exceed 300 feet (91 meters) above sea level. Most of the development along the coast is concentrated within just 40 to 50 feet (12 to 15 meters) of sea level, however.

The flat, relatively shallow Florida plateau extends 20 to 40 miles (32 to 64 kilometers) out from the coastline, which means divers must venture relatively far out into the Gulf to find depths in excess of 80 to 90 feet (24.5 to 27.5 meters).

The history of Northwest Florida

Archaeologists have found evidence that pre-Clovis humans butchered mastodons in northern Florida almost 15,000 years ago. These findings helped confirm that humans not only migrated into North America earlier than 13,000 years ago, which was previously believed based on the "Clovis Hypothesis," but that mastodons frequented what is now coastal Northwest Florida.

Evidence of large earthworks and mounds dating from between 800 AD and 1550 AD have been identified in the region, including around Pensacola and Fort Walton Beach. These mounds speak to the history of occupation that predated the arrival of Europeans. From at least 1000 AD, a tribe of native American farmers known as the Apalachee lived in the eastern portion of Northwest Florida. Meanwhile, the Creek Indians controlled most of this region, with their territory stretching from modern-day Pensacola in the west to the Apalachicola River in the east. Their territory also stretched into modern-day Alabama and Georgia to the north. Farther to the west was the Choctaw tribe, in what is now coastal Alabama.

The first European explorers may have reached Pensacola Bay from Cuba as early as 1516. However, the first multi-year settlement was not established until 1559 – this predates the establishment of St. Augustine, Florida, which is

the oldest, continuously inhabited city in the U.S. The Spanish expedition, led by Don Tristán de Luna y Arellano, sailed out of Vera Cruz, Mexico, with 1,500 colonists on 11 ships. They settled in modern-day Pensacola, but within weeks of landing, the fledgling colony was decimated by a powerful hurricane that sank six of the ships, ruined supplies and resulted in the death of many colonists and sailors. The settlement struggled on for two years before it was abandoned in 1561. The Spanish deemed the region too dangerous for future settlement, and the area remained largely ignored until the end of the 17th century.

In 1698, the Spanish refounded what is now Pensacola as a buffer to the French presence in Louisiana. The buffer failed, however, and the French captured the lightly defended Spanish fort at Pensacola in 1719 – the garrison commander was unaware that Spain and France were at war when the French forces showed up to take the fort. The French held the town for just three years before a hurricane devastated the area. The French left Pensacola in 1722 and the Spanish reoccupied it. This occupation lasted just two decades, but it saw the development of Pensacola as an important port in the region thanks to its deep-water harbor. It also marked the beginning of a centuries-long pattern of Pensacola changing hands among various European superpowers. It was never fully abandoned during this period, however, in part due to its strategic importance.

10

The sun sets on the Okaloosa Fishing Pier in Fort Walton Beach.

The British were the next to take control of Pensacola, taking it over in 1763 at the conclusion of the Seven Years War (known in America as the French and Indian War) under the Treaty of Paris. The town was named the capital of British West Florida and saw further development of the harbor and shipyards. During the American Revolution, Florida (which included West Florida and East Florida at the time) remained loyal to the crown. In support of the revolution, Spain's Bernardo de Gálvez (who was the Spanish equivalent of the better-known Marquis de Lafayette) led an attack on Pensacola in 1781, capturing both the town and West Florida for the Spanish, who held the region for the next 40 years.

The original prop of the *Empire Mica* now sits outside the Capt. Anderson's Restaurant in Panama City Beach.

11

An aerial view of Destin Harbor in Okaloosa County.

In 1802, France forced Spain to cede control of the Louisiana territory. Only a year later, France sold the entire territory to the United States (the famous Louisiana Purchase) after financial difficulties following a slave revolt in Haiti. The U.S. acquisition of Louisiana effectively doubled the size of the fledgling nation. The U.S. then proceeded to annex the Spanish region from the Mississippi River to Pensacola between 1810 and 1819, incorporating this area into the existing states of Mississippi and Alabama.

After additional pressure, Spain eventually ceded all of Florida to the U.S. in 1821, and the decision was made at that time to leave Pensacola as part of the new state of Florida. This decision is why modern-day Florida includes a panhandle, and why Alabama has access to only a small section of the Gulf of Mexico coastline.

Recent history

Pensacola remained the economic center for the region well into the middle of the 20th century thanks in part to an economic boom from 1880 to 1920 due to timber harvesting. Nearby Destin, a town settled in 1845 by Leonard Destin, a fisherman, and his family from Connecticut, was primarily a subsistence fishing community until ice machines allowed fish to be shipped and sold at larger inland markets, thus increasing the scale of the nascent industry. To the east, Panama City enjoyed its own economic growth due to a combination of the timber trade and commercial fishing. As a region, however, Northwest Florida did not experience real economic development until the industrial boom following the Second World War.

During the postwar era, many servicemen returned to the U.S. and chose to settle in Florida because of the mild climate. From 1950 to 1980, the region's population more than doubled. Okaloosa County more than tripled, from 27,500

pisaphotography/Shutterstock©

Pensacola in Escambia County, the Destin-Fort Walton Beach area in Okaloosa County, and Panama City in Bay County.

The basics

English is the official language in Northwest Florida, as it is in the continental U.S. Spanish is less commonly heard than in other parts of Florida given the region's geographic and cultural distance from the Latin-influenced southeast. The official currency is the U.S. dollar and there are plenty of bank branches, ATMs and foreign exchange counters in all the major cities.

The electricity in Northwest Florida is the North American standard 110 volts / 60 hertz with flat-bladed plugs and a rounded grounding pin. WiFi is available at most hotels and in many coffee shops, eateries and other local businesses – sometimes free, sometimes paid. Tap water is safe to drink here. The region operates in the Central Standard Time (CST) zone, which is one hour behind the rest of the state. Daylight Savings Time (CDT) is in effect from March to November.

Visitors

There are nearly 30 million visitors to Northwest Florida each year. Many come from surrounding states in the south and southeast U.S. Visitors come for the sandy beaches, the sport fishing opportunities and for the diving and snorkeling. Most visitors are from elsewhere in the U.S., but there is a growing international presence.

Getting there and getting around

Getting there

There are no direct international flights to the region, but many U.S. international hubs connect to one of the three commercial airports in the region: Pensacola International Airport (PNS), Destin-Fort Walton Beach Airport (VPS), and Northwest Florida Beaches International Airport (ECP) in Panama City. The region is also easily accessible via the U.S. system of interstate highways.

Getting around

Driving is the most common way of getting around Northwest Florida. Most major car rental companies operate in the region. U.S. Route 98 represents the primary east-west highway as it runs along the coast and passes through all three major population centers. The highway starts at the state border between Alabama and Florida and runs along the coast before turning southeast and crossing the Florida peninsula, terminating in West Palm Beach on the Atlantic coast. Drivers also have the option of using

to 109,900, during this period. As the economy of the region developed, it became largely focused on its economic relationship with the three major military bases located here, including the Naval Air Station in Escambia County, Eglin Air Force Base in Okaloosa County, and Tyndall Air Force Base in Bay County. Tourism makes up the other main component of the region's economy. The rise of industrialization across the U.S. led to a growing middle class with discretionary income, and tourists flocked to the region to take advantage of Northwest Florida's sandy beaches and pleasant weather.

Northwest Florida today

Population

Today, the five counties of Escambia, Santa Rosa, Okaloosa, Walton and Bay have a combined population of nearly 1 million, with Escambia and Okaloosa accounting for the lion's share. The region's main population centers are

Interstate 10 to navigate through the region, but this major highway sits inland from the coast, paralleling Route 98. Although I-10 passes through the city of Pensacola, it is situated well north of Panama City and Destin, which is why U.S. 98 is a more popular option.

Public transportation systems operate in many of the individual counties without much overlap from county to county. The Escambia County transit system, known as ECAT, centers around Pensacola (**www.goecat.com**), while the system operating in Okaloosa County is called the Emerald Coast Rider (**www.ecrider. com**). The latter only goes as far west as the Fort Walton Beach area, however. Walton County has a free shuttle service named GoWal (**www. gowaltransit.com**), but this service primarily operates along a north-south route that services residents and visitors traveling between the northern part of the county and the coast. Panama City and Panama City Beach are serviced by Bay County's Bay Town Trolley system (**www. baytowntrolley.org**). Taxis and ride-share companies such as Uber and Lyft operate across the region as well, but visitors looking to dive across multiple counties during their stay should consider renting a car. Just be sure to leave extra time for traffic during rush hour from 6am to 9am on weekday mornings, and 4pm to 6pm on weekday evenings.

Pensacola Beach's iconic water tower is a landmark you can see for miles.

Located just outside of Destin, Florida, Crab Island is a popular sandbar where people gather to unwind.

Environment

Weather

Northwest Florida has a mild climate relative to much of the continental U.S., but temperatures tend to be cooler here than in southern Florida. The winter season, which stretches from December to February, can approach freezing temperatures with overnight lows of 35°F to 40°F (2°C to 4.5°C). Daytime temperatures are generally much more comfortable, with highs ranging from 62°F to 65°F (16.5°C to 18.5°C). Fall (October and November) and spring (March and April) are relatively dry months with mild temperatures. May is the unofficial start of the summer season in Northwest Florida with the arrival of warm and humid air masses from the tropics. During the summer months, daytime highs typically average between 85°F and 90°F (29.5°C and 32°C) while nighttime lows stay comfortably in the 70°F to 77°F range (21°C to 25°C). Humidity is higher during the summer than in the winter. Water temperatures generally align with the seasons, with summertime sea surface temperatures averaging around 85°F (29.5°C) while wintertime

temperatures can get down to a chilly 64.5°F (18°C). Wetsuits are often recommended outside of the summer season.

Northwest Florida is the most hurricane-prone area of the state due to the warm, shallow waters of the Gulf of Mexico, which tends to favor their development. The official hurricane season stretches from June to November, with the peak in activity typically occurring between August and November. Over the years, hurricanes have caused a lot of damage in the region. One of the most devastating storms of recent years was Hurricane Michael – the first Category 5 hurricane on record to impact Northwest Florida. It made landfall near Panama City in 2018 and caused 59 fatalities in the U.S. and over $25 billion USD in damages. Many hurricanes that enter the Gulf of Mexico make landfall farther to the west, in nearby Louisiana or Texas. These storms may cause little physical damage to Northwest Florida, but they can cause high waves, strong currents and reduced visibility due to the shallow waters and sandy bottom along the coast.

DID YOU KNOW?

When the weather is "blown-out" along the Gulf Coast, which is the term used by locals for wave action that restricts access to the ocean, many people head inland to explore the area's many freshwater springs. While some of the better-known springs are located farther to the east, there are some 40 diveable springs in Northwest Florida. Due to the geology of the area, these springs are mostly limited to Walton and Bay counties, as well as nearby Washington and Holmes counties. Two of the most accessible and popular springs, Vortex Spring and Morrison Springs, are described on page 294 in greater detail. Many local dive shops visit these springs regularly and may conduct some of their training dives there.

Waves and visibility

In general, the Gulf of Mexico experiences moderate waves and decent visibility, however conditions can deteriorate quickly. Wind direction plays a big role in determining wave height. For instance, winds from the south can create large, offshore waves across the entire region, while conditions tend to be better when winds come from the north. An easterly wind favors diving off of Panama City, which receives shelter from the shore, while a northwesterly wind can favor diving out of Pensacola or Destin.

Visibility can vary from day to day as winds and currents disturb the sandy sediment. Typical visibility is 30 to 50 feet (9 to 15 meter) although it can range from 10 feet (3 meters) to 100 feet or more (30 meters). In general, visibility declines close to major rivers and passes, particularly where Mobile Bay and Perdido Bay empty into the Gulf to the west of Pensacola. And while offshore sites tend to have better visibility than inshore sites, there is no guarantee.

Grass covered dunes border much of the Gulf along Northwest Florida, like this stretch near Panama City Beach.

Currents and tides

Currents in the Gulf of Mexico are generally mild. The large ocean basin is cut off from the stronger oceanic currents of the Atlantic. However, a large storm system in the region can trigger strong currents, including powerful longshore and riptide currents. Tides in the Gulf of Mexico are relatively mild compared to the rest of Florida. The shift in sea level from high to low tide is usually less than a foot in height (0.3 meters). The biggest impact of tides in the region is on dive and snorkel sites located near passes. Visibility is at its best on an incoming tide, and at its worst during an outgoing tide as the waters of the various bays and sounds empty into the Gulf. Despite generally moderate conditions in the Gulf, divers and snorkelers should take all necessary precautions before entering the water from the shore or when diving without the support of a boat.

Ecosystems

Natural reefs

The Gulf of Mexico along the coast of Northwest Florida does not feature many hard-bottom areas, and the colder temperatures mean the region does not feature the typical coral reefs – whether living or relic reefs – that are common along the coasts of southeast Florida or the Florida Keys. However, there are natural limestone ledges ranging in height from just 2 feet (0.6 meters) to more than 10 feet (3 meters). These natural ledges are important habitat for reef fish in this region, and support everything from sea fans to colorful sponges and soft corals. These ledges are popular with divers and fishers as they support a high diversity of reef creatures. But they are also susceptible to concentrated fishing and diving pressures. The extensive deployment of artificial reefs in this region is, in part, an attempt to relieve fishing and diving pressure on these natural reefs. In support of this effort, we have chosen to feature artificial reefs in this guidebook rather than the natural ledges in the area. The one exception is White Hill Ledge (see page 168) which is already well known to the public and is located around 500 feet (150 meters) north of the *Destin Liberty Ship*.

Artificial reefs

Artificial reefs started appearing in Northwest Florida in the 1950s and '60s, when fishers began placing all manner of structures in the water to attract fish. Today, the deployment of artificial reefs follows a strict permitting process. It reflects the science of what

makes for a good reef and where it should be deployed to enhance the local ecosystem while also providing support to recreational activities such as diving. Each county has its own artificial reef coordinator who works in partnership with the state artificial reef program, which is part of the Florida Fish & Wildlife Conservation Commission (FWC). Artificial reefs feature large vessels and other structures that have been cleaned of potential contaminants and sunk off shore, including tanks, tugboats, hovercraft, bridges and even an aircraft carrier. But they can also be piles of concrete, including rubble, culverts and old concrete military targets, which can stretch across many acres. County reef coordinators also deploy specific reef module designs depending on the characteristics of the site and the goals for the reef. These modules can range from towering pyramids to 10-foot (3-meter) pylons featuring multiple discs to support a variety of marine life. Many of these artificial reef modules are built and deployed by regional artificial reef contractor Reefmaker/Walter Marine. Visit: **Reefmaker.com**.

Estuaries

Barrier islands are an important feature along the coast of Northwest Florida. These long, narrow stretches of accumulated sand not only buffer the adjacent land from the impacts of powerful hurricanes, but they shelter estuaries and bays on the "sound" side, opposite the Gulf waters. These estuaries are important nursery habitats for a variety of juvenile commercially, recreationally and ecologically important fish species. These young fish shelter and forage in shallow seagrass beds, oyster habitat or mud flats until they grow large enough to venture out into the Gulf of Mexico. There are multiple shore-accessible snorkel and diving sites located in the sound and bay side of the barrier islands, particularly in Escambia and Santa Rosa counties. These sites generally have lower visibility than those found in the Gulf and are generally less popular with divers and snorkelers as a result. They still offer plenty of interesting reef life to observe. Many organizations work to protect the various bays and estuaries in Northwest Florida, including the Pensacola Perdido Bay Estuary Program (in Escambia County), the Choctawhatchee Bay Estuary Program (in Okaloosa County) and the St. Andrews Bay Estuary Program (in Bay County).

Marine management, research and conservation

As one might expect for a region so closely tied to the marine environment, Northwest Florida has a full complement of aquariums, rehabilitation centers and marine conservation organizations. Visitors to the region have plenty to keep them busy when they are not spending time in the water. Here are just a few of the local organizations that are helping protect Northwest Florida's ecosystems.

Emerald Coast Wildlife Refuge

Based in Navarre, the refuge is active across all five counties, focusing its efforts on the rehabilitation and release of wildlife. Visitors can stop in and tour the grounds, visiting with the refuge's handful of species ambassadors. The education and outreach center is open Wednesday through Saturday from 9am to 3pm, and Sunday 11am to 3pm. If you see an injured or stranded animal, you can call the refuge at 850-684-1485, or report it on their website. Visit: **Emeraldcoastwildliferefuge.org**

Emerald Coast Science Center

An interactive museum based in the Fort Walton Beach region of Okaloosa County, the Emerald Coast Science Center provides families with an opportunity to learn more about the marine environment. The center is generally open Wednesdays through Saturdays from 10am to 3pm. Visit: **Ecscience.org**

Navarre Beach Sea Turtle Conservation Center

This sea turtle conservation center aims to support the local sea turtle population through a variety of measures, including monitoring nesting beaches, rehabilitating injured sea turtles and conducting public education and outreach. The center is open to visitors, but hours vary. Visitors should check online for upcoming events. Visit: **Navarrebeachseaturtles.org**

Navarre Marine Science Station

This small Navarre-based science station is an interactive center launched by local students. The station offers environmental programs for school groups and provides education about everything from plankton and whales to watershed issues. Hours vary, so visitors should go online to see when the station is open. Visit: **Navarresciencestation.org**

Choctawhatchee Basin Alliance-Northwest Florida State College

The CBA works to improve and protect the water quality in local waterways in the Choctawhatchee Bay watershed – the large bay located in Okaloosa and Walton counties. The organization does research, education and outreach and hosts volunteer efforts to clean up the waterways, including the removal of invasive species. For volunteer opportunities or more information, visit: **Basinalliance.org**

Science Discovery Center of Northwest Florida

Based in Panama City, this local science center offers children and adults the opportunity to experience hands-on, interactive exhibits about science and technology. For more information, visit: **Scienceanddiscoverycenter.org**

SCIENTIFIC INSIGHT

Invasive lionfish pose a real threat to marine ecosystems in the Caribbean and Atlantic Ocean. Lionfish are indigenous to the Indo-West Pacific oceans and are now established in the Western Atlantic, including the Caribbean Sea and Gulf of Mexico. They were first spotted near Dania Beach in southeast Florida in 1985. The most likely theory behind their origin is the intentional release of aquarium fish into local waterways. Since then, the lionfish population has expanded south throughout the Caribbean and north into the Carolinas, as well as west into the Gulf of Mexico. Initial genetic testing suggested that the current Caribbean-wide population originated from just 10 individuals, but more recent studies place the original number of colonists at closer to 120, likely released over multiple instances.

The main threat posed by lionfish is that they are voracious predators. They feed on fish and crustaceans and are not picky about what species they target. According to the National Oceanic and Atmospheric Administration (NOAA), an adult lionfish's diet includes more than 160 different species, including many that are ecologically or economically important. They also reproduce incredibly rapidly, producing on average thousands of eggs every few days throughout the entire year. Without any consistent natural predators outside of the Indo-West Pacific region, they have the potential to cause significant changes to the reef ecosystems they have invaded.

Lionfish are unlikely to ever be fully removed from the Western Atlantic at this point – there are just too many of them and they are too well established. However, there are many long-term efforts underway to help control their numbers. Divers have become particularly effective at removing lionfish through spearfishing. Lionfish derbies (fishing competitions) have become popular in Northwest Florida, as well as throughout the Caribbean, and many restaurants are now serving lionfish dishes, sometimes using fish that customers have caught themselves.

Nature is helping fight back as well. Starting in 2017, lionfish began appearing with skin lesions that were deep enough to expose the fish's underlying muscle tissue. Instances of the lesion became increasingly common through 2018, and the lionfish population in the Northwest Panhandle plummeted.

By 2019, dive sites that once hosted dozens of lionfish might have just one or two. Most experts believe the virus will not be enough to eliminate the invasive species, although it might help control their numbers. However, by 2020, there was evidence that the population was once again increasing.

Many non-profit organizations are working to help tackle the lionfish invasion as part of broader mandates to help protect marine ecosystems and the reef resources. Part of these efforts include raising public awareness, but also looking to build public-private partnerships to incentivize the removal of lionfish through fishing competitions and creating demand for these invasive and delicious creatures. For more information on some of these organizations, visit: **CoastWatch Alliance.org**, **Lionfishuniversity.org**, **Reef. org, Sealeg.org**

The invasive lionfish.

Northwest Florida beaches

Northwest Florida is known for its fantastic sugar-white beaches consisting of fine quartz crystals originating from the nearby Appalachian Mountains. The entire stretch of coast from Pensacola to Panama City is essentially one long sandy beach, broken up by a few passes. There are well over 100 public access points along the coast (too many to attempt to list here), and visitors can check on the various county's websites to identify the nearest public access to wherever they are staying. In the pages below, we have highlighted some of the major beaches that visitors might want to visit, including ones that feature access to the snorkel reefs described later in this guidebook.

Escambia County

Perdido Key State Park Beach
The rolling sand dunes and dense covering of dune grass help visitors appreciate what this area might have looked like when the Spaniards first arrived on their ill-fated colonization trip. Located just east of the state border with Alabama, this state park features picnic tables and nearby restrooms. There is a charge per vehicle to access the park.

Johnson's Beach National Seashore
Part of the National Park system, Johnson's Beach offers a swimming beach and picnic facilities. There is a fee to enter the park unless you have a National Park Pass.

Casino Beach
Located just across the causeway from Gulf Breeze, which itself is just across the bridge from downtown Pensacola, Casino Beach is right next to the Pensacola Gulf Pier, and it combines a gorgeous sandy beach with plenty of restaurants, bathroom facilities and even a new snorkel reef (see page 66 for more information).

Pensacola Beach Park East
Located within the National Seashore, but freely accessible and offering facilities and ample parking, this beach features a snorkel reef located just off shore (see page 68 for more information).

Opal Beach
This stretch of beach is also part of the National Seashore, although it charges no fee for access. It was created when Hurricane Opal flattened the nearby sand dunes in 1995. The beach has ample parking and restroom facilities.

Santa Rosa County

Navarre Beach Marine Park
Santa Rosa's main public beach is next to the Navarre fishing pier. It is also located next to the Marine Science Station, the Navarre Beach Sea Turtle Conservation Center and the Navarre Beach Snorkel Reefs (see pages 114 and 116 for more information). The beach here is wide open with ample parking and plenty of facilities.

Wide open public beaches pepper the coastline, such as this one in Pensacola Beach.

DID YOU KNOW?

Florida law states that all beaches are public below the average high-tide mark. So, visitors are free to walk up and down the beach provided they do not stray too far from the water's edge. That said, some counties have established ordinances permitting beachgoers to set up blankets and beach umbrellas above the high-water mark along certain stretches of beach. It remains a fairly contentious issue, however, so visitors should check on the county website or with their hotel's concierge about local ordinances if they plan to visit a beach not included in the list above.

Okaloosa County

Wayside Park

This stretch of beach is located next to the Okaloosa fishing pier and is associated with the nearby boardwalk with its many restaurants and bars. A large parking lot means ample parking, but this beach does get crowded in season.

Beasley Park Beach

Located just to the east of the Okaloosa fishing pier, this park offers showers and restrooms, ample parking and access to the Beasley Park Snorkel Reef (see page 126 for more information).

Eglin Matterhorn Beach

This beach is the first (when arriving from the west) of two sections of beach owned by the Eglin AFB on Okaloosa island that are open to the public. There are numerous paths that cut through the dunes, requiring a short walk from the parking area to the beach. There are no facilities on site – just a gorgeous sandy beach.

Princess Beach

The second (from the west) of two sections of beach owned by the Eglin AFB that are open to the public, this beach offers visitors a similar kind of sandy beach to Eglin Matterhorn Beach, and is a slightly shorter walk from the parking area than its neighbor to the west.

Norriego Point

Located on a spit of land opposite the entrance to the Destin Harbor, Norriego Point has no facilities for visitors, but does offer plenty of people- and boat-watching opportunities, and a snorkeling area (see page 128 for more information).

Henderson State Park Beach

This state park features trails, restrooms, cold showers for day users, as well as a campground, a pavilion and picnic areas. There are two snorkel reefs located just off the beach. (See pages 132 and 134 for more information.) There is a charge per vehicle to access the park.

James Lee Park Beach

This beach and associated picnic area are managed by Okaloosa County. It features restrooms and ample parking, as well as access to a lovely stretch of Gulf Coast beach. There is no fee for access.

Walton County

Topsail Hill State Park Beach

This state park features trails, restrooms, cold showers for day users, as well as a campground, a pavilion and picnic areas. A snorkel reef in the shape of a seahorse is located just off the beach. (See page 206 for more information.) There is a charge of per vehicle to access the park.

Grayton Beach State Park Beach

This state park features a one-mile (2-kilometer) nature trail, restrooms, cold showers for day users, as well as a campground, a pavilion and picnic areas. A snorkel reef in the shape of a turtle is located just off the beach. (See page 208 or more information.) There is a charge per vehicle to access the park.

Bay County

Russell Fields Pier Beach

This is the city pier located to the west of Panama City Beach – it is one of two piers in Bay County. This fishing pier has ample parking, free access to the beach, and a public restroom. There is a fee to access the pier itself.

Half-Hitch MB Miller Pier Beach

The county pier is located just a few miles (5 kilometers) east of the city pier. It has multiple public restrooms with ample parking and free access to the beach. There is a fee charged to access the pier itself.

St. Andrews State Park Beach

This state park features two half-mile (one-kilometer) trails, restrooms, cold showers for day users, as well as a campground, a pavilion and picnic areas. The park features one of the most popular shore diving sites in Bay County - the St. Andrews jetty. (See page 222 for more information.) There is a charge per vehicle to access the park.

In case of emergency

There are many organisms that can put a damper on a visit to Northwest Florida, from jellyfish to stingrays to the invasive lionfish that have made the Gulf of Mexico their home. Many of these potentially dangerous marine creatures are listed in a special section toward the back of the book (pages 306–309). We have included information in that section on the harm these species can cause and some of the common treatments that might help. That said, this book is not intended as a substitute for professional medical help. There is also the ever-present risk of decompression sickness (DCS). In the event of a dive-related incident, consider calling the 24-hour emergency number for the Divers Alert Network (DAN) for support (919-684-9111).

For visitors unfortunate enough to become injured while enjoying their time in Northwest Florida, there are many high-quality medical facilities they can visit to receive care. If an injury is not an emergency, consider visiting the nearest walk-in clinic or urgent care clinic during its normal operating hours – most open at 7am or 9am. Given the geographic region, there is a limit to how many clinics and emergency rooms we can list in this guidebook, so visitors would do well to familiarize themselves with the nearest

emergency resources to where they are staying before an emergency arises. Divers should do their own research and develop their own emergency action plan based on where they are staying and where they are diving ahead of time – as well as ensuring their dive operator has equipped their vessel with appropriate emergency equipment, including access to oxygen.

The American healthcare system is effective, but it can also be expensive. International visitors should acquire appropriate health insurance coverage prior to their arrival. Without coverage, an accident could be potentially expensive.

Should the unthinkable happen, here are some important numbers and places for visitors to keep in mind if they need to seek help:

Emergency contacts

Police:	911
Fire:	911
Ambulance:	911
U.S. Coast Guard:	VHF 16
Divers Alert Network (DAN):	919-684-9111

Divers training on emergency procedures.

Emergency and Urgent Care

Escambia County
Ascension Sacred Heart Emergency (24-hr ER)
5151 North 9th Avenue, Pensacola
850-416-7000
Healthcare.ascension.org

Baptist Hospital (24-hr ER)
1000 West Moreno Street, Pensacola
850-434-4011
Ebaptisthealthcare.org/BaptistHospital

Gulf Breeze Hospital (24-hr ER)
1110 Gulf Breeze Parkway, Gulf Breeze
850-934-2000
Ebaptisthealthcare.org/GulfBreezeHospital

Santa Rosa County
Baptist ER and Urgent Care (24-hr ER)
8888 Navarre Parkway, Navarre
850-446-5687
Baptisteruc.org

Okaloosa County
Emerald Coast Urgent Care
12598 Emerald Coast Parkway, Destin
850-654-8878
Emeraldcoasturgentcare.com

Fort Walton Beach Medical Center (24-hr ER)
200 Tequesta Drive, Destin
850-837-9194
Fwbmc.com

Walton County
Ascension Sacred Heart Emergency (24-hr ER)
7800 U.S. 98, Miramar Beach
850-278-3000
Healthcare.ascension.org

Emerald Coast Urgent Care
13625 Emerald Coast Parkway, Inlet Beach
850-588-1843
Emeraldcoasturgentcare.com

Bay County
Ascension Sacred Heart Emergency (24-hr ER)
615 North Bonita Avenue, Panama City
850-769-1511
Healthcare.ascension.org

Emerald Coast Urgent Care
2704 Thomas Drive, Panama City Beach
850-236-8655
Emeraldcoasturgentcare.com

Gulf Coast Regional Medical Center (24-hr ER)
449 W 23rd Street, Panama City
850-769-8341
Gcmc-pc.com

Decompression / Hyperbaric chambers

The closest hyperbaric chamber accessible to divers for treatment of DCS is located across state lines in Alabama. Other chambers in the region will not treat DCS nor will the military bases accept civilian divers.

Hyperbaric Medicine Program
Springhill Medical Center
3719 Dauphin Street, Mobile
251-344-9630
Springhillmedicalcenter.com

If you think you might be experiencing DCS, contact Divers Alert Network's emergency 24-hour number (919-684-9111) to identify the nearest operational chamber.

EMERGENCY INFORMATION

Surfing

The best surfing sites in the Florida panhandle are located between Gulf Shore, Alabama and St. Andrews Pass near Panama Beach, Florida, which coincides with the five counties covered in this guidebook. This stretch of coastline is dotted with a number of recognized breaks. While the beaches are stunning and easy to access, the swells tend to be irregular and unpredictable. As such, most of these sites are unlikely to appear on any list of top surf breaks in the continental United States. However, when conditions are right, the Gulf Coast can easily compete with the breaks on Florida's east coast.

Winter is often the best time to surf in Northwest Florida and Alabama. When southeastern swells combine with northern winds, conditions can produce hollow, overhead waves at places like Alabama Point and Amazons – perhaps the two best sites in the region. Wetsuits are necessary at this time of year because water temps drop to around 68°F (20°C) – some surfers even break out their hoodies and boots. Hurricane season can also produce some decent surf in the Gulf, although conditions can get dangerous depending on how close the system is to shore. In short, the key to surfing this region is to monitor ocean conditions and jump in the water when conditions are right. Timing is everything, and ideal conditions rarely last long.

Our three-star rating system indicates the quality of the site in most conditions. And while the wave varies from day to day, we have attempted to provide as much information as we can about its quality, consistency and the direction of the break, to help you get the most out of your surfing experience.

We have also provided information on access to the break and local conditions, including potential dangers, where they exist. Be sure to check up-to-date conditions online at any one of the many surf report sites available, such as:
Magicseaweed.com and **Surfline.com**.

Surfing and other services

Escambia County

Innerlight Surf Shop - Downtown
114 Palafox Place, Pensacola
Tel: 850-495-3507
Email: jayden@innerlightsurf.com
Innerlightsurf.com

Innerlight Surf Shop - 9th Avenue
6307 North 9th Avenue, Pensacola
Tel: 850-434-6743
Email: jacob@innerlightsurf.com
Innerlightsurf.com

Maverick Board Riding Company
69b Via De Luna Drive, Pensacola Beach
Tel: 850-677-8021
Maverickboards.com

Pure Life Surf
7831 Tippin Avenue E-17, Pensacola
Tel: 970-238-6387
Purelifesurf.business.site

Waterboyz
380 North 9th Avenue, Pensacola
Tel: 850-433-2929
Email: help@waterboyz.com
Waterboyz.com

Santa Rosa County

Innerlight Surf Shop - Gulf Breeze
203 Gulf Breeze Parkway, Gulf Breeze
Tel: 850-932-5134
Email: bill@innerlightsurf.com
Innerlightsurf.com

Maverick Board Riding Company
2547 Gulf Breeze Parkway, Gulf Breeze
Tel: 850-677-8127
Maverickboards.com

Sage's Surf Shack
8228 Gulf Boulevard (Unit 2), Navarre
Tel: 850-396-3044
Sages-surf-shop.business.site

Okaloosa County

All-A-Board Surf School
3290 Scenic Highway 98, Destin
Tel: 850-699-2455
Email: allaboardsurf@gmail.com
Allaboardsurf.com

Fluid Surf Shop
158 Miracle Strip Parkway Southeast
(Unit C), Fort Walton Beach
Tel: 850-244-3554
Email: info@fluidsurfshop.com
Fluidsurfshop.com

Innerlight Surf Shop - Destin
4135 Legendary Drive (Suite F116), Destin
Tel: 850-650-5509
Email: blake@innerlightsurf.com
Innerlightsurf.com

Jetsurf Destin
4607 Legendary Marina Drive, Destin
Tel: 850-900-7873
Email: ride@jetsurfdestin.com
Jetsurfdestin.com

Ride On Surf School
3796 Scenic Highway 98, Destin
Tel: 850-240-7822
Email: rideonsurfschool@cox.net
Rideonsurf.com

Yolo Board & Beach
11610 US Highway 98, Destin
Tel: 850-424-6852
Email: info@yoloboard.com
Yoloboard.com

Walton County

Austin Magee's Surf School
2236 East County Highway 30A (Suite 1),
Santa Rosa Beach
Tel: 850-217-4042
Email: austin.magee@rocketmail.com
Amsurfschool.com

Gulf Wind Paddle & Surf
4552 US Highway 98, Santa Rosa Beach
Tel: 850-502-4357
Email: store@paddleboards30a.com
Paddleboards30a.com

LD Surf Shop
5311 E County Highway 30A (Suite 1),
Santa Rosa Beach
Tel: 850-213-3475
Email: liquiddreams@gmail.com
Ldsurfshop.com

Yolo Board & Bike
95 Laura Hamilton Boulevard, Santa Rosa Beach
Tel: 850-267-0602
Email: info@yoloboard.com
Yoloboard.com

Bay County

Jetsurf Panama City Beach
312 Bayshore Drive, Panama City Beach
Tel: 850-832-9367
Email: info@jetsurfpcb.com
Jetsurfpcb.com

Mr. Surfs Surf Shop
7220 Thomas Drive, Panama City Beach
Tel: 850-235-2702
Email: mrsurfs@gmail.com
Mrsurfs.com

Salty Dog Surf Shop
11930 Front Beach Road, Panama City Beach
Tel: 850-230-3430
Email: saltydogpcb@yahoo.com
Facebook.com/SaltyDogPCB

Javier Garcia/Shutterstock ©

Surfing is popular along the Gulf of Mexico coast when the conditions are right.

Surf breaks

Alabama Point

Located in Orange Beach, Alabama, this break is one of the more consistent surf spots in the area. The best waves are usually found in front of the resorts and condominiums just west of Perdido Pass. On a good day, with a decent southeastern swell and an offshore wind, this spot can produce 6-foot (2-meter) barrels, but they are usually short-lived. Hurricane season can also provide some action. Decent waves are also found on the eastern side of the pass when conditions are right.

Swell direction

Perdido Pass

Pensacola
Alabama Point

SAFETY TIP

Rip currents flow from the shore to the open sea and can be incredibly strong, particularly in stormy weather and at low tide. Surfers use rip currents as a quick and easy passage through the waves to the lineup. But they can be extremely dangerous for swimmers, and are known to kill approximately 100 people every year in the United States. If you are caught in a rip current, always swim perpendicular to the current to free yourself, rather than against it.

Start

Name:	Alabama Point, also known as Orange Beach		**Level:**	all
Location:	Orange Beach, AL		**Best tide:**	all
Wave direction:	left		**Best season:**	winter
Wave length:	short		**Popularity:**	crowded
Sea bed:	sand			
Type:	jetty/beach break			

The Bungalows

The Bungalows is located inside the Perdido Key State Park on the Perdido Key barrier island. Beach breaks occur along much of the park's shoreline, but the best spots are accessible from the eastern end of the park, where there is plenty of parking and a simple boardwalk provides access to the beach. As with most surf spots in Northwest Florida, Bungalows needs the right conditions to be worth the effort – generally a southeast swell with offshore winds. One benefit: The Bungalows is often less crowded than the busier breaks at Pensacola Beach and Alabama Point.

Swell direction

Start

Pensacola
The Bungalows

THE BUNGALOWS

Name:	The Bungalows		**Level:**	all
Location:	Perdido Key, FL		**Best tide:**	all
Wave direction:	left and right		**Best season:**	winter
Wave length:	short		**Popularity:**	quiet
Sea bed:	sand			
Type:	beach break			

Pensacola Beach

The stretch of Pensacola Beach that extends one mile (1.6 kilometers) from The Cross surf site to the Pensacola fishing pier has some decent rideable waves when conditions allow. These beach breaks are fairly consistent, producing left and right-handers that are possible to surf even when the swell is relatively small. The best conditions usually come in winter when southeast swells and offshore winds combine to produce clean lines.

The Cross

★★☆

Pensacola
Pensacola Beach

DID YOU KNOW?

The Cross surf site on Pensacola Beach is named after the 10-foot (3-meter) cross located on top of one of the nearby sand dunes, about one mile (1.6 kilometers) east of the Pensacola Pier. The cross was placed overlooking the Gulf of Mexico to mark the location of the first Catholic Mass in the United States, which was held on Pensacola Beach in 1559. The cross is sometimes referred to as the "indestructible cross" as it has survived every hurricane since it was erected.

Pensacola Pier

Swell direction

Start

Name:	The Cross and Pensacola Pier	Level:	all
Location:	Pensacola Beach, FL	Best tide:	all
Wave direction:	left and right	Best season:	winter
Wave length:	short	Popularity:	crowded
Sea bed:	sand		
Type:	beach/jetty break		

Navarre Beach

Navarre Beach is a relatively quiet beach break located on the barrier island just south of Navarre. The best place to surf is around the pier – usually along the beach to the east – where small spilling breakers can become hollow tubes when conditions align. As with most other surf spots along the coast here, the best conditions are usually in winter and during hurricane season when a storm is off shore and producing decent swells. At most other times, the waves are usually too small for experienced surfers, but beginners love this spot and it is also popular with kids.

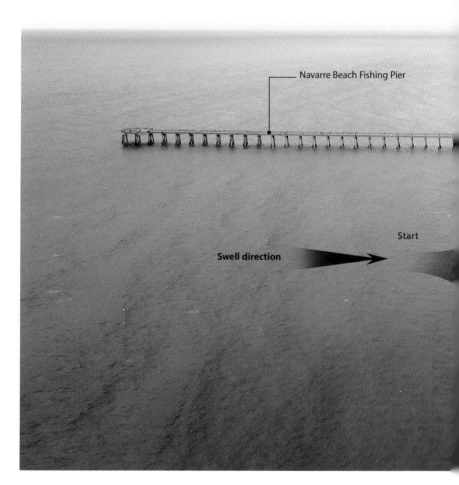

Navarre Beach Fishing Pier

Start

Swell direction

Pensacola
Navarre Beach

ECO TIP

Most people consider surfers to be an eco-friendly bunch but some of the products they use are far from good for the environment. For example, almost all the board wax available on the market today is made from petrochemical-based paraffin. Natural and organic waxes made from various plants and beeswax are now starting to appear, and surfers are taking notice. Surfers also tend to pile-on the sunscreen, which has been shown to damage coral reefs. Biodegradable sunscreens that are free of ingredients such as parabens, cinnamate, oxybenzone, benzophenone and camphor derivatives have been available for years. Always read the label to ensure what you are buying is safe for the marine environment and safe for reefs; it usually means it is better for your body too.

Name:	Navarre Beach	**Level:**	novice
Location:	Navarre Beach, FL	**Best tide:**	all
Wave direction:	left and right	**Best season:**	winter
Wave length:	short	**Popularity:**	quiet
Sea bed:	sand		
Type:	jetty/beach break		

Fort Walton Beach

Fort Walton Beach is located on Okaloosa Island. It is a stretch of relatively consistent surf that runs from the Okaloosa Island Fishing Pier in the east to the Breakers condominiums, which are located just under one mile (1.6 kilometers) to the west. This jetty and beach break produces decent lefts and rights, mostly during the winter months. The spot can get crowded at times, as there is plenty of entertainment around the pier after a day spent in the water.

The Breakers

Fort Walton Beach Destin

DID YOU KNOW?

Several species of shark are found in Florida waters, including tiger and bull sharks. Although attacks on snorkelers, bathers, surfers and divers do occur, it is important to keep in mind that deliberate attacks by sharks are very rare. Most shark bites are accidental, brought about by the limited visibility close to shore.

On average, there is less than one fatality each year from shark attacks in the U.S. Consider that statistic relative to the following: According to data provided by the Consumer Product Safety Commission, more than twice as many people die annually in the U.S. from vending machines falling on top of them. Moreover, 20 people are killed by cows each year, according to the Centers for Disease Control and Prevention.

Okaloosa Island fishing Pier

Start

Swell direction

Start

		Type:	jetty/beach break
Name:	Fort Walton Beach, also known as Breakers and Okaloosa Pier	**Level:**	all
Location:	Fort Walton Beach, FL	**Best tide:**	all
Wave direction:	left and right	**Best season:**	winter
Wave length:	short	**Popularity:**	quiet
Sea bed:	sand		

Amazons

Amazons, or The Pass as it is often called, is widely regarded as the best wave in Northwest Florida. The site is located in St. Andrews State Park, about 8 miles (13 kilometers) east of Panama City Beach. Amazons tends to overshadow the modest but workable beach breaks that can be found to the west next to the nearby fishing piers. The swell at Amazons often begins south of the pass that separates St. Andrews park from Shell Island on the other side of the pass; incidentally, Shell Island is considered another decent surf spot, although somewhat harder to reach without a boat. As the wave at Amazons begins to break, it curves around the breakwater to produce a long, hollow left-hander that can generate plenty of coverage and hit 8 feet (2.5 meters) in ideal conditions. Amazons is reasonably consistent and starts working at only a few feet in height. The downside of this spot is that it is often quite crowded.

Swell direction

Start

Shell Island

Panama City
Amazons

SAFETY TIP

Access to the surf spot on nearby Shell Island can be challenging without a boat. It is tempting for many surfers to access this site by paddling across the pass, but this can be particularly dangerous for a number of reasons including the strong tidal currents, the possibility of bull sharks, and the significant boat traffic that passes through the channel. If all that wasn't reason enough to stay out of the pass, Coast Guard officials are quick to write hefty tickets for those caught in the act.

St Andrews State Park Pier

Name:	Amazons, also known as The Pass	**Sea bed:**	sand
		Type:	jetty/beach break
Location:	St. Andrews State Park, Panama City, FL	**Level:**	intermediate to advanced
		Best tide:	all
Wave direction:	left	**Best season:**	winter
Wave length:	medium to long	**Popularity:**	crowded

37

Diving and snorkeling

Northwest Florida offers an amazing array of diving and snorkeling experiences for visitors and locals alike. From shore-accessible artificial reefs and jetties to open water wrecks and natural ledges, the region boasts something for everyone regardless of their level of experience.

Most artificial reefs in Northwest Florida are strategically positioned around one of three passes or inlets: Pensacola Pass, Destin East Pass and St. Andrews Pass. The reefs range in size from small modules, often deployed as part of a larger reef system, all the way up to massive wrecks measuring over 800 feet (240 meters) in length. While some of the region's artificial reefs are deployed in less than 50 feet (15 meters) of water just a short boat ride from a pass, others lie 20 to 40 miles (32 to 64 kilometers) off shore at depths of more than 200 feet (60 meters).

ECO TIP

This guidebook focuses mostly on Northwest Florida's artificial reefs. The region does have a number of natural limestone ledges, but the primary habitat for divers and snorkelers to explore are the area's artificial reefs. Ledges represent an important biological resource that can be easily disturbed, so divers should be particularly careful to minimize their impact when visiting these ecosystems. Divers who wish to visit Northwest Florida's natural ledges can reach out to local dive shops, most of whom schedule trips out to these ledges on a semi-regular basis.

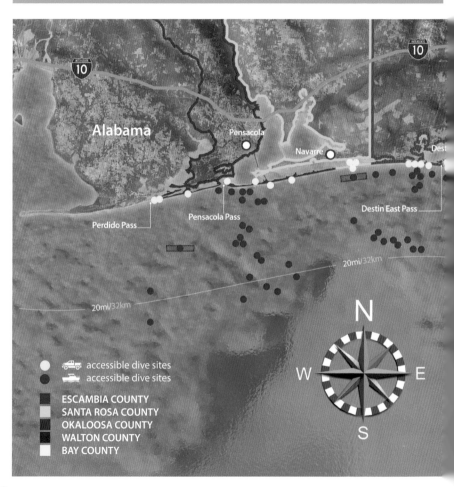

We have highlighted 59 of the region's most popular dive and snorkel sites in this guidebook, many of which are accessible from shore. We also provide a list of dive-oriented artificial reefs so that visitors can explore some of the less popular sites as well. Even so, this secondary list represents just a subset of the total list of artificial reefs deployed in the Gulf of Mexico along this stretch of coastline. Many of these other artificial reefs are geared toward the fishing community, based on their depth, location or other characteristics but are still interesting to explore.

For each site described in detail in this guidebook, we provide the history of the reef (if available) to give divers some interesting context during their visit. Our three-star rating system offers insight into the difficulty level, strength of the current, depth, and the quality of the reef and fauna that divers and snorkelers are likely to encounter. We offer a suggested route and point out some of the key information to enhance the in-water experience, such as what species to look for and what key features to observe. When coupled with detailed 3D renderings of wrecks and reefs, divers and snorkelers will have an idea of what to expect before they venture into the water.

The counties of Northwest Florida have invested significant time money and resource in developing these sites over the years and are still actively adding new artificial reefs when budgets permit. This guidebook is accurate as of its publication date, and divers and snorkelers should check with local dive operators to see what new and exciting artificial reefs there are to visit. We will continue to revise and expand our guidebook in the future to help ensure we offer the most up-to-date information possible. Each county manages its own list of reef sites and we provide the websites in the introduction pages for each county.

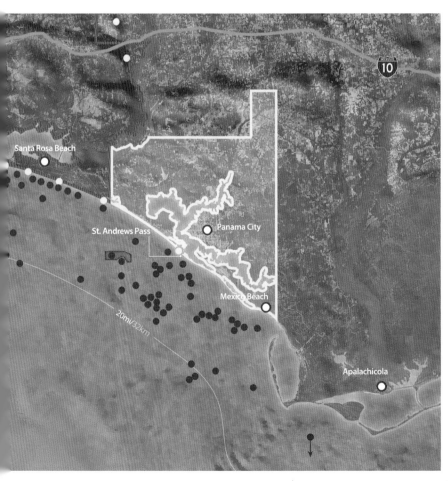

Diving and snorkeling services

Businesses are listed alphabetically by county:

Escambia County

Dive Pros
7203 West Highway. 98, Pensacola
Tel: 850-456-8845
Email: info@florida-divepros.com
Florida-divepros.com

Due South Custom Charters
Southwind Marina
10121 Sinton Drive, Pensacola
Tel: 850-565-7247
Email: duesouthcharters@gmail.com
Duesouthcustomcharters.com

Emerald Ocean Dive Charters, LLC
3009 Barrancas Avenue, Pensacola
Tel: 850-512-8701
Email: emeraldoceandivers@gmail.com
Emeraldoceandivers.com

H20 Below
Southwind Marina
10121 Sinton Drive, Pensacola
Tel: 850-291-3501
Email: h2obelow@cox.net
Ussoriskanydiver.com

High Ty'd Charters
Southwind Marina
10121 Sinton Drive, Pensacola
Tel: 231-855-0396
Hightydcharters.com

MBT Divers
3920 Barrancas Avenue, Pensacola
Tel: 850-455-7702
Email: mbtdivers@gmail.com
Mbtdivers.com

Niuhi Dive Charters
Southwind Marina
10121 Sinton Drive, Pensacola
Tel: 850-529-2475
Email: sharkman58@gmail.com
Niuhidivecharters.com

Six Shooter Charters
Southwind Marina
10121 Sinton Drive. Pensacola
Tel: 850-292-1105
Email: captdoug73@gmail.com
Sixshootercharter.com

Viking Diving
3009 Barrancas Ave, Pensacola
Tel: 850-916-3483
Email: vikingdivingpensacola@outlook.com
Vikingdivingpensacola.com

Santa Rosa County

Bay Breeze Dive Center
49 Gulf Breeze Parkway, Gulf Breeze
Tel: 850-934-8363
Email: diveshop@baybreezescuba.com
Baybreezescuba.com

Shark Quest
5614 Gulf Breeze Parkway, Gulf Breeze, FL 32563
Tel: 850-516-6800
Email: sharkquestdiveshop@gmail.com
Scuba-dive-pensacola.com

Under Pressure Divers
Tel: 850-723-4104
Email: updivers.fl@gmail.com

Okaloosa County

Benthic Ocean Sports
501 Harbor Boulevard, Suite G, Destin
Tel: 850-837-3315
Email: info@benthicoceansports.com
Benthicoceansports.com

Destin Snorkel
10 Harbor Boulevard, Destin
Tel: 850-269-2329
Destinsnorkel.com

Discovery Dive World
92 South John Sims Parkway, Valparaiso
Tel: 850-678-5001
Email: support@discoverydiveworld.com
Discoverydiveworld.com

DreadKnot Charters
Tel: 850-542-8700
Email: dreadknot850@gmail.com
Dreadknotcharters.com

Emerald Coast Scuba
503-b Harbor Boulevard, Destin
Tel: 850-837-0955
Email: ecsdivedestin@gmail.com
Divedestin.net

Fort Walton Beach Scuba
425 Page Bacon Road, Mary Esther

Tel: 850-716-0867
Email: fortwaltonbeachscuba@gmail.com
Fortwaltonbeachscuba.com

ScubaTech of NWFL
301 Harbor Boulevard, Destin
Tel: 850-837-2822
Email: scubatech@scubatechnwfl.com
Scubatechnwfl.com

Sea Pal Dive Charters
104 Miracle Strip Parkway, Fort Walton Beach
Tel: 850-716-0867 (via Fort Walton Beach Scuba)
Tel: 850-678-5001 (via Discovery Dive World)
Seapaldivecharters.com

Walton County

Dive 30A
133 Defuniak Street, Santa Rosa Beach
Tel: 850-460-1442
Email: info@dive30a.com
Dive30a.com

Bay County

Dive Locker
1010 Thomas Drive, Panama City Beach
Phone: 850-230-8006
Email: divelocker@divelocker.net
Divelocker.net

Diver's Den
3120 Thomas Drive, Panama City Beach
Phone: 850-234-8717
Email: kim@diversdenpcb.com
Diversdenpcb.com

Kitchen Pass Charters
St. Andrews Marina
3151 West 10th Street, Panama City
Tel: 850-896-6476
Email: kitchenpasscharters1@gmail.com
Kitchenpasscharters.com

Panama City Dive Center
4823 Thomas Drive, Panama City Beach
Tel: 850-235-3390
Email: pcdc1983@gmail.com
Pcdivecenter.com

Panama City Diving
106 Thomas Drive, Panama City Beach
Phone: 850-588-8077
Email: Pat@PanamaCityDiving.com
Panamacitydiving.com

Red Alert Diving
1619 Moylan Road, Panama City Beach
Tel: 850-238-8760
info@redalertdiving.com
Redalertdiving.com

Try Scuba Diving
Panama City Beach
Tel: 850-304-7079
Email: pcb@tryscubadiving.com
Tryscubadiving.com

Spring

Vortex Spring Adventures
1517 Vortex Springs Lane, Ponce De Leon
Tel: 850-836-4979
Email: vsareserve@gmail.com
Vortexspring.com

Courtesy of Panama City Diving

Access to the Gulf requires going through one of three main passes in the area. 41

ESCAMBIA COUNTY

Escambia County diving is primarily accessed via the Pensacola Pass, which sits southwest of the city. The county has been deploying artificial reefs since the late 1970s, starting with the *Joseph L Meek Liberty Ship* and the Three Coal Barges. They have continued to invest in artificial reefs, adding dozens of new wrecks, bridge rubble and reef modules over the decades. Today, divers can explore a variety of reefs ranging from army tanks to airplanes and even an aircraft carrier. The *Oriskany* is the most famous artificial reef in Escambia County – and

possibly all of the U.S. – as well as the largest artificial reef in the world (see page 100 for more information). Many of the dive shops operating out of Pensacola Pass also cross into Alabama state waters to visit the popular wrecks of that region too.

In the pages that follow, you will find detailed information and 3D-rendered maps for six popular Escambia County wrecks and two wrecks found in Alabama waters. Escambia County has its share of shore-accessible dive

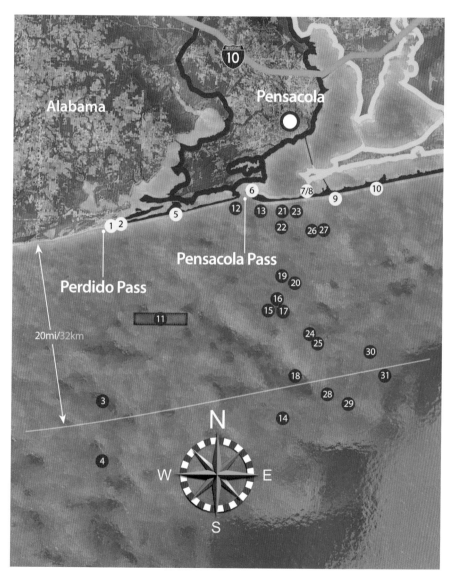

and snorkel sites as well, and we provide information about six of these sites, some featuring our unique 3D-rendered models. The visibility of shore sites decreases toward the west as Gulf waters mix with the muddier waters of the Mississippi River and those exiting Mobile Bay, but we have added two popular Alabama shore-accessible sites to this section, as they are frequented by Pensacola-based divers.

Escambia County keeps an up-to-date list of all of its artificial reef sites online. To see if new reefs have been added since publication, please visit:
Myescambia.com/our-services/natural-resources-management/marine-resources/artificial-reefs

Dive and snorkel sites

ALABAMA and ESCAMBIA COUNTY

1	Alabama Point Jetties	
2	Alabama Point Circalittoral Reef	
3	LuLu	
4	New Venture	
5	Perdido Key Reef	
6	Fort Pickens Jetty	
7	Park West Reef	
8	Capt Bob Quarles Reef	
9	Casino Beach Reef	
10	Park East	
11	I-10 Bridge Rubble (#1 through #6)	
12	USS Massachusetts	
13	Catherine	
14	Avocet	
15	Tug Born Again	
16	Pete Tide II	
17	LCM and Heron	
18	Knicklebine Barge	
19	San Pablo (aka Russian Freighter)	
20	Ocean Wind	
21	Lane Gilchrest Reef	
22	Joe Patti Memorial Reef	
23	Three Coal Barges	
24	YDT-14	
25	YDT-15	
26	Tex Edwards Barge	
27	Joseph L. Meek Liberty Ship	
28	Antares	
29	Tenneco Platform	
30	Chevron Platform	
31	Oriskany	

Alabama Point Jetties

Difficulty ● ○ ○
Current ● ● ○
Depth ● ○ ○
Reef ★★★☆
Fauna ★★☆

Pensacola
Alabama Point
Jetties

Access 🚙 about 41 mins from downtown Pensacola
🏊 about 2 mins from shore

Level Open Water

Location
Orange Beach, Alabama
GPS 30°16.176'N, 87°33.383'W

Getting there
From downtown Pensacola, head west along US-98 Business. Shortly after the road merges onto East Garden Street, turn left to take Barrancas Avenue headed southwest.

West Route

1,800ft / 550m

Perdido Pass

550ft / 168m

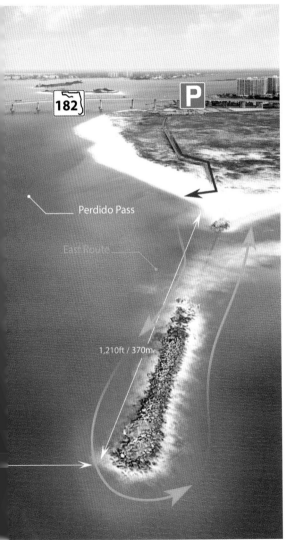

Barrancas Avenue becomes FL-292, which crosses Chico Bayou, and then continues for 14 miles (22.5 kilometers) in a mostly western direction. The name of the road will change multiple times, from Barrancas to Gulf Beach Highway to Sorrento Road, before a final change to Perdido Key Highway. As it nears the beaches of Perdido Key, FL-292 veers sharply west again and runs along the length of Perdido Key. The road becomes Route 182 at state border, that sits just 5.4 miles (8.7 kilometers) along the beach from this final turn. The jetties are 1.7 miles (2.4 kilometers) beyond the border.

To dive the eastern jetty, exit to the right just before the bridge and follow the service road under the bridge to the public parking lot of the Alabama Point East State Park. To dive the western jetty, exit to the right immediately after the bridge and circle around beneath the overpass to the free parking lot there.

Access

Diving the jetties on either side of Perdido Pass requires a bit of a hike with your gear, but it is worth it. Some divers opt to park in an abandoned parking lot off Gulf Road, which is the second street after the bridge, as this dramatically shortens the walk to the west-side jetty. Visitors should scout the location for themselves and park at their own risk. On the east side of the pass, a long boardwalk takes visitors out to the sandy beach. The best time to access the Alabama Point jetties is in the hour just before high slack tide so that your dive time straddles the period when visibility is at its best and the currents are at their lowest. Currents can be very strong through the pass except during low or high slack tide.

Description

The jetties on either side of Perdido Pass represent multiple dive sites in one. On the west side of the pass, divers can explore either the seawall or the jetty, while snorkelers may have a better experience on the gulf side of the jetty, sheltered from the currents in the pass. On the east side, divers can explore the jetty while snorkelers can check out the gulf side or the pass side of the jetty. These are all shallow sites, with maximum depths of approximately 30 feet (9 meters).

It is very important for divers and snorkelers to close to shore as there is regular boat traffic through the channel. Staying close to the seawall or jetties should be easy, however, since these are the most interesting areas to explore. Sheepshead, spadefish, flounders and rays are commonly spotted at these sites.

Alabama Point Circalittoral Reefs

Difficulty ● ○ ○
Current ● ○ ○
Depth ● ○ ○
Reef ★★☆
Fauna ★☆☆

Pensacola
Alabama Point
Circalittoral
Reefs

Access 🚙 about 40 mins from downtown
Pensacola
🏊 about 5 mins from shore

Level Open Water

Location
Orange Beach, Alabama
GPS 30°16.420'N, 87°32.520'W

Getting there
From downtown Pensacola, head west along US-98 Business. Shortly after the road merges onto East Garden Street, turn left to take Barrancas Avenue heading southwest. Barrancas Avenue becomes FL-292, which crosses Chico Bayou, and then continues for 14 miles (22.5 kilometers) in a mostly western direction. The name of the road will change multiple times, from Barrancas to Gulf Beach Highway to Sorrento Road, before a final change to Perdido Key Highway. As it nears the beaches of Perdido Key, FL-292 veers sharply west again and runs along the length of Perdido Key. The state border sits just 5.4 miles (8.7 kilometers) along the beach from this final turn, and the public parking lot for the Alabama Point Circalittoral Reef sits just 1.5 miles (2.4

kilometers) beyond the state border. Turn left into the public beach access parking lot. There are no facilities located here, but there are plenty of parking spaces.

Access

A boardwalk runs from the parking lot to the beach, which can vary greatly in width from year to year and season to season, measuring as little as 200 feet (61 meters) and as much as 400 feet (122 meters). Divers and snorkelers should check the conditions before entering the water, including potential riptides, as well as checking on the surf which can be strong at times.

Two sets of posts are located on either side of the boardwalk, 700 feet (213 meters) apart. These mark the eastern and western borders of the reef modules that make up this site. Surface swimming out to the reefs is possible by staying in between these sets of posts. There are no buoys that mark the reef itself.

Description

This reef is the easternmost of three sets of circalittoral reefs that Alabama deployed in 2018. In total, there are 160 modules deployed at this reef. The first line of modules sits about 500 feet (152 meters) off the beach, although they might be closer if the beach has a higher volume of sand. The modules are positioned so they are a minimum of six feet (1.8 meters) below the surface of the water to ensure they do not interfere with navigation. The sandy seafloor is typically at a depth of between 10 and 15 feet (3 and 4.5 meters).

The reef modules are posts topped with concrete and limestone discs. Each post holds between two and four discs, which offers a hard surface for soft corals, sponges and other marine life to colonize. Divers and snorkelers are likely to see juveniles of many reef fish, including young snapper, grouper, grey triggerfish, Atlantic spadefish, sheepshead and blue runners. As they explore the site, divers should watch out for arrow crabs, octopus and even sea turtles.

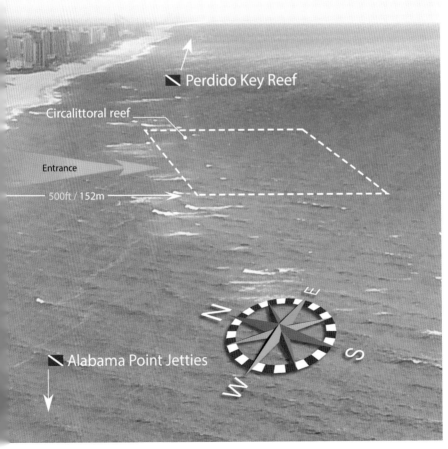

Perdido Key Reef

Circalittoral reef

Entrance

500ft / 152m

Alabama Point Jetties

LuLu

Difficulty ● ● ○
Current ● ● ○
Depth ● ● ●
Reef ★★☆
Fauna ★★☆

Access 🚤 about 19.5mi (31.5km) south of Perdido Pass

Level Open Water

Location
Orange Beach, Alabama
GPS 29°59.520'N, 87°33.037'W

Getting there
Given the distance from shore, *LuLu* should only be visited by operators and private vessels with experience operating in the Gulf. There are no surface mooring buoys at this site, so operators typically tie in to the wreck or anchor in the sand nearby.

Access
The top of the wreck sits at a depth of just 61 feet (18.5 meters) making it accessible to open water divers with more experience. As with most coastal freighters, *LuLu* is a relatively open wreck. The layout makes the site relatively easy to explore, however she rests on a sandy seabed at a depth of 114 feet (34.5 meters), which means only advanced divers with experience at depth will get to explore the entire artificial reef. This wreck is primarily visited by dive charters and shops operating out of coastal Alabama.

Description
LuLu was a cargo freighter originally built in Bergum, Netherlands in 1972. Christened the *Ingeborg*, she had multiple names and changed hands many times before ending her career as *Yokamu*, under the flag of the Saint Vincent and the Grenadines. She was acquired for the purpose of deploying her as an artificial reef through a joint effort by public and private interests. These included local reef maker Walter Marine, the Alabama Gulf Coast Reef and Restoration Foundation, and Mac McAleer, who was the title sponsor of the project. The vessel was renamed *LuLu* after Mr. McAleer's wife and local restauranteur, Lucy Buffett.

LuLu was successfully scuttled on a sunny day in May 2013, amid a floating party replete with a live band playing music with the help of a generator. She was surrounded by more than 200 personal and private charter boats. The sinking went off without a hitch and without the need for explosives. The controlled nature of the scuttling meant that viewers were able to stay within 100 feet (30.5 meters) of the vessel as she went down, which is much closer than the normal safety perimeter.

She came to rest upright on a sandy seabed at a depth of between 114 and 116 feet (34.5 and 35.5 meters). The top of her superstructure sits at 61 feet (18.5 meters) now that the roof of the wheelhouse has been torn off. Although that is pretty much the limit to her damage. The four-leveled superstructure and massive cargo hold are largely intact, affording divers with wreck penetration experience plenty of opportunities for exploration. Meanwhile, open water divers can spend their time exploring the outside of the ship.

The wreck has been well-colonized by reef creatures, from small cocoa damselfish and sharpnose puffers, up to larger species such as grey snapper and scamp grouper. Divers will

Atlantic spadefish are common across many of the sites in Northwest Florida.

Lureen Ferretti ©

49

see tomtates and other grunts sheltering in the hold, while Atlantic spadefish and greater amberjacks swim about in the water column above the wreck.

Route

A typical dive route will depend on the current and a diver's level of experience. Those able to explore the deeper areas of the site generally start the dive by exploring the hold and the outside of the hull. From there, they investigate

106ft
32.5m

80ft
24.5m

62

19

114ft
34.5m

Bow

Name:	*LuLu*	**Length:**	271ft (82.5m)
Type:	Coastal freighter	**Tonnage:**	1,388grt
Previous names:	*Ingeborg, Topr Avon,*	**Construction:**	Bodewes Hoogezand,
	Blue Scan, Myrberg,		Bergum, Netherlands, 1972
	Mer Sun, Saga Sub,	**Last owner:**	Walter Marine
	Scorpio, Yokamu	**Sunk:**	May 26, 2013

-80ft
24.5m

19

106ft
32.5m

62

Bow

114ft
34.5m

the bow before heading back toward the stern and the four levels of the superstructure. Gradually ascending while touring the superstructure will allow divers plenty of time to explore the now-exposed wheelhouse. Less-experienced divers focus on the superstructure at the stern of the ship, which is the shallowest part of the wreck.

90ft
27.5m

61ft
18.5m

88

Stern

38

56

54

116ft
35.5m

Other species commonly found at this site:

L **16** **17** **20** **32** **33** **39** **45** **50**

60 **69** **80** **81** **82**

New Venture

Difficulty ● ● ●
Current ● ● ○
Depth ● ● ●
Reef ★★☆
Fauna ★★☆

Pensacola
New Venture

Access 🚤 about 25mi (41km) south of Perdido Pass

Level Open Water

Location
Orange Beach, Alabama
GPS 29°54.052'N, 87°32.896'W

Getting there
Given the distance from shore, *New Venture* should only be visited by operators and private vessels with experience operating in the Gulf. There are no surface mooring buoys at this site, so operators typically tie in to the wreck or anchor in the sand nearby.

Access
The top of the wreck sits at a depth of just 62 feet (19 meters) making it accessible to open water divers, although she sits on a sandy seafloor with a maximum depth of 121 feet (37 meters) which means only advanced divers will be able to fully explore the site. *New Venture* is a complex wreck with multiple overhead environments, which should only be explored by those divers with wreck penetration experience. This wreck is primarily visited by dive charters and shops operating out of coastal Alabama and those based in Pensacola, Florida.

Description
New Venture was originally built for Alpha Marine Services as a seismic survey vessel in February 1986. She was later sold to Fairfield Industries, Inc. and renamed the *Fairfield New Venture*. The nearly 250-foot-long (76-meter) research vessel was primarily used to survey the seafloor for minerals and oil. She was ultimately acquired by the Alabama Marine Resources Division thanks in part to a grant from the National Fish and Wildlife Foundation in Alabama that originated with oil spill funds. The grant helped cover the $970,000 USD price tag for the project, which included intensive cleaning efforts and preparing the vessel for deployment as an artificial reef.

New Venture was sent to the seafloor on June 20, 2018 after a delay of a couple of days due to bad weather. While the overall length and beam

New Venture offers divers a complex dive site to explore.

may be similar to the large freighters that often find a second life as artificial reefs, *New Venture's* tall sides and five-level superstructure make this artificial reef far more complex than many of its peers. Holes cut into her hull at all levels permit easy penetration and access to the interior of the wreck, and divers with wreck penetration experience will need multiple dives to truly explore every nook and cranny. Yet, some of the interior space, particularly near the stern, permit partial swim-throughs that are suitable even for less experienced divers.

The wreck is a newer deployment relative to its neighbor, *LuLu*, as well as many of the wrecks

Virgil Zetterlind ©

farther to the east in Florida waters, including the massive aircraft carrier, *Oriskany*. Even so, colonization by soft corals, algae and sponges is well underway. Numerous fish species have taken up residence in the wreck. Divers are likely to see damselfish, sea bass and puffers close to the structure, while large jacks, snapper and grunts can be found sheltering in open spaces within the wreck or above the top deck. The reef life is interesting enough to be worth the trip, but it is the complexity of the wreck itself that keeps divers coming back time and again to this site.

Route

The recommended dive route will depend on a diver's level of experience and their comfort in overhead environments. Divers should not exceed their level of experience when diving this wreck. Most divers begin at the stern, dropping down into the open bay that was once the helicopter landing pad. From there, they can make their way forward, weaving in and out of the numerous access points to the wreck's interior. Many divers make their way to the surface of the main deck at a depth of 76 feet (23 meters). From there, they typically head toward the bow, circling the outside of the wheelhouse before exploring inside, if comfortable doing so. Although not

80

62ft
19m

92

Bow

121ft
37m

extremely deep, the wreck is large so divers will need to monitor their depth and bottom time carefully. Fortunately, the complexity of the wreck means there is plenty of opportunity to shift to a shallower depth profile to gain back bottom time while still having interesting things to explore.

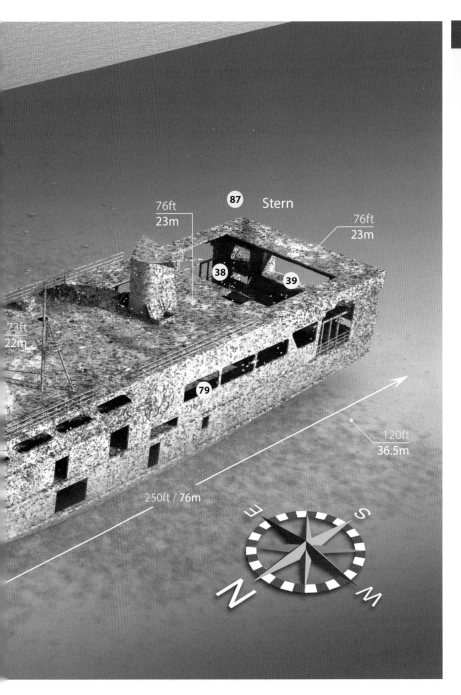

Name:	*New Venture*	Larose, LA, 1986
Type:	Research/survey vessel	**Last owner:** Fairfield Industries, Inc.
Previous names:	*Fairfield New Venture*	**Sunk:** June 20, 2018
Length:	250ft (76m)	
Tonnage:	2,912grt	
Construction:	North American Shipbuilding,	

76ft
23m

87

76ft
23m

39

38

Stern

120ft
36.5m

62ft
19m

92

73ft
22m

80

Bow

79

121ft
37m

W

N

S

E

Other species commonly found
at this site:

J   **2**   **10**   **14**   **16**   **20**   **21**   **25**   **28**

33   **43**   **77**   **78**   **88**

05 Perdido Key Reef

Pensacola

Perdido Key Reef

Difficulty ● ○ ○
Current ● ○ ○
Depth ● ○ ○
Reef ★☆☆
Fauna ★★☆

Access 🚙 about 30 mins from downtown Pensacola
🏊 about 5 mins from shore

Level Open Water

Location
Perdido Key, Escambia County
GPS 30°17.675'N, 87°25.600'W

Getting there

From downtown Pensacola, head west along US-98 Business. Shortly after the road merges onto East Garden Street, turn left to take Barrancas Avenue headed southwest. Barrancas Avenue becomes FL-292, which crosses Chico Bayou, and then continues for 14 miles (22.5 kilometers) in a mostly westerly direction. The name of the road changes multiple times, from Barrancas to Gulf Beach Highway to Sorrento Road, before becoming Perdido Key Highway as it turns and heads south toward the beach. Just 0.9 miles (1.5 kilometers) after crossing onto Perdido Key, and just before FL-292 veers right to head west along the key, turn left onto Johnson Beach Road and take an immediate right onto Sandy Key Drive. Follow this to the narrow parking lot for Escambia Beach Access #1. The official address for the site is 13549 Sandy Key Drive, Pensacola, Florida, 32507.

Access

A narrow path allows visitors to access the beach between the hotel and condo buildings along this stretch of coastline. There are no facilities here. There are two range markers at the end of the path that divers and snorkelers can use to navigate to the reef. The shoreward post has a blue square on top

while the seaward post, which is occasionally missing, has a yellow triangle. Divers and snorkelers can navigate to the reef by keeping these posts lined up as they surface swim out. If the yellow triangle post is missing, divers and snorkelers can use a bearing of 168° from the blue square

Sighting pole

60

post to reach the reef. The surf can be high at times, so divers should be careful entering and exiting the water with their gear. Divers and snorkelers are required to fly a "diver down" flag while in the water.

Description

The reef modules are the standard design featuring a central post that supports multiple limestone and concrete discs. The modules here are arranged in three rows of eight that extend directly out from the shore. The first modules are less than 500 feet (150 meters) from shore, which makes for a relatively easy swim out for divers and snorkelers. The space between modules ranges from 20 to 25 feet (6

to 7.5 meters). The reefs are not particularly deep, with the bottom of the posts ranging in depth from 12 to 15 feet (3.5 to 4.5 meters). The tops of the posts are generally within 6 feet (1.8 meters) from the surface and should be readily visible to snorkelers at the surface. However, visibility can be as little as 10 feet (3 meters) depending on ocean conditions, which could make navigating from module to module a little tricky.

Visitors are likely to see everything from sea turtles to damselfish. Juvenile grouper and snapper are often present on the modules, while cryptic toadfish may be seen closer to the sand, along with a stingray or two.

Fort Pickens Jetty

ESCAMBIA COUNTY

Difficulty	● ○ ○
Current	● ● ○
Depth	● ○ ○
Reef	★★★☆
Fauna	★★★☆

Pensacola

Fort Pickens
Jetty

Access 🚐 about 33 mins from downtown
Pensacola
🏊 about 2 mins from shore

Level Open Water

Location
Pensacola, Escambia County
GPS 30°19.880'N, 87°17.727'W

Getting there
From downtown Pensacola take US-98 across the Pensacola Bay Bridge to Gulf Breeze. About a mile (1.6 kilometers) after crossing the bridge, turn right to exit onto Pensacola Beach Road toward Pensacola Beach and Fort Pickens. The bridge to the barrier island has a toll. Once across the sound, continue along past marinas and stores until the road begins to veer left. Turn right onto Fort Pickens Road. This road will take you 9.7 miles (15.6 kilometers) west along the barrier island to the Fort Pickens State Park. The park entrance is located 2.5 miles (4 kilometers) after the turn, and the ranger station, where you will need to pay an entrance fee, is located another 0.85 miles (1.4 kilometers) down the road. There is a per vehicle fee to pay, and you want to consider an annual pass if you plan on diving multiple days. Continue along Fort Pickens Road past the battlements and out-buildings until it curves north and ends in a parking lot at the edge of Pensacola Bay. Turn left and drive along the edge of the water until the road starts to curve back south.

Access
There is a set of stairs at the corner of the road that leads down to the waters edge in between the jetty and the fishing pier. The best entry point is due north from the base

of the stairs, and not to the west on the jetty itself. However, divers and snorkelers may find it interesting to explore the jetty as well. The focus of this site begins 80 feet (24 meters) from shore on a northern heading. Given the site's proximity to Pensacola Pass, it is best accessed during the hour before

120ft / 36.5

and after high slack tide when the currents and visibility are generally most suitable. Conditions can deteriorate quickly at other points in the tidal cycle. Tide data are listed under the name Fort McRee Breakwater.

Description

Fort Pickens is widely regarded as the best shore dive in the Pensacola area, and one of the best in all Northwest Florida. The waters are part of the Fort Pickens Aquatic Preserve which has helped the area develop a relatively high level of biodiversity, with visitors likely to see sheepshead, red drum, porcupinefish, flounder and several species of snapper and grouper. Many tropical reef fish use the rocky seabed here as a nursery, so juvenile damselfish, blennies and wrasses are a common sight as well.

The site is a popular location for training dives with many of the local operators using the jetties for their open water sessions. Depths at the site range from 10 feet (3 meters) closer to shore, to 42 feet (13 meters) roughly 200 feet (61 meters) from shore. The bottom is mostly covered with rocks, while a few key features, such as large and small cages, an overturned Jeep and even aircraft debris, provide plenty of structure to explore.

80ft / 24.5m

Park West and Captain Bob Quarles Reefs

		Pensacola
Difficulty	● ○ ○	
Current	● ○ ○	Park West and
Depth	● ○ ○	Captain Bob
Reef	★★☆	Quarles Reefs
Fauna	★☆☆	

Access 🚙 about 15 mins from downtown Pensacola
🏊 about 3 mins from shore

Level Open Water

Location
GPS (Park West) 30° 19.672'N, 87° 10.874'W
(Capt Bob Quarles) 30°19.738'N, 87°10.871'W

Getting there
From downtown Pensacola, take US-98 across the Pensacola Bay Bridge to Gulf Breeze. About one mile (1.6 kilometers) after crossing the bridge, turn right to exit onto Pensacola Beach Road toward Pensacola Beach and Fort Pickens. The bridge to the barrier island has a toll. Once across the sound, continue past marinas and stores until the road begins to veer left. Turn right onto Fort Pickens Road and drive for 2.5 miles (4 kilometers). The parking lot closest to the two adjacent artificial reef deployments is on the right, just before the entrance to the Fort Pickens park. There is no fee to park here.

Fort Pickens Jetty

Access

The walk to the water is just 160 feet (50 meters) across the beach. This sheltered spot provides protection from waves and currents, even during weather that might prevent divers from venturing into the Gulf. However, this location is also known for its limited visibility, which can drop as low as 5 to 10 feet (1.5 to 3 meters) at times. The Park West Reef is easy to identify by the large pylons sticking out of the water marking the four corners of the site. The closest pylon sits less than 300 feet (91.5 meters) from the beach. Captain Bob Quarles Reef is farther out into the bay and thus potentially harder to reach – it represents an additional swim of 330 feet (100 meters) from the outer pylons of the Park West Reef. The center of this second reef is roughly in line with the two pylons that mark the eastern edge of the Park West Reef. A dive flag is required by law for all snorkelers and divers visiting these reefs.

Description

Escambia County deployed two tons of concrete to create Park West Reef in September 2017, mostly in the form of reef balls. The concrete structures sit in a square measuring roughly 100 by 100 feet (30.5 by 30.5 meters). The average depth of the site is just 12 feet (3.5 feet) with the deepest point not much more than 14 feet (4.5 meters). By comparison, Captain Bob Quarles Reef, which was named after a local research diver, boat captain, surfer and fishing guide, was deployed in 2011. It consists of 270 tons of deck spans and other bridge rubble from the old Gulf Breeze bridge, and it features a ledge-like structure that rises as much as 7 feet (2 meters) off the seabed, which is approximately 14-feet (4.5 meters) deep. These sites provide habitat for a variety of fish, including juvenile grouper and snapper. Lobsters are frequent visitors to Captain Bob Quarles Reef, and are often found sheltering beneath the rubble.

Captain Bob Quarles Reef

ark West Snorkel Reef

330ft / 100m

300ft / 91.5m

Casino Beach Snorkel Reef

Difficulty ●○○
Current ●○○
Depth ●○○
Reef ★☆☆
Fauna ★★☆

Access: about 10 mins from downtown Pensacola; about 5 mins from shore

Level Open Water

Location

Pensacola Beach, Escambia County
GPS 30°19.729'N, 87°08.321'W

Getting there

From downtown Pensacola take US-98 across the Pensacola Bay Bridge to Gulf Breeze. About a mile (1.6 kilometers) after crossing the bridge, turn right to exit onto Pensacola Beach Road toward Pensacola Beach and Fort Pickens. The bridge to the barrier island has a toll. Once across Santa Rosa Sound, continue past marinas and stores until the road begins to veer left. Take a right on Casino Beach Boardwalk – the turn just after Fort Pickens Road. Drive along the Boardwalk until the third entrance to the large parking lot on the right. That entrance aligns with the access point to the beach closest to the snorkel reef. This large parking lot also serves the Fishing Pier and the nearby restaurants.

Access

There are two range markers to the east of the beach access path – on the left-hand side of the path, approaching the water. The shoreward post has a blue square on top while the seaward post has a yellow triangle. Divers and snorkelers can navigate to the reef by keeping these posts lined up as they surface swim out. Divers and snorkelers are required by law to fly a diver down flag while in the water. There are public restrooms here.

Description

Escambia County deployed this set of 17 reef modules in June 2020. The site's formal name is the Charles Fennel Gonzalez, IV, Casino Beach Reef in memory of a county employee of 20 years who worked on the project and who died unexpectedly just before its deployment. The reef modules are the standard design for snorkel reefs along this stretch of coast, featuring a central post that supports multiple limestone and concrete discs. The narrow formation of reef modules starts between 600 and 700 feet (183 and 213 meters) from shore, depending on the tide and the size of the beach at the time. The tops of the modules are at or below a depth of 6 feet (1.8 meters) to avoid impacting navigation, but the depth of the seafloor varies based on where the

sandbar is sitting. Depth generally ranges from 12 feet (3.5meters) near the first module from shore, to around 17 feet (5 meters) at the final set of modules. The modules are spaced roughly 25 feet (7.5 meters) apart and support a variety of reef creatures. Divers and snorkelers will likely see damselfish, blennies and juvenile grouper and snapper, while small jacks can be seen flitting about the site. There is even a chance to see an octopus or sea turtle.

SAFETY TIP

The surf can sometimes be high at this site, so snorkelers and divers, particularly with their heavy gear, should be careful entering and exiting the water. The safest way to enter the water is to first ensure that both buddies are fully geared up and have completed their buddy check. Only then should they enter the water, with air already in their BCDs and without fins attached. Once in the water, buddies should use each other for the support, if necessary, to attach their fins and push through the surf as quickly as possible. When exiting, divers should remember to keep their mask and regulator in place, their BCD inflated and remove their fins in the water so they can walk up the beach.

Sighting poles

650ft / 200m

3.5m

4m

70m

17ft
5m

Park East Snorkel Reef

Pensacola

Difficulty ● ○ ○
Current ● ○ ○
Depth ● ○ ○
Reef ★☆☆
Fauna ★★☆

Park East
Snorkel Reef

Access 🚐 about 20 mins from downtown
Pensacola
🏊 about 5 mins from shore

Level Open Water

Location
Pensacola, Escambia County
GPS 30°20.745'N, 87°03.153'W

Getting there
From downtown Pensacola take US-98 across the Pensacola Bay Bridge to Gulf Breeze. About one mile (1.6 kilometers) after crossing the bridge, turn right to exit onto Pensacola Beach Road toward Pensacola Beach and Fort Pickens. The bridge to the barrier island has a toll. Once across the sound, continue past marinas and stores until the road begins to veer to the left. Continue for another 5 miles (8 kilometers) past the Casino Beach Boardwalk until the parking lot on the right – it is nothing but sand dunes on both sides of the road for the last mile (1.6 kilometers). About 0.4 miles (0.65 kilometers) after the first lot is the entrance to Parking Lot H, which is the closest to the Park East Snorkel Reef.

Access
A wooden boardwalk leads from the middle of Parking Lot H to the beach. In addition, there are multiple narrow, sandy paths that run parallel to the boardwalk, providing alternate, and sometimes more direct, paths to the beach from the parking lot. Two range markers are located in the sand dunes, approximately 330 feet (100 meters) east of the southeastern corner of this parking lot. The shoreward post has a blue square on top while the seaward

post has a yellow triangle. Divers and snorkelers can navigate to the reef by keeping these posts lined up as they surface swim out. The surf can be high at times, so divers should be careful entering and exiting the water with their gear. Divers and snorkelers require a diver down flag while in the water at

this site. There are public restrooms in the small building located between the two parking lots.

between 12 and 15 pairs of modules during their visit.

Description

Escambia County deployed this set of 38 reef modules in 2011. The reef modules are the standard design for dive and snorkel reefs along this stretch of coast, featuring a central post that supports multiple limestone and concrete discs. The line of paired modules, which are approximately 25 feet (7.5 meters) apart, starts at about 500 feet (150 meters) from shore and extends to about 950 feet (287 meters) from shore. The first few pairs of modules are often buried by the shifting sandbar so divers and snorkelers may only see

The tops of the modules are at, or below, a depth of 6 feet (1.8 meters) to avoid impacting navigation. The depth of the seafloor varies based on the location of the sandbar but is generally 12 feet (3.5meters) close to shore and around 15 feet (4.5 meters) deep at the final set of modules. This site supports a variety of reef creatures, including damselfish, blennies and juvenile grouper and snapper. Flounder and stingrays are often seen in the sand, while sea turtles regularly cruise through the area.

Sighting poles

500ft / 152m

Buried modules

3.5m

14 Avocet

Difficulty ● ● ●
Current ● ● ○
Depth ● ● ●
Reef ★★☆
Fauna ★★☆

Pensacola

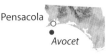

Avocet

Access 🚤 about 25mi (40km) south of
Pensacola Pass

Level Advanced

Location
Pensacola, Escambia County
GPS 29°58.411'N, 87°12.621'W

Getting there
Avocet is one of the deeper, offshore dive sites accessible through the Pensacola Pass. It is located to the west of the popular *Antares* and *Oriskany* wrecks. These three sites are far enough out to sea that access is usually limited to local charter boats and boat operators who have experience handling the changing weather of the Gulf of Mexico. There are no surface mooring buoys at this site, so operators typically tie in to the wreck itself or anchor in the sand nearby.

Access
This wreck is recommended for advanced divers due to its depth. The small section of superstructure still standing tops out at 96 feet (29.5 meters) deep, which means most of the wreck sits below 100 feet (30.5 meter). The site is best reached via one of the dive shops operating out of the Pensacola Pass, although it is well within reach of operators from coastal Alabama and even those operating out of Destin East Pass to the east.

Description
Avocet is a 247-foot (76-meter) long clamshell dredger that sits on a sandy seafloor at a depth of 114 feet (35 meters). Not much is known about the massive dredge except that she was originally built in 1943 and was sunk as an artificial reef in May 1991. At one point, her multi-level structure topped out at a depth of 60 feet (18.5 meters), but the many decades spent underwater has collapsed her upper levels. The debris field that sits to the south of the wreck is all that remains of that upper structure. Despite her degraded state, Avocet is still considered one of the best dives in the area due to her size and depth.

The bulk of her 55-foot (16.5-meter) wide main deck remains largely intact, although a crack

runs across her beam near the stern. The crack is up to 7 feet (2 meters) wide near the port side and narrows to just a few inches on the starboard side. The main deck sits at a depth of 107 feet (32.5 meters) and sports a mix of debris, holes and twisted poles that are still anchored to it. The bow is marked by a raised deck and angled frame that sticks out over the bow.

The dredge's massive fore and aft holds are open and accessible to divers. They are deep and some contain debris that could constitute an entanglement risk, so divers should proceed with caution. The forward holds are partly covered by what is left of the upper level. The center part of the wreck is full of partial walls, support studs and

RELAX & RECHARGE

Choice is on the menu at **The Tin Cow** located at 102 South Palafox Place in Pensacola. They have a "crazy amount" of burgers because customers can build their own from the wide range of customizable options, starting with the meat, which includes wild boar, venison, tuna, chicken and lamb, among others. You can go the "made to order" route or opt for one of their signature burgers, which includes the half pound Spam Monster, complete with egg and bacon, and the Cowboy, which combines bison and pulled pork. A large selection of canned craft beer, cocktails and their award winning spiked and regular milkshakes, which are essentially a decadent dessert in a glass, will keep you refreshed. There is a "mini moo" menu for kids, and happy hour for adults (Monday to Friday from 3pm to 6pm) that includes half-off canned beers and a quarter-off all starters. There are also specialty nights all week long, like Whiskey & Wings Wednesday, which is a must if you are a fan of either… or both! Visit: **Thetincow.com.**

incomplete upper decking that provides shelter to a variety of fish species and gives divers with good trim and buoyancy control plenty to explore.

Divers are almost guaranteed to see plenty of jacks and snapper schooling around this deep, offshore wreck. Grey, cubera and lane snapper are common, while almaco jacks and greater amberjacks of impressive size are also regularly encountered, which makes this site very popular with spearfishers. African pompanos and rainbow runners are also frequently seen in the waters above the artificial reef, while bull sharks occasionally patrol the area just off the wreck. Closer in to the wreck itself, divers will see blue and French angelfish, sergeant majors, and even a spotted moray eel that is often seen in the debris-filled crack that divides the wreck into unequal parts. This is also a popular spot for lionfish, with divers regularly collecting dozens of these invasive creatures on each dive.

Avocet supports a variety of reef fish, including angelfish, despite having lost its upper structure.

Route

The depth of this site means there is not a lot of bottom time for divers to explore the entire wreck. The debris field is interesting enough, but given it mostly tops out at 110 feet (33.5 meters) divers are likely to use up a lot of bottom time if they are not careful. For that reason, most divers start out on the main deck, touring the holds and weaving in and out of the structure that remains standing. There is plenty to explore despite her degraded state. Most divers like to visit this site on successive dives after a suitable

107ft
32.5m

Stern

L

37

75

115ft
35m

Name:	*Avocet*	**Last owner:**	n/a
Type:	Clamshell dredge	**Sunk:**	May 15, 1991
Previous names:	n/a		
Length:	247ft (76m)		
Tonnage:	2,640grt		
Construction:	1943		

96ft
29m

107ft
32.5m

75

37

Stern

115ft
35m

surface interval. That strategy is the best way to
fully experience this site.

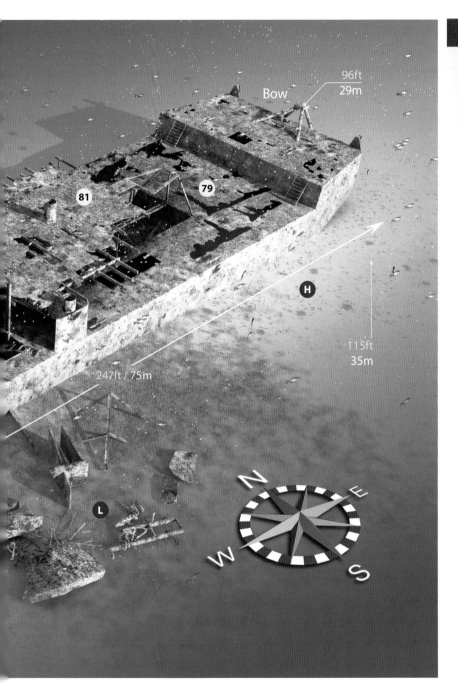

Bow

96ft
29m

81

79

H

115ft
35m

247ft / 75m

L

N
E
W
S

Other species commonly found
at this site:

1   3   4   18   35   38   54   62   63

80   82   87   88   92

Pete Tide II

Difficulty	●	●	○
Current	●	●	○
Depth	●	●	○
Reef	★	☆	☆
Fauna	★	★	☆

Pensacola

Pete Tide II

Access 🚤 about 13mi (21km) southeast of Pensacola Pass

Level Open Water

Location

Pensacola, Escambia County
GPS 30°08.775'N, 87°14.052'W

Getting there

Pete Tide II is considered a mid-shore dive site among local operators, as it is located closer to shore than the distant sites of *Oriskany*, *Antares* and *Avocet*. Even so, it is still far enough out to sea that access is generally limited to local charter boats or boat operators who have experience handling the changing weather of the Gulf of Mexico. There are no surface mooring buoys at this site, so operators typically tie in to the wreck itself or anchor in the sand nearby.

Access

This wreck is accessible to a wide range of divers. Located in line with Pensacola Pass and the offshore dive sites, *Pete Tide II* makes for a good second dive. It is best reached via one of the dive shops operating out of the Pensacola Pass, although it is well within reach of operators from coastal Alabama and even those operating out of Destin East Pass to the east.

Description

Pete Tide II had a career servicing oil fields in the Gulf of Mexico that lasted two decades. Measuring 165 feet (50.5 meters) in length, she was originally built in 1973 by Halter Marine in Lockport, Louisiana. She was designed as an AHTS, or anchor-handling tug supply vessel.

Lureen Ferretti ©

A diver swims across a wreck as a school of fish passes by.

SAFETY TIP ⓘ

Like most artificial reefs, *Pete Tide II* was thoroughly prepped before sinking, which involved the removal of objects that could pose a danger to recreational SCUBA divers, such as electrical wiring, which represents an entanglement risk, and doors and porthole covers, which could close and trap a diver inside a room. Despite this preparation work, wrecks can still be potentially dangerous to explore. As they age, wrecks naturally start to collapse, producing sharp edges and loose elements. Artificial reefs are also popular for fishing and, as a result, can become covered in monofilament line and torn sections of netting that can be particularly hard for divers to see. Divers should proceed with extreme caution when exploring a shipwreck. Do not take unnecessary risks, always dive with a buddy, and consider bringing a dive knife or other cutting device in case of entanglement. Professional training can vastly improve safety, so consider taking a wreck specialty course with a local dive operator.

These sturdy boats were designed to tow large oil rigs out to their drilling locations in the Gulf, as well as providing other supply services.

She was deployed as an artificial reef in May 1993 and is one of the original members of the Florida Panhandle Shipwreck Trail. The trail was established in 2012 and helped popularize the many artificial reefs available for divers in the region.

Pete Tide II is in excellent shape despite her many years underwater. She is well colonized with soft corals, sponges and algae, and hosts a variety of reef fish. She sits upright on a sandy bottom at a depth of 102 feet (31 meters), with the top of her wheelhouse reaching 62 feet (19 meters). She offers divers three deck levels to explore as well as three large holds that sit open and accessible in the main deck area toward the stern. There are penetration opportunities for those divers with experience in overhead environments, while the open wheelhouse is accessible to those with good buoyancy control and adequate trim.

Visitors to this site are almost guaranteed to see schools of Atlantic spadefish swarming around the wreck. Large snapper, including red and lane snapper, are also common, as are barracuda and king mackerel in the waters above the wreck. Looking more closely at the wreck itself, divers are likely to see angelfish, particularly blue angelfish, as well as cocoa damselfish, sharpnose puffers and even spotfin butterflyfish.

Route

Divers commonly start their exploration in the holds or the outer hull of the wreck. After circling the artificial reef, there is plenty to check out along the main deck and in the three levels of structure at the bow. Those divers with penetration experience can make their way into the superstructure at either the main deck level or the level of the first deck. The wheelhouse itself is relatively open and provides swim-through opportunities for divers. However, there are wires hanging down from the ceiling and other entanglement risks, so divers should proceed with caution.

PETE TIDE II

92ft
28m

82ft
25m

Stern

C

1

35

102ft
31m

165ft / 50.5m

N
E
W
S

Name:	*Pete Tide II*	**Construction:**	Halter Marine, Rockport, LA, 1973
Type:	Oilfield tug		
Previous names:	n/a	**Last owner:**	Tidewater Resources, Inc
Length:	165ft (50.5m)	**Sunk:**	May 23, 1993
Tonnage:	278grt		

68ft
21m

76ft
23m

86

88

69

Bow

102ft
31m

Other species commonly found
at this site:

J   **2**   **3**   **9**   **12**   **13**   **19**   **32**   **38**

40   **45**   **54**   **56**   **87**

Ocean Wind

Pensacola

Ocean Wind

Difficulty	● ● ○		
Current	● ○ ○		
Depth	● ● ○		
Reef	★★☆		
Fauna	★★★		

Access 🚤 about 11.5mi (18.5km) southeast of Pensacola Pass

Level Open Water

Location
Pensacola, Escambia County
GPS 30°10.995′N, 87°12.017′W

Getting there
Given the distance from shore, *Ocean Wind* should only be visited by operators and private vessels with experience operating in the Gulf. There are no surface mooring buoys at this site, so operators typically tie in to the wreck or anchor in the sand nearby.

Access
Due to its relatively shallow depth, the wreck is accessible to most divers. It is relatively close to the pass and makes for a good second dive for boats on their way back home after diving one of the deeper sites farther off shore. It is best reached via one of the dive shops operating out of the Pensacola Pass, although it is well within reach of operators from coastal Alabama and even those operating out of Destin East Pass to the east.

Description
Little is known about *Ocean Wind* and her history as a utility tugboat. Ironically, she was tasked with towing many of the vessels that were deployed as artificial reefs in the surrounding area. It is therefore fitting that she joined them on the sandy seafloor.

As with many of the tugs deployed in the northeastern Gulf of Mexico, *Ocean Wind* is in excellent shape. She has already been colonized by soft corals, sponges and algae, although some of the white coloration on her wheelhouse and superstructure can still be seen in patches. She sits upright on a sandy bottom at a depth between 82 and 84 feet (25 and 25.5 meters). She has a slight list to port but remains mostly intact with plenty of penetration opportunities. And at just 87 feet (26.5 meters) in length, divers have plenty of bottom time to explore the wreck before returning to the surface.

Divers looking to enter the wheelhouse area may need to ask permission first from the resident goliath grouper who is often spotted here.

Above the wreck, divers will likely encounter a typical assortment of jacks, snapper and reef fish, including patrolling barracuda. Closer to the wreck structure, whitespotted soapfish, sharpnose puffers and a variety of damselfish species can be seen defending territories or warily watching divers as they swim by.

SAFETY TIP

Goliath grouper are often found on the wreck of the *Ocean Wind*. While the species is not generally considered aggressive and is usually quite tolerant of divers, it is known to exhibit territorial behavior near its preferred shelter. A cornered goliath grouper may initially warn an approaching diver by producing a loud "booming" sound with its swim bladder and surrounding muscles. This can be startling to an unsuspecting diver. Additional threat displays consist of opening the mouth wide and shaking the body. As a last resort, a threatened Goliath grouper may charge a diver, which can result in serious injury. If you plan to penetrate a wreck, it is often wise to peek inside before fully entering to ensure that you are not blocking the escape route of a large reef fish.

Goliath grouper are regularly seen on specific wrecks in the region, including in *Ocean Wind*'s wheelhouse.

DID YOU KNOW?

Tugboats make excellent artificial reefs because they are structurally robust enough to push and pull much larger ships. As a result, these vessels can withstand the ravages of being underwater for prolonged periods of time. While tugboats often lack the exciting backstories of their larger peers – think dramatic drug busts for a coastal freighters or wartime service for military vessels – they still provide excellent habitat for reef creatures.

59ft
18m

80

64

70ft
21.5m

69

Bow

82ft
25m

Route

As a relatively small artificial reef, divers have free range when it comes to choosing a route that will help them fully explore *Ocean Wind*. Most divers start by exploring the main deck and the hull of the vessel before exploring the openings in the middle of the ship. There are plenty of penetration access points for divers with experience in overhead environments. The intact wheelhouse is generally one of the last areas that divers visit before touring the wreck's upper level.

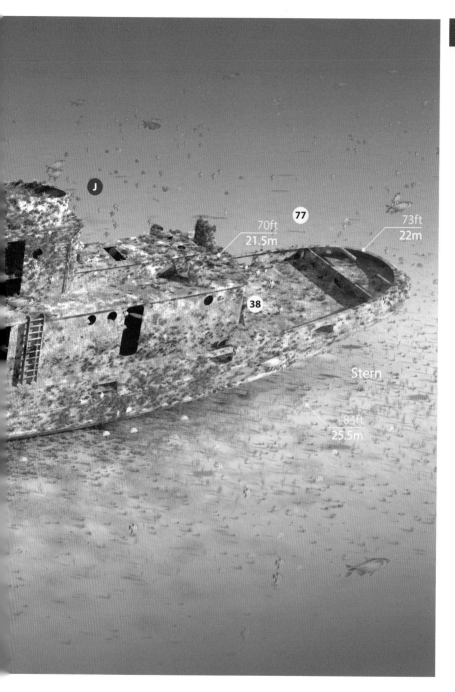

70ft
21.5m

73ft
22m

38

Stern

84ft
25.5m

Name:	Ocean Wind	Last owner:	n/a
Type:	Utility tugboat	Sunk:	Jan 12, 2016
Previous names:	n/a		
Length:	87ft (26.5m)		
Tonnage:	141grt		
Construction:	n/a		

73ft
22m

70ft
21.5m

77

38

Stern

70ft
21.5m

59ft
18m

80

64

69

J

Bow

82ft
25m

84ft
25.5m

Other species commonly found at this site:

6   8   11   15   19   20   21   23   30

33   43   56   78   81

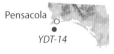

			Pensacola
Difficulty	● ● ○		
Current	● ● ○		YDT-14
Depth	● ● ○		
Reef	★★★☆		
Fauna	★☆☆		

Access 🚤 about 18.5mi (29.5km) southeast of Pensacola Pass

Level Open Water

Location
Pensacola, Escambia County
GPS 30°05.330'N, 87°09.640'W

Getting there
YDT-14 is considered an offshore dive site among local operators, even though it is located closer to the pass than the *Oriskany*, *Antares* and *Avocet* wrecks. It is far enough out in the Gulf that access is generally limited to local charter boats or boat operators who have experience handling the changing weather of the Gulf of Mexico. There are no surface mooring buoys at this site, so operators typically tie in to the wreck itself or anchor in the sand nearby.

Access
This wreck is accessible to most divers. However, given deck level is around 85 feet (26 meters), it is perhaps best suited to divers with deep diving experience. YDT-14 is best reached via one of the dive shops operating out of the Pensacola Pass, although it is well within reach of operators from coastal Alabama and even those operating out of Destin East Pass.

Description
YDT-14 was a U.S. Navy Yard Diving Tender (YDT) built during World War II. Originally designated YF-294, she was part of a series of "covered lighter, self-propelled" vessels used by the Navy in a supporting role during the war. "Lighters," as they are sometimes known, are basically barges used to carry cargo and other materials, and YFs were a design that could move under their own power. Historical records suggest YF-294 played a role as an inter-island supply vessel in the Caribbean during World War II as part of the 10th Naval District. She was stationed at various times in San Juan Harbor, Key West and Norfolk Harbor.

After the war, she was transferred to Norfolk and the 5th Naval District. In 1965 she was renamed *Phoebus*, before being redesignated YDT-14 and assigned to the Washington, D.C.-

based U.S. Navy Diving and Salvage Training Center in 1974. In 1980, she relocated to Panama City, Florida, along with the Training Center. She remained in the region until she was decommissioned in 1980. The Escambia County artificial reef program acquired her and eventually deployed her as an artificial reef in April 2000 along with her sister ship, YDT-15. The latter sits over 500 feet (150 meters) to the southeast of YDT-14 although the two are rarely explored on the same dive.

YDT-14 is one of the original members of the popular Florida Panhandle Shipwreck Trail and remains in excellent condition. Her bow faces south and is tilted upwards so that it sits slightly higher than her stern. The deck is just a few feet above the sandy seafloor, while the wheelhouse is largely intact, topping out at 69 feet (21 meters). YDT-14 offers divers two main swim-throughs from the back deck through to the front deck on either side of her superstructure. These spaces are mostly clear, although divers should watch out for potential entanglements from the debris that is present. The main cargo hold is open and accessible, as is the bridge.

The site hosts a variety of reef fish, including barracuda, snapper and butterflyfish. Amberjacks and Atlantic spadefish are often seen schooling above the wreck, while angelfish patrol the deck among a scattering of territorial damselfish. Divers often see grouper here as well, including gag and scamp.

Route

Divers commonly start their exploration at the deepest point, which is the stern, choosing to head toward the bow along the outside of the hull

Striped burrfish are found throughout many of the sites along the coast of Northwest Florida.

David Bailey ©

RELAX & RECHARGE

The **original McGuire's Irish Pub & Brewery** opened in Pensacola (600 E Gregory St) in 1977. An additional location, just east of the Destin Bridge (29 Harbor Boulevard), opened nearly 20 years later, in 1996. Together, these establishments have become favorites for both locals and visitors alike. They are so popular, you will probably need to get on the waiting list, but it is worth it. The menu includes seafood specialties such as tuna steaks, mahi mahi, and ale-battered shrimp. There are pasta dishes, killer steaks and chops, and 29 different types of burger. Even the appetizers are talking points: the 18 cent Senate Bean Soup is a must and is still made using the same recipe as it was a century ago in Washington DC – and sold at the same price!

McGuire's even serves classic Irish Boxtys – a traditional Irish potato pancake whose recipe certainly predates that of the bean soup. The beer at McGuire's is brewed on site and ranges from fine ale's to porters and stouts. They have rotating seasonals, which may include a raspberry wheat ale, Octoberfest, Hefeweizen and a popular Christmas ale, to name just a few. Billed as the oldest brewery in Florida, they love to give tours and will even provide yeast samples to budding homebrewers who visit. The Destin location is paired with a pizzeria called **Vinny McGuire's** where you can build your own pizza from a range of classic and gourmet toppings that include smoked prime rib, Cajun sausage, meatballs and prosciutto. Visit: **Mcguiresirishpub.com** and **Vinnymcguires.com.**

85ft
26m

88

38

73ft
22m

78ft
24m

Bow

92ft
28m

or through the swim-throughs located on either side of the superstructure. After exploring the main cargo hold and the raised bow area, divers often return to the superstructure to explore the enclosed spaces there. The bridge is intact, allowing divers with good buoyancy control to enter the wheelhouse and look out through the bridge's windows. From here, divers can complete their dive by exploring the top of the main structure before heading to the surface.

Name:	YDT-14	**Construction:**	Eerie Concrete & Steep
Type:	Yard Diving Tender		Supply, Eerie, PA 1942
Previous names:	Phoebus, YF-294	**Last owner:**	U.S. Navy
Length:	132ft (40m)	**Sunk:**	April 1, 2000
Tonnage:	300grt		

80

80ft
24.5m

85ft
26m

72

Stern

92ft
28m

Other species commonly found
at this site:

I **3** **5** **9** **12** **19** **27** **42** **53**

54 **59** **63** **69** **86**

Antares

Pensacola

Difficulty ● ● ●
Current ● ● ○
Depth ● ● ●
Reef ★★☆
Fauna ★★★

Antares

Access 🚤 about 23.5mi (38km) southeast of Pensacola Pass

Level Advanced

Location
Pensacola, Escambia County
GPS 30°00.594'N, 87°07.775'W

Getting there
Antares is considered an offshore dive site among local operators, as it is located between the *Oriskany* and the *Avocet,* out in the deeper waters off Pensacola Pass. As a result, access is typically limited to local charter boats or boat operators who have experience handling the changing weather of the Gulf of Mexico. There are no surface mooring buoys to tie to, so operators typically tie in to the wreck or drop anchor in the sand.

Access
The wreck is accessible to advanced divers with experience diving at depth. The site is best reached via one of the dive shops operating out of the Pensacola Pass, although it is within reach of operators from coastal Alabama and even those operating out of Destin East Pass to the east.

Description
Antares was a massive cargo freighter deployed as an artificial reef in September 1995. Originally measuring 387 feet (118 meters) in length and displacing 4,258 tons, she was built in 1968 by Spanish shipbuilder Euskalduna de Construcción Naval, in Bilbao and christened *Mirenchu* at the time of her launch. She was the second vessel built for Spanish shipping company Clemente Campos to carry that name. The first was half the size and built nine years earlier. The smaller *Mirenchu* was lost at sea in 1986 after her cargo shifted in a storm and the vessel sank before authorities could stabilize her, with the loss of all crew members.

Antares had its own fraught history, although none of her crew perished. In 1972, she was sold to another Spanish shipping company, Maritima Del Norte, and renamed *Sierra Jara.* She was resold in 1980 to Panama-based Ferilpis Shipping, reflagged and renamed *Acmi*. A year later, she ran aground in the Berbice River in Guyana, allegedly due to confusion around the local tidal schedule. The accident caused extensive damage to her hull and after she was refloated and towed to the Dominican Republic, she was deemed a total loss.

Her story does not end there, however. She was repaired, resold to Altair Maritime and renamed *Altair I* in 1983. She changed names again in 1991 to *Galazio Kyma*, but only lasted one year with that name before her final name change to *Antares*. Even that did not last long, as she was decommissioned just a year later, in 1993. Acquired by the Escambia County artificial reef program, she was deployed at a depth of 130 feet (39.5 meters) as an artificial reef on September 27, 1995 – just one week ahead of the arrival of a major hurricane.

Hurricane Opal made landfall near Pensacola on October 4, 1995. A Category 4 hurricane as she transited the Gulf of Mexico, Opal thankfully weakened to a Category 2 hurricane just before making landfall. Even so, she packed enough punch to cause major damage to the newly deployed *Antares* reef. The superstructure held its own against the currents, but the hull broke into large pieces that now lie scattered around the site. Since that initial damage, the *Antares* superstructure has further deteriorated, losing a large portion of the port side to the debris field that surrounds her. Despite lying in many pieces, *Antares* remains a popular dive site with locals and visitors alike.

The highest point of the site is the starboard corner of the bow section lying on its port side at the northern end of the site. The bow reaches a depth of 94 feet (28.5 meters) with the sandy seafloor at around 120 feet (36.5 meters). The bottom is deeper in the middle of the site, closer to the superstructure, where it reaches 130 feet (39.5 meters). The large difference in depth profile is due to sand having accumulated over time on one side of the keel section and not the other.

The site itself is highly complex and offers plenty for divers to explore, although at this depth, there is limited bottom time. The sheer size of the hull pieces, superstructure and intact keel section will make a diver feel small by comparison. The site supports a wide array of large reef species, including bull sharks, large snapper and even a resident goliath grouper than can often be seen in the bridge section of the superstructure. Amberjacks, spadefish and smaller grouper are also regular visitors to the site.

Route

The wreck is large enough that it is unlikely divers will be able to properly explore the whole site before running out of bottom time. *Antares* is worth taking the necessary time to fully explore, even if that means diving it more than once. Most dive boats will anchor at the southern end of the site where the superstructure, stern section and large engine provide easy reference points for navigation. From there, many divers choose to follow the keel section north to where it is covered by a section of the collapsed starboard hull.

Bull sharks are commonly seen patrolling the *Antares* wreck.

Fiona Ayerst/Shutterstock ©

116ft
35m

120ft
36.5m

H

94ft
28.5m

C

63

Bow

Continuing north will take divers toward the bow section, where they can turn southwest and make their way back toward the superstructure sections by navigating along the large section of portside hull that marks the western edge of the site. If time remains, divers can continue to the eastern edge of the site, with the large starboard hull section that collapsed outwards.

Stern

108ft
33m

64

39

410ft 125m

130ft
39.5m

40

Name:	Antares	**Construction:**	Euskalduna de Construcción
Type:	Cargo freighter		Naval, Bilbao, Spain, 1968
Previous names:	Mirenchu, Sierra Jara,	**Last owner:**	n/a
	Acmi, Altair I, Galazio Kyma	**Sunk:**	September 27, 1995
Length:	387ft (118m)		
Tonnage:	4,258grt		

64

39

106ft
32.5m

Engine

Stern

130ft
39.5m

130ft
39.5m

40

108ft
33m

115ft
35m

C

94ft
28.5m

63

Bow

120ft
36.5m

H

116ft
35m

117ft
35.5m

N

W

E

S

Other species commonly found at this site:

L   1   4   9   13   37   41   47   48

52   62   79   85   86

Oriskany

Difficulty	●	●	●
Current	●	●	○
Depth	●	●	●
Reef	★	★	★
Fauna	★	★	★

Pensacola

Oriskany

Access 🚤 about 26mi (42km) southeast of Pensacola Pass

Level Advanced

Location
Pensacola, Escambia County
GPS 30°02.569'N, 87°00.399'W

Getting there
Oriskany is far enough away from shore that access is generally limited to local charter boats or boat operators who have enough experience in handling the changing weather of the Gulf of Mexico to safely navigate that far from land. There are no surface mooring buoys on this site, so operators typically tie in to the wreck itself or, when the current is low, they may drop divers into the water while holding position near the wreck without anchoring or tying in.

Access
Oriskany is best accessed by advanced divers and technical divers because the shallowest part of the wreck is 81 feet (24.5 meters) and descends to a depth of 212 feet (64.5 meters) on the sandy seafloor. Even the flight deck of the massive aircraft carrier sits outside of recreational SCUBA limits, at 146 feet (44.5 meters) deep. The carrier's conning tower, sometimes referred to as the "island," is the most accessible part of the wreck for divers and is consequently the most explored.

Description
Oriskany is the largest artificial reef in the world – some call her the "Great Carrier Reef." Originally a 911-foot (278-meter) aircraft carrier, *Oriskany* was sent to the bottom on May 17, 2006 with the help of 26 charges and $19 million USD in funding. Her deployment as an artificial reef in Northwest Florida capped off an illustrious career that began in the dockyards of New York in May 1944. Originally designed as an Essex-class aircraft carrier, the U.S. Navy changed its plans for the *USS Oriskany* when World War II ended, and the vessel was just 85% complete. Refitted with upgrades to help her handle the new era of jet fighters, she was relaunched and commissioned in 1950.

After starting out in the Mediterranean, she was eventually sent to the Pacific (via the long route south rather than through the Panama Canal). Once there, she provided supported to the United Nations in the Korean War starting in 1952. In early 1957, she was back in the San Diego naval dockyards to receive more upgrades, including an angled

flight deck. After two years, she was recommissioned and redeployed to the eastern Pacific, eventually finding action in support of American forces during the Vietnam War in 1965.

A massive fire in October 1966 caused her to return to San Diego for repairs, but she was soon back in Vietnam, this time carrying navy pilot John McCain, the future senator and presidential candidate. In total, *USS Oriskany*

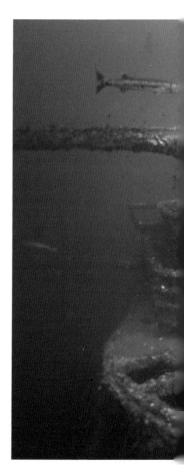

completed six tours in Vietnam, earning 10 battle stars for her service – in addition to the two she earned for her service in the Korean War.

After a few more upgrades and overhauls, as well as additional service in the Far East, *Oriskany* was ultimately decommissioned in 1976 due to budget cuts and old age. She was sold for scrap in 1995, although ultimately reclaimed by the Navy in 1997 and moved to Texas. In 2004, she was made available to the state of Florida for deployment as an artificial reef. And after being cleaned and prepared for sinking, she was sent to the bottom 26 miles (42 kilometers) off the coast of Pensacola. She became the marquee name on the Florida Panhandle Shipwreck Trail that launched in the region in 2012.

DID YOU KNOW?

Much time and effort went into figuring out how to sink *Oriskany*, as she was designed to be unsinkable. The decision was made to blow the ship's sea chests, which are the valves that allow the water to enter the ship's ballast tanks. Dozens of holes were cut between various tanks and chambers in the bowels of the ship to allow the water to pass throughout the structure and sink the vessel.

Approximately 500 pounds (230 kilograms) of C-4 explosives were placed at 22 locations and then detonated simultaneously to ensure the flooding occurred evenly and rapidly throughout the entire ship. Any miscalculation could have been disastrous and potentially sent *Oriskany* to the bottom on her side, putting the spectacular conning tower out of reach of all but technical divers. The ship sank stern first and took approximately 37 minutes to slip beneath the waves.

The iconic tower and bridge of the *Oriskany*.

Virgil Zetterlind ©

Stern

81ft
24.5m

146ft
44.5m

212ft
64.5m

N
W — E
S

The deployment originally targeted a depth of 130 feet (40 meters) for the flight deck, but over time, the wreck has gradually settled another 15 feet (5 meters) into the soft Gulf seafloor. Despite the depth, she is still one of the most popular diving sites in the region, if not the entire United States. The accessible conning tower offers divers the chance to explore the primary flight bridge, navigational bridge and Flag bridge, as well as multiple doorways, walkways and swim-throughs. Meanwhile, experienced technical divers can access the hangar bay via the escalator at the base

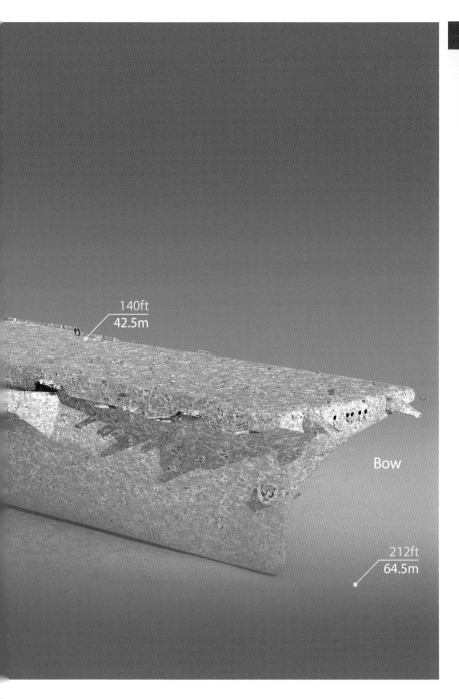

140ft
42.5m

Bow

212ft
64.5m

Name:	*USS Oriskany (CV-34)*	**Last owner:**	U.S. Navy
Type:	Essex-class aircraft carrier	**Sunk:**	May 17, 2006
Previous names:	n/a		
Length:	911ft (278m)		
Tonnage:	32,000grt		
Construction:	Brooklyn Navy Yard, NY, 1944		

of the conning tower, spending their dive time exploring the carrier's interior.

The wreck itself is in good shape, with the biggest change from her original condition taking place in 2009, when currents associated with Tropical Storm Ida caused the central section of the conning tower to collapse, creating a tall, narrow swim-through in the process. The complex structure of the wreck supports a wide array of large pelagic species. Large grouper, jacks, snapper and amberjacks frequent the conning tower, while sharks are often seen patrolling below the edge of the flight deck. Smaller

wrasses, blennies, angelfish and damselfish have also colonized the wreck. Divers are almost guaranteed to see large barracuda, jacks and other pelagics on *Oriskany,* and they may even spot the occasional whale shark or manta ray cruising by.

Route

The recommended dive route will depend on the currents and conditions. Most divers descend to the lowest point of their depth profile, which is generally not below the navigational bridge at a depth of 125 feet (38 meters). From there, they can circle the

84ft
25.5m

81ft
24.5m

83

107ft
32.5m

62

125ft
38m

146ft
44.5m

J

Access to the hangar bay
via the escalator
For experienced tech divers only

Enlarged area

Bow

Stern

conning tower, exploring the walkways that pass between its two sections, while watching out for debris and any entanglements in this space. The most common route continues as a spiral, gradually getting shallower in profile and encompassing the primary flight deck and the twisted remains of the exhaust funnel before reaching the observation platform that extends out over the flight deck. Bottom time is often limited on this dive, which is why many divers opt for nitrox.

Other species commonly found at this site:

4   6   11   15   16   29   30   53   61

64   81   85   87   92

Other Escambia County Sites

The following list represents other popular dive sites in Escambia County visited by local operators.

11 I-10 Bridge Rubble

GPS (#1) 30°06.750'N, 87°24.250'W
GPS (#2) 30°06.700'N, 87°25.300'W
GPS (#3) 30°06.700'N, 87°26.300'W
GPS (#4) 30°06.600'N, 87°27.500'W
GPS (#5) 30°06.600'N, 87°28.600'W
GPS (#6) 30°06.550'N, 87°29.550'W

Difficulty ● ● ○
Current ● ○ ○
Depth ● ● ○
Reef ★★☆
Fauna ★★☆

When Hurricane Ivan wrecked the I-10 bridge in 2004, the rubble from its demolition was spread across six sites in an east-west line starting at the border with Alabama. The resulting artificial reefs range in depth from 75 feet (23 meters) to 93 feet (28.5 meters), with the rubble rising to as high as 30 feet (9 meters) above the seabed.

13 Catherine

GPS 30°18.710'N, 87°15.940'W

Difficulty ● ○ ○
Current ● ● ○
Depth ● ○ ○
Reef ★☆☆
Fauna ★☆☆

This shallow wreck sits in 15 feet (4.5 meters) of water just over 1,000 feet (300 meters) from the beach opposite Fort Pickens. *Catherine* was originally a three-masted, wooden sailing ship built in Canada in 1869 with the name *Eliza*. She was sold to a Norwegian company and renamed *Catherine* just a few years before she ran aground in a storm just outside of Pensacola Pass in 1894. She is too far out in the Gulf to reach from shore. Parts of her hull are often visible but the shifting sands make it hard to predict what debris will be visible on any given day.

12 USS Massachusetts

GPS 30°17.795'N, 87°18.720'W

Difficulty ● ● ○
Current ● ● ●
Depth ● ○ ○
Reef ★☆☆
Fauna ★☆☆

USS Massachusetts was originally a 350-foot (107-meter) battleship first launched in 1893. She was sunk in less than 30 feet (9 meters) of water just outside of Pensacola Pass as part of a military target practice exercise in 1921. She is one of Florida's Underwater Archaeological Preserves, and she represents a challenging snorkel or dive due to her placement in the middle of the pass. Currents are often strong here and visibility is typically low.

15 Tug Born Again

GPS 30°08.222'N, 87°14.218'W

Difficulty ● ○ ○
Current ● ○ ○
Depth ● ○ ○
Reef ★★☆
Fauna ★★☆

This 65-foot (20-meter) tugboat sits at a depth of 95 feet (29 meters). Deployed as an artificial reef in 1991, her hold is full of metal pipes. She has started to deteriorate after multiple decades spent underwater, but she remains an interesting reef to explore.

17 LCM and Heron

GPS 30°08.187'N, 87°13.684'W

Difficulty ● ○ ○
Current ● ● ○
Depth ● ● ○
Reef ★☆☆
Fauna ★★☆

These two wrecks originally sat one on top of the other when they were first deployed in 1990. The 56-foot (17-meter) *LCM* (landing craft mechanized) vessel known as *Elsie* now sits next to the 53-foot (16-meter) steel tugboat called the *Heron* (or *Herron*) at a depth of 92 feet (28 meters). *Elsie* has deteriorated over the years, while the *Heron*'s superstructure has suffered damage from various hurricanes.

18 Knicklebine Barge

GPS 30°01.970'N, 87°11.495'W

Difficulty ● ● ○
Current ● ● ○
Depth ● ● ●
Reef ★★☆
Fauna ★☆☆

This 117-foot (35.5-meter) barge sits at a depth of 122 feet (37 meters). A total of 14 pieces of concrete ballast are stacked on top of the barge to provide it with some structure.

19 San Pablo (aka the "Russian Freighter")

GPS 30°11.333'N, 87°13.070'W

Difficulty ● ● ○
Current ● ○ ○
Depth ● ● ○
Reef ★★☆
Fauna ★★☆

A member of the Florida Panhandle Shipwreck Trail, *San Pablo* was not actually a Russian freighter as its nickname implies. She was a Panamanian-flagged transport ship originally torpedoed by a German U-boat in Costa Rica in 1942. She was refloated and towed to Panama City in 1943. What is left of the 315-foot (96-meter) cargo ship now sits at a depth of 84 feet (25.5 meters) just off the coast of Pensacola.

21 Lane Gilchrest Reef

GPS 30°17.467'N, 87°13.773'W

Difficulty ● ○ ○
Current ● ○ ○
Depth ● ○ ○
Reef ★★☆
Fauna ★★☆

This artificial reef consists of 8,000 tons of concrete rubble from the Gulf Breeze fishing bridge spread across 60 acres of seafloor. It has a maximum depth of 50 feet (15 meters).

22 Joe Patti Memorial Reef

GPS 30°17.329'N, 87°13.755'W

Difficulty ● ○ ○
Current ● ○ ○
Depth ● ○ ○
Reef ★★☆
Fauna ★☆☆

This 175-foot (53.5-meter) barge was deployed in 50 feet (15 meters) of water in July 2013. She was decked out with 120 pieces of metal artwork before she was deployed as a memorial reef to honor the Patti family.

23 Three Coal Barges

GPS 30°17.473'N, 87°13.278'W

Difficulty ● ○ ○
Current ● ○ ○
Depth ● ○ ○
Reef ★☆☆
Fauna ★★☆

These three barges were purposefully sunk in 50 feet (15 meters) of water in 1972. The barges have not held up well during their time underwater, and a new round of concrete rubble has since been deployed in the middle of the site to help supplement it. This site was an early addition to the Florida Panhandle Shipwreck Trail.

25 YDT-15

GPS 30°05.309'N, 87°09.622'W

Difficulty ● ● ○
Current ● ● ○
Depth ● ● ○
Reef ★☆☆
Fauna ★☆☆

Located just 500 feet from her sister ship, *YDT-14* (see pg 88), this Navy diving tender sits at a depth of almost 90 feet (27.5 meters).

She has deteriorated more than her sister ship, however, having suffered extensive damage to her superstructure.

26 Tex Edwards Barge

GPS 30°16.138'N, 87°10.157'W

Difficulty ● ○ ○
Current ● ○ ○
Depth ● ● ○
Reef ★☆☆
Fauna ★☆☆

This barge sits at a depth of 75 feet (23 meters). It has settled into the sandy seafloor since it was first deployed in 1982, although it still offers plenty for divers to explore and supports a variety of marine life.

Alex Fogg – Destin-Fort Walton Beach ©

27 Joseph L. Meek Liberty Ship

GPS 30°16.384'N, 87°09.574'W

Difficulty ● ● ○
Current ● ○ ○
Depth ● ● ○
Reef ★★☆☆
Fauna ★★☆

One of multiple Liberty Ships deployed as artificial reefs across the region in the 1970s, the *Joseph L Meek Liberty Ship* sits at a depth of 95 feet (29 meters). Only the hull and lower deck remain from this mass-produced vessel that was a key part of the Allied wartime trans-Atlantic supply chain.

Many tanks have been deployed as artificial reefs across Northwest Florida.

29 Tenneco Platform

GPS 29°59.713'N, 87°05.118'W

Difficulty ● ● ●
Current ● ● ○
Depth ● ● ●
Reef ★★☆
Fauna ★★★

An offshore site, this artificial reef is one of the original rigs-to-reef deployments. A deep site, this old oil rig platform bottoms out at a depth of 175 feet (53.5 meters). The reef attracts large snapper and jacks, which makes it a popular dive with spearfishers.

DID YOU KNOW? ❓

Converting old oil platforms to artificial reefs is not a new concept, it has been done over 420 times in the waters around the U.S. The Rigs-To-Reefs program, which is run by the U.S. Department of the Interior, is popular with both the oil and gas industry and the fishing industry. However, it generates mixed feelings among environmental organizations, some of whom simply see this as a way for oil and gas companies to reduce their decommissioning expenses, even though a percentage of the savings is sometimes donated by these companies to environmental initiatives.

30 Chevron Platform

GPS 30°04.244'N, 87°02.118'W

Difficulty ● ● ○
Current ● ● ○
Depth ● ● ●
Reef ★★☆
Fauna ★★☆

The Chevron Platform site features two oil rig jackets lying side by side at a depth of 137 feet. Deployed in 1993, these structures are great habitat for large fish species, including large red snapper and greater amberjacks.

SANTA ROSA COUNTY

Santa Rosa County does not have a pass, so there is less of a focus on diving than in the neighboring counties of Escambia and Okaloosa. Even so, there are still a handful of dive shops in the county, which often have boats that operate out of either the Pensacola or Destin East passes.

Despite the lack of pass, the county has collaborated with its neighbors to improve habitat and recreational opportunities through the deployment of artificial reefs in its waters. Santa Rosa participated in the Natural Resource Damage Assessment Early Restoration Phase III – Northwest Florida Artificial Reef Creation and Restoration Project that resulted in the deployment of more than 500 modules, weighing

over 1,400 tons, across 27 patch reef sites from late 2018 to 2019. These reefs, located about one mile (1.6 kilometers) off shore, complemented the artificial reefs deployed as shore-accessible dive and snorkeling sites on both the Gulf and Santa Rosa Sound sides of Navarre Beach. More information on these shore-accessible sites are included in the pages that follow.

Santa Rosa County also has its own Liberty Ship, the *Joseph E. Brown Liberty Ship*. This artificial reef was deployed in the late 1970s along with the Liberty Ships found in neighboring counties. In the pages that follow, you will find detailed information for the popular Gulf-side and sound-side artificial reefs off Navarre Beach.

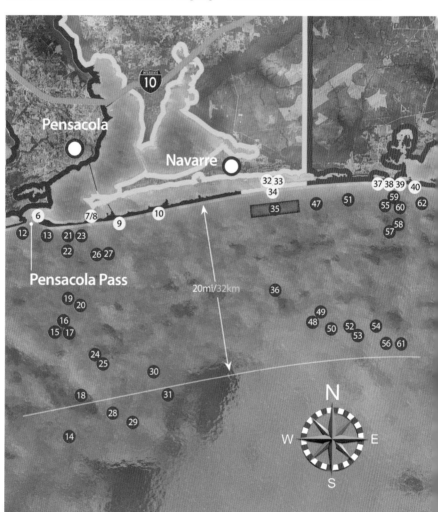

Santa Rosa County keeps an up-to-date list of all of its artificial reef sites online. To see if new reefs have been added since publication, please visit: **Navarrebeachmarinesanctuary.org**

Dive and snorkel sites

SANTA ROSA COUNTY

Other Santa Rosa County Sites

35 SR-27 Artificial Reef sites

SR-27 Patch Reef 1	30°21.402'N, 86°52.724'W
SR-27 Patch Reef 2	30°21.410'N, 86°52.582'W
SR-27 Patch Reef 3	30°21.442'N, 86°52.443'W
SR-27 Patch Reef 4	30°21.495'N, 86°51.984'W
SR-27 Patch Reef 5	30°21.515'N, 86°51.845'W
SR-27 Patch Reef 6	30°21.534'N, 86°51.704'W
SR-27 Patch Reef 7	30°21.555'N, 86°51.562'W
SR-27 Patch Reef 8	30°21.630'N, 86°51.033'W
SR-27 Patch Reef 9	30°21.650'N, 86°50.893'W
SR-27 Patch Reef 10	30°21.670'N, 86°50.751'W
SR-27 Patch Reef 11	30°21.267'N, 86°52.699'W
SR-27 Patch Reef 12	30°21.287'N, 86°52.559'W
SR-27 Patch Reef 15	30°21.376'N, 86°51.930'W
SR-27 Patch Reef 16	30°21.398'N, 86°51.789'W
SR-27 Patch Reef 17	30°21.418'N, 86°51.649'W
SR-27 Patch Reef 18	30°21.438'N, 86°51.508'W
SR-27 Patch Reef 19	30°21.457'N, 86°51.367'W
SR-27 Patch Reef 20	30°21.529'N, 86°50.870'W
SR-27 Patch Reef 21	30°21.549'N, 86°50.729'W
SR-27 Patch Reef 22	30°21.157'N, 86°52.678'W
SR-27 Patch Reef 23	30°21.164'N, 86°52.535'W
SR-27 Patch Reef 24	30°21.198'N, 86°52.398'W
SR-27 Patch Reef 25	30°21.257'N, 86°51.887'W
SR-27 Patch Reef 26	30°21.277'N, 86°51.748'W
SR-27 Patch Reef 27	30°21.297'N, 86°51.606'W
SR-27 Patch Reef 28	30°21.318'N, 86°51.466'W
SR-27 Patch Reef 29	30°21.427'N, 86°50.706'W

Difficulty	● ○ ○
Current	● ○ ○
Depth	● ● ○
Reef	★☆☆
Fauna	★★☆

These 27 patch reefs range in depth from 60 to 70 feet (18.5 to 21.5 meters) and rise from the seabed between 8 and 18 feet (2.5 or 5.5 meters) depending on the type of reef module deployed. Most sites feature more than one module and support a variety of reef life.

36 Joseph E. Brown Liberty Ship (aka Navarre Liberty Ship)

GPS 30°12.777'N, 86°49.327'W

Difficulty	● ● ○
Current	● ○ ○
Depth	● ● ○
Reef	★☆☆
Fauna	★★☆

Joseph E. Brown Liberty Ship (aka *Navarre Liberty Ship*) was one of the many Liberty Ships deployed as artificial reefs across all five Northwest Florida counties in the 1970s. She was named after a Georgia senator. The wreck now rests at a depth of 85 feet (26 meters). Only the hull and lower deck remain from this mass-produced 440-foot (134-meter) vessel that was a key part of the Allied wartime trans-Atlantic supply chain.

Navarre Sound-Side West Reef and East Reef

Difficulty ● ○ ○
Current ● ○ ○
Depth ● ○ ○
Reef ★☆☆
Fauna ★☆☆

Pensacola

Navarre
Sound-Side
East Reef and
West Reef

Access 🚙 about 32 mins from downtown
Pensacola
🏊 about 3 to 5 mins from shore

Level Open Water

Location
Navarre Beach, Santa Rosa County
GPS (West) 30°23.184′N, 86°51.514′W
(East) 30°23.117′N, 86°51.383′W

Getting there
From downtown Pensacola, head east on US-98 across the Pensacola Bay Bridge to Gulf Breeze. Once across the bridge, continue on US-98 for 19.7 miles (31.7 kilometers). The road will change from the Gulf Breeze Highway to the Navarre Beach Highway as it passes through Navarre. Turn right onto FL-399/Navarre Beach Causeway and cross the Santa Rosa Sound to reach the barrier island of Santa Rosa. At the four-way intersection, turn left into the Navarre

Santa Rosa Island

Beach Marine Park. West Reef is best accessed from Red Drum Pavilion, which is the first left after the park entrance. East Reef is farther along, and best accessed from the Sandpiper Pavilion, which involves following the main park road to the point where it curves north toward the sound.

Access

These sound-side reefs require a short walk from their respective parking lots to the beach. Both the East and West reefs are accessible to divers and snorkelers alike, but West Reef will likely be more interesting to divers as it is slightly deeper and larger than East Reef. Both reefs are clearly marked with large pylons at each corner. West Reef is located about 300 feet (91 meters) from shore, while East Reef is just 150 feet (45.5 meters) out. Visibility in the sound can be much lower than in the Gulf but currents are generally much milder. Divers and snorkelers must use a surface marker buoy while in the water.

Description

Santa Rosa County deployed these two reefs in May 2012. They both feature reef modules with central posts that support three limestone concrete discs at the top. West Reef features a total of 77 modules that bottom out at an average depth of 15 feet (4.5 meters). East Reef includes 28 modules with an average depth of 12 feet (3.5 meters). The modules are spaced roughly 10 feet apart, which makes them relatively easy to navigate through in the reduced visibility of the Sound. Divers and snorkelers commonly report seeing juvenile reef species at these sites, including sheepshead, grouper and mangrove snapper, as well as damselfish and blennies.

West Reef

Entrance

East Reef

P

P

N

W

E

S

34 Navarre Gulf-Side Reef

Pensacola

Navarre
Gulf-Side Reef

Difficulty	● ○ ○		
Current	● ○ ○		
Depth	● ○ ○		
Reef	★☆☆		
Fauna	★★☆		

Access — about 32 mins from downtown Pensacola
about 5 mins from shore

Level Open Water

Location
Navarre Beach, Santa Rosa County
GPS 30°22.758'N, 86°51.229'W

Getting there
From downtown Pensacola, head east on US-98 across the Pensacola Bay Bridge to Gulf Breeze. Once across the bridge, continue on US-98 for 19.7 miles (31.7 kilometers). The road will change from the Gulf Breeze Highway to the Navarre Beach Highway as it passes through Navarre. Turn right onto the FL-399/Navarre Beach Causeway and cross the sound onto the barrier island. At the four-way intersection, turn left into the Navarre Beach Marine Park. Follow

Posts

Four modules

Three modules

the main road for 0.4 miles (0.65 kilometers) and turn into the parking lot for the Sea Oak Pavilion – the third of three parking lots on the right.

Access

The easternmost boardwalk leads visitors down to the sandy beach directly in front of the where the Gulf-side snorkel reef is located. If visitors make their way to the beach via the main boardwalk, which passes by the restrooms, they will need to walk east about 150 feet (45 meters) along the beach to reach the snorkel reef. Four large posts anchored in the dunes mark the east and west boundaries of the snorkel reef. The reef modules start around 350 feet (107 meters) from the beach. There are no buoys located in the water. The surf can be high at times, so divers and snorkelers should be careful entering and exiting the water. A surface marker buoy is required by law while in the water.

Description

Santa Rosa County deployed the first phase of this reef in September 2012, which involved three rows of 10 reef modules spaced 20 feet (6 meters) apart and arranged in a rectangle extending 275 feet (84 meters) into the Gulf. The county expanded the reef in 2017, deploying an additional 48 modules in three rows of eight on either side of the original reef. The shallowest modules in the initial deployment are often buried by the sandbar that extends outward from the beach, so the county decided to eliminate the shallowest modules for their expansion plan. The uncovered modules bottom out at depths between 11 and 12.5 feet (3.5 and 4 meters) and all have at least 6 feet (1.8 meters) of clearance for navigation. Divers and snorkelers are likely to see damselfish, blennies, triggerfish and snapper at this site, while flounder and stingrays are often seen in the sand.

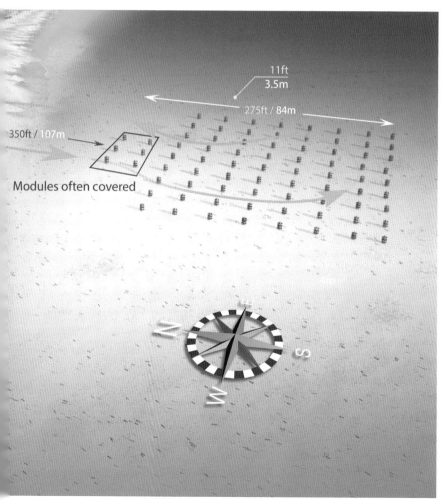

350ft / 107m

Modules often covered

11ft
3.5m

275ft / 84m

OKALOOSA COUNTY

Okaloosa County is home to the Destin-Fort Walton Beach area, which is one of the main population centers in Northwest Florida. It also features the Destin East Pass, which provides access to the Gulf of Mexico for the entire Choctawhatchee Bay, the eastern side of Santa Rosa County and all of Okaloosa and Walton counties. There are many dive operators based in Destin-Fort Walton Beach, as well as the nation's largest charter fishing fleet.

The county has invested heavily – and continues to do so – in its artificial reef program, with the Destin-Fort Walton Beaches Wreck Alley program launching in 2021 and featuring dozens of wrecks off shore. The development of artificial reefs supports diving and snorkeling activities as well as fishing. Okaloosa County has over 380 official reef sites, with more added each year. Many deployments involve multiple reef modules. The county's artificial reefs range from concrete reef modules of varying sizes to small barges and large freighters. Many sites feature reef modules close to shore, while others are found far out in the Gulf in deeper water.

The pages that follow contain detailed information for many of the shore-accessible dive and snorkel sites in the county as well as details, for nine large wrecks, one complex artificial reef and a natural ledge site very popular with local and visiting divers.

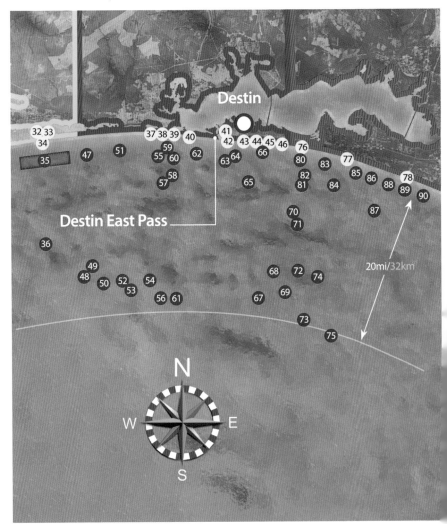

Okaloosa County keeps an up-to-date list of all of its artificial reef sites online. To see if new reefs have been added since publication, please visit:
Destinfwb.com/explore/ecotourism-hotspots/artificial-reefs/

Dive and snorkel sites

OKALOOSA COUNTY

37 Beach Access #6..
38 Beach Access #4..
39 Beach Access #2..
40 Beasley Park..
41 Norriego Point...
42 Destin Jetties...
43 Henderson Park West..
44 Henderson Park East...
45 Pompano Street..
46 Crap Trap Destin..
47 FH-16...
48 *Burgess Barge*..
49 *Zuess*..
50 *Mohawk Chief*...
51 FH-15...
52 *Sea Barb*...
53 *Belize Queen*...
54 *Chepanoc*..
55 FH-14...
56 *Angelina B*..
57 *Thomas Heyward Liberty Ship*..............................
58 White Hill Ledge..
59 *Barrel Barge*..
60 *Brown Barge*..
61 *Deborah*..
62 Mac's Reef...
63 Main Stack (Bridge rubble)....................................
64 *Eglin Barge*...
65 *Phoenix Barge*...
66 *Miss Louise*...
67 *Tully*..
68 A.J.'s/Carey Ricks Memorial Reef.........................
69 *Dylan*..
70 *Eglin LCM-8*..
71 *Janet*...
72 *Monica Lee*..
73 *Baskins Barge*..
74 *Eglin LCM-1*..
75 *Prewitt*..

119

Beach Access #6 Reef

Difficulty ● ○ ○
Current ● ○ ○
Depth ● ○ ○
Reef ★☆☆
Fauna ★☆☆

Destin ●
Beach Access
#6 Reef

Access 🚗 about 12 mins from downtown Destin
🏊 about 8 mins from shore

Level Open Water

Location
Fort Walton Beach, Okaloosa County
GPS 30°23.631'N, 86°37.575'W

Getting there
From downtown Destin, head west on US-98 across the Destin Bridge toward Fort Walton Beach. Once on Okaloosa Island, continue along US-98 for 4.5 miles (7.2 kilometers) to the set of traffic lights before Brooks Bridge, which connects back to Fort Walton Beach from the island. Turn left onto Santa Rosa Boulevard and continue for 1.7 miles (2.8 kilometers) to reach the Beach Access #6 parking area. The lot is located on the left and has a few dozen parking spots available. The official address is 820 Santa Rosa Boulevard, Fort Walton Beach, Florida, 32548.

Access
The beach is accessible via a short walk down a wooden boardwalk that crosses the barrier island's sand dunes. There are simple restroom facilities available on site, but the beach is only accessible from sunrise to sunset. A gate closes to block the entrance after hours.

The reef modules start around 800 feet (243 meters) from the beach. There are no buoys in the water to mark the site, so divers and snorkelers will need to navigate to the reef using the yellow navigational poles anchored next to the boardwalk. To navigate using the poles, keep them in line, one in front of the other, as you swim out to the reef facing back to shore. If you can see both poles at the same time (meaning they are no longer one in front of the other) then you have drifted off course. It is important to keep the poles in line in order to make your way successfully out to the area where the reef modules are deployed.

The surf can be high at times, so divers and snorkelers should be careful when entering and exiting the water. A diver down flag is required by law for both divers and snorkelers at this site.

Description
This is one of four shore-accessible reefs deployed by Okaloosa County in the spring of 2021. The Beach Access #6 Reef features a total of 90 four-disc reef modules that form a series of concentric circles surrounded by a square. Three clusters of six modules each form stars at the seaward edge of the reef complex. The shallowest modules are embedded in the sandy seafloor at a depth of 16 feet (5 meters), while the deeper ones bottom out at 22 feet (6.5 meters).

All modules are at least 6 feet (2 meters) below the surface of the water to ensure safe navigation. Meanwhile, the tops of the deepest modules sit just over 10 feet (3 meters) deep. Divers and snorkelers are likely to see damselfish, blennies, snapper, triggerfish and grouper here, along with the occasional octopus and sea turtle. Stingrays and flounder are also sometimes seen on the sand around the modules.

A close-up render of a four-tiered reef module.

120

800ft / 244m

N

W E

S

16ft
5m

800ft / 116m

73m

22ft
6.5m

Beach Access #4 Reef

Difficulty ● ○ ○
Current ● ○ ○
Depth ● ○ ○
Reef ★★☆
Fauna ★☆☆

Destin

Beach Access
#4 Reef

Access 🚙 about 11 mins from downtown Destin
🏊 about 6 mins from shore

Level Open Water

Location
Fort Walton Beach, Okaloosa County
GPS 30°23.655'N, 86°37.018'W

Getting there
From downtown Destin, head west along US-98 across the Destin Bridge toward Fort Walton Beach. Once on Okaloosa Island, continue along US-98 for 4.5 miles (7.2 kilometers) to the set of traffic lights before Brooks Bridge, which connects back to Fort Walton Beach from the island. Turn left onto Santa Rosa Boulevard and continue for 1.2 miles (1.9 kilometers) to reach the Beach Access #4 parking area. The lot is located on the left with two dozen spots available. The official address is 600 Santa Rosa Boulevard, Fort Walton Beach, Florida, 32548.

Access
The beach is accessible via a short walk down a wooden boardwalk that crosses the barrier island's sand dunes. There are simple restroom facilities available on site, but the beach is only accessible from sunrise to sunset. A gate closes to block the entrance after hours.

The reef modules start around 630 feet (192 meters) from the beach. There are no buoys

in the water to mark the site, so divers and snorkelers will need to navigate to the reef using the yellow navigational poles anchored next to the boardwalk. To navigate using the poles, keep them in line, one in front of the other, as you swim out to the reef facing back to shore. If you can see both poles at the same time (meaning they are no longer one in front of the other) then you have drifted off course. It is important to keep the poles in line in order to reach the reef.

A diver down flag is required by law for both divers and snorkelers at this site.

Description
This is one of four shore-accessible reefs deployed by Okaloosa County in the spring of 2019. The Beach Access #4 Reef features a total of 22 four-disc reef modules and six three-disc modules that form the shape of a swirl with two nearby stars. The shallowest modules feature the three-disc format and are embedded in the sandy seabed at a depth of 11 feet (5 meters), while the deeper ones bottom out at closer to 14 feet (4 meters). All modules are at least 6 feet (2 meters) below the surface of the water. Divers and snorkelers are likely to see damselfish, blennies, snapper, triggerfish and grouper here, along with the occasional octopus and sea turtle.

SAFETY TIP

Conditions along the Gulf of Mexico coast can vary widely from day to day, and are not always easy to predict based on the weather. A storm out in the Gulf can generate large swells that can make beaches unsafe for snorkelers and divers. Winds can shift throughout the day as well, resulting in conditions that are fine in the morning but change quickly to becoming unsafe.

Public beaches feature a warning flag system that helps beachgoers know whether

conditions are safe to enter the water. These flags include:

GREEN: low hazard, calm conditions, exercise caution
YELLOW: medium hazard, moderate surf or currents
RED: high hazard, high surf or strong currents
RED over **RED** (two flags): water closed to the public
PURPLE: dangerous marine organisms may be present

630ft / 192m

11ft
3m

2m

14ft
4m

92ft / 28m

163ft / 49.5m

Beach Access #2 Reef

Difficulty ● ○ ○
Current ● ○ ○
Depth ● ○ ○
Reef ★ ☆ ☆
Fauna ★ ☆ ☆

Destin
Beach Access
#2 Reef

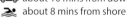

Access 🚙 about 10 mins from downtown Destin
🏊 about 8 mins from shore

Level Open Water

Location
Fort Walton Beach, Okaloosa County
GPS 30°23.553'N, 86°36.491'W

Getting there
From downtown Destin, head west along US-98 across the Destin Bridge toward Fort Walton Beach. Once on Okaloosa Island, continue along US-98 for 4.5 miles (7.2 kilometers) to the set of traffic lights before Brooks Bridge, which connects the island back to the mainland. Turn left onto Santa Rosa Boulevard and continue for 0.6 miles (1 kilometer) to reach the Beach Access #2 parking area. The lot is located on the left and has nearly two dozen spots available. The official address is 2nd Beach Park, Fort Walton Beach, Florida, 32548.

Access
The beach is accessible via a short walk down a wooden boardwalk that crosses the sand dunes. There are simple restroom facilities available on site, but the beach is only accessible from sunrise to sunset. A gate closes to block the entrance after hours.

The reef modules start around 800 feet (243 meters) from the beach. There are no buoys in the water to mark the site, so divers and snorkelers will need to navigate to the reef by using the yellow navigational poles anchored next to the boardwalk. To navigate using the poles, keep them in line, one in front of the other, as you swim out to the reef facing back to shore. If you can see both poles at the same time (meaning they are no longer one in front of the other) then you have drifted off course. A diver down flag is required by law when divers and snorkelers enter the water at this site.

Description
This is one of four shore-accessible reefs deployed by Okaloosa County in the spring of 2021. The Beach Access #2 Reef features a total of 97 four-disc reef modules in the shape of a swirl with three "stars" placed on the inshore side of the swirl, and another three placed on the seaward side. The shallowest modules are embedded in the sandy seabed at a depth of 15 feet (4.5 meters), while the deeper ones bottom out at closer to 22 feet (6.5 meters). All modules are at least 6 feet (2 meters) below the surface of the water while the tops of the deepest modules are just over 10 feet (3 meters) deep. Divers and snorkelers are likely to see damselfish, blennies, snapper, triggerfish and grouper here, along with the occasional octopus and sea turtle.

Sea turtles are frequent visitors to the coastal snorkel reefs.

Beasley Park Reef

Difficulty ● ○ ○
Current ● ○ ○
Depth ● ○ ○
Reef ★☆☆
Fauna ★☆☆

Destin
Beasley Park
Reef

Access 🚙 about 9 mins from downtown Destin
🏊 about 8 mins from shore

Level Open Water

Location
Fort Walton Beach, Okaloosa County
GPS 30°23.411'N, 86°35.099'W

Getting there
From downtown Destin, head west along US-98 across the Destin Bridge toward Fort Walton Beach. Once on Okaloosa Island, continue along US-98 for 3.6 miles (5.8 kilometers) before turning left into the entrance of John Beasley Park. The park has ample parking available and an official address of 1550 Miracle Strip Parkway Southeast, Fort Walton Beach, Florida, 32548.

The park is located right next to the Destin-Fort Walton Beach Visitor's Center that offers additional information about all of the snorkel reefs in Okaloosa as well as many of the other dive and snorkel sites in the area.

Access
John Beasley Park is a county park with picnic areas, restroom facilities and two large pavilions. The park is accessible from sunrise to sunset. Two wooden boardwalks offer access to the wide beach, and the reef modules are located seaward of the western boardwalk. The first modules are located in the sand around 865 feet (264 meters) from the water's edge. There are no buoys in the water to mark the site, so divers and snorkelers will need to navigate out to the reef using the yellow navigational poles anchored to the westernmost boardwalk.

To navigate using the poles, keep them in line, one in front of the other, as you swim out to the reef facing back to shore. If you can see both poles at the same time (meaning they are no longer one in front of the other) then you have drifted off course. It is important to keep the poles in line in order to reach the reef.

The surf can be high at times, so divers and snorkelers should be careful when entering

and exiting the water. A diver down flag is required by law when divers and snorkelers enter the water at this site.

Description
This is one of four shore-accessible reefs deployed by Okaloosa County in the spring of 2019. The Beasley Park Reef features a total of 69 four-disc reef modules in the shape of a cross surrounded by a square, with four sets of three modules each located at the inside corners of the cross. The shallowest modules are embedded in the sandy seabed at a depth of 15 feet (4.5 meters), while the deeper ones bottom out at closer to 23 feet (7 meters). All modules are at least 6 feet (2 meters) below the surface of the water while the tops of the deepest modules sit closer to 16 feet (5 meters) deep. Divers and snorkelers are likely to see snapper, triggerfish and grouper here.

These yellow poles act as navigational aids when swimming out to the reef modules.

Alex Fogg – Destin-Fort Walton Beach ©

Norriego Point

Difficulty ● ○ ○
Current ● ● ○
Depth ● ○ ○
Reef ★☆☆
Fauna ★☆☆

Destin
Norriego Point

Access 🚙 about 9 mins from downtown Destin
🚶 about 10 mins from parking
🏊 about 1 mins from shore

Level n/a

Location
Destin, Okaloosa County
GPS 30°23.563'N, 86°30.741'W

Getting there
From downtown Destin, head east along US-98. Turn right onto Gulf Shore Drive and then follow the road as it curves back toward the west. Just over 1 mile (1.8 kilometers) past this curve, follow Gulf Shore Drive as it turns right and then keep following the road as it veers left shortly thereafter. The modestly sized parking area for Norriego Point is at the end of Gulf Shore Drive, just 0.6 miles (1 kilometer) past the split in the road. It sits at the tip of the sandy peninsula with Destin Harbor to the east and Destin East Pass to the west.

Access
There are no restroom facilities at this site, although the county has plans to build limited facilities by the end of 2022. The snorkeling at Norriego Point is focused around the small protected bays on the western side of the peninsula, in the waters of the Destin East Pass.

To access the four shallow swimming areas along the western side of the Norriego Point peninsula, head northwest from the parking lot at the end of Gulf Shore Drive. The swimming areas are located between 600 feet (180 meters) and 0.4 miles (0.6 kilometers) from the parking, each evenly spaced along the shoreline. Visitors should not walk on the sand dunes as those are part of

an active conservation and restoration effort. The best time to access this site is at either slack high or slack low tide since the currents can be fairly strong through the pass on the incoming and outgoing tides.

Courtesy of Taylor Engineering ©

Description

Norriego Point supposedly gets its name from a prominent Spanish family that lived in Pensacola back when that city was under Spanish rule. The sheltered swimming areas are popular with snorkelers as they are often easier to access than the waters of the Gulf of Mexico. The small jetties and sheltered waters of the four lagoons provide habitat to a variety of small fish species, including pinfish, snapper, damselfish, sandfish, toadfish and Atlantic spadefish. Snorkelers may even encounter a juvenile green sea turtle if they venture out to the pass-side of the rocks.

SAFETY TIP ❗

The northeast side of Norriego Point offers visitors a fun beach walk and great views of the Destin Harbor Boardwalk, but please refrain from snorkeling along this side of the point. Boat traffic in and out of the harbor is significant, particularly during weekends and holidays, and during the busy summer months. Stick to the southwest side of the point with its dedicated swim areas and the rock jetties that border the pass. There is also far more interesting marine life to see on that side.

0.4mi / 640m

0.4mi / 640m

P

N

41

OKALOOSA COUNTY

NORRIEGO POINT

129

Destin Jetties

Difficulty	● ○ ○		
Current	● ● ○		
Depth	● ○ ○		
Reef	★☆☆		
Fauna	★★☆		

Destin

Destin Jetties

Access   about 8 mins from downtown Destin
about 15 mins from parking
about 1 mins from shore

🤿 **Level** Open Water

🤿 **Location**
Destin, Okaloosa County
GPS 30°23.057'N, 86°30.426'W

Getting there
From downtown Destin, head east along US-98, also called Harbor Boulevard. Turn right onto Gulf Shore Drive and then follow the road as it curves back toward the west. Just over 1 mile (1.8 kilometers) past this curve, follow Gulf Shore Drive as it turns right and then keep following the road as it veers left shortly thereafter. The limited parking area for the beach access is on the right side of the road, just 0.4 miles (0.6 kilometers) past the split in the road. This is the O'Steen Public Beach Access, with an official address of 320 Gulf Shore Drive, Destin, Florida, 32541. Many charter boats and snorkel tours also visit this site.

Access
There are no restrooms at this site, but there is a shower head near the parking area suitable for rinsing off. The diveable site at this location is the finger jetty that sticks out from the side of the pass, not the jetties sticking out into the Gulf. To access this site, cross the road and head toward the beach via the public beach access path. Once at the beach, turn left and walk south toward the jetty. The total walk is nearly 0.3 miles (450 meters) across mostly unpacked sand. This site is best accessed at slack high and low tide since the current through the pass can be strong when the tide is coming

in our going out. Visibility is generally best at, or just prior to, high tide. A diver down flag is required by law when diving or snorkeling at this site.

Description
The finger jetty is located on the eastern side of the Destin East

0.3mi/450m

Courtesy of Taylor Engineering ©

Pass. It extends over 300 feet (91 meters) into the pass and reaches a depth of 50 feet (15 meters) at its deepest point, although shifting sands in the pass can make this a shallower dive at times. This is a popular site with divers when conditions make it difficult to dive in the Gulf. The jetty supports plenty of reef creatures, including damselfish, sergeant majors, angelfish, sheepshead and belted sandfish. Some divers have even reported seeing sharks swimming through the pass.

ECO TIP

It is not uncommon to see sharks and other large marine life, such as spotted eagle rays, cruising through the relatively shallow waters of Destin East Pass and other passes in Northwest Florida. The reason divers and snorkelers are more likely to spot these majestic creatures in a pass compared to anywhere else along the beach is because these corridors provide access to the bays and estuaries that sit inside the region's barrier islands. These nutrient-rich coastal waters are full of life, and sharks and rays and other predators are simply traveling to where food can be found. Since there are only a handful of access points to these productive areas, the odds are higher that swimmers will see these large creatures as they come and go.

Destin jetty

Henderson Park West Reef

Difficulty ● ○ ○
Current ● ○ ○
Depth ● ○ ○
Reef ★ ☆ ☆
Fauna ★ ☆ ☆

Destin

Henderson
Park West Reef

Access about 11 mins from downtown Destin
about 3mi (5km) east of Destin East Pass
about 8 mins from shore

Level Open Water

Location
Destin, Okaloosa County
GPS 30°22.828'N, 86°27.169'W

Getting there
From downtown Destin, head east along US-98. After close to 3 miles (5 kilometers) turn right into Henderson Beach State Park. Follow Henderson Beach Road into the park and stay right to access the western parking area – there are two major sections of the park, a western section and an eastern section. Henderson Park West Reef is located off the beach adjacent to the westernmost section of parking. The park has an official address of 17000 Emerald Coast Parkway, Destin, Florida, 32541.

Access
Henderson Beach State Park has picnic areas, restroom facilities and an overnight campground. The park is open from 8am to sundown and there is a vehicle fee to enter. A wooden boardwalk provides access to the wide sandy beach opposite the buildings visible from the parking lot. The reef modules are located nearly 800 feet (244 meters) from the beach.

There are no buoys in the water or navigational poles on the beach to help mark the site, so divers may have difficulty navigating out to the reef. As a result, most visitors to this site arrive by boat and anchor in the sand near to one of the reef modules.

The surf can be high at times, so divers and snorkelers should be careful when entering and exiting the water. A diver down flag is required by law for any diver or snorkeler who enters the water at this site.

Description
Henderson Park West Reef is more accessible than its neighbor, Henderson Park East Reef, as it is located closer to the state park's parking lots. The Park West Reef is one of four shore-accessible reefs deployed by Okaloosa County in the spring of 2021, and it features 78 four-disc modules in the shape of a jet fighter firing reef-module missiles toward shore.

The reef is located just off the runway of the nearby Destin Executive Airport. The shallowest modules are embedded in the seafloor at a depth of 12 feet (3.5 meters), while the deeper ones bottom out at closer to 23 feet (7 meters). All modules are at least 6 feet (2 meters) below the surface of the water while the tops of the deepest modules sit closer to 16 feet (5 meters) deep.

Divers and snorkelers are likely to see damselfish, blennies, snapper, triggerfish and grouper here, along with the occasional octopus and sea turtle.

SCIENTIFIC INSIGHT

The juveniles of many reef fish look nothing like their adult form. This is particularly noticeable among damselfish species, where juveniles often sport vibrant, almost fluorescent colors compared to the dull and dark coloration of adults. Some scientists believe this difference in coloration is to help the juveniles avoid the territorial aggression adults exhibit toward each other. That way they can forage on an adult's territory when though they are too small to properly defend themselves. While studies haven't prove the reason why, it is clear that adults are less aggressive to individuals with juvenile coloration.

In fact, the difference in color is so pronounced that some juveniles were misidentified as a separate species altogether until they were placed in an aquarium and the color transformation was observed by researchers as the individuals matured.

800ft / 244m

16ft
5m

128m

22ft
6.5m

240ft / 73m

Henderson Park East Reef

Difficulty ● ○ ○
Current ● ○ ○
Depth ● ○ ○
Reef ★ ☆ ☆
Fauna ★ ☆ ☆

Destin

Henderson
Park East Reef

Access 🚗 about 11 mins from downtown Destin
🚤 about 4.5mi (7km) east of Destin East Pass
🚶 about 20 mins from parking
🏊 about 8 mins from shore

Level Open Water

Location
Destin, Okaloosa County
GPS 30°22.811'N, 86°26.101'W

Getting there
From downtown Destin, head east along US-98. After close to 3 miles (5 kilometers), turn right into Henderson Beach State Park. Follow Henderson Beach Road toward the water and then turn left to access the eastern parking area – there are two major sections of the park, a western section and an eastern section. Henderson Park East Reef is located farther down the beach from the easternmost section of parking. The park has an official address of 17000 Emerald Coast Parkway, Destin, Florida, 32541.

Access
Henderson Beach State Park has picnic areas, restroom facilities and an overnight campground. The park is open from 8am to sundown and there is a vehicle fee to enter. Wooden boardwalks provide access to the wide, sandy beach opposite the buildings located next to the eastern lots. The reef modules are located nearly 0.5 miles (800 meters) down the beach from the easternmost boardwalk of this parking lot, and they are located 735 feet (224 meters) off shore. There are no buoys in the water or navigational posts on land to help mark the site, so divers and snorkelers may find it challenging to navigate out from shore. A diver down flag is required by law for divers and snorkelers who enter the water at this site.

Description
Henderson Park East Reef is less accessible than its neighbor to the west, known as Henderson Park West Reef as it requires a long walk down the beach. The Park East Reef is one of four shore-accessible reefs deployed by Okaloosa County in the spring of 2019, and it features 40 four-disc modules in the shape

of a diamond featuring two rows of modules along its sides, and four modules at its center. The shallowest modules are embedded in the sandy seabed at a depth of 15 feet (4.5 meters), while the deeper ones bottom out at closer to 17 feet (5 meters). All modules are at least 6 feet (2 meters) below the surface of the water while the tops of the deepest modules sit closer to 10 feet (3 meters) deep. Divers and snorkelers are likely to see damselfish, blennies, snapper, triggerfish, sea bass and grouper here, along with the occasional octopus and sea turtle.

SAFETY TIP

The surf can sometimes be high at this site, so snorkelers and divers, particularly with their heavy gear, should be careful entering and exiting the water. The safest way to enter the water is to first ensure that both buddies are fully geared up and have completed their buddy check. Only then should they enter the water, with air already in their BCDs and without fins attached. Once in the water, buddies should use each other for the support, if necessary, to attach their fins and push through the surf as quickly as possible. When exiting, divers should remember to keep their mask and regulator in place, their BCD inflated and remove their fins in the water so they can walk up the beach.

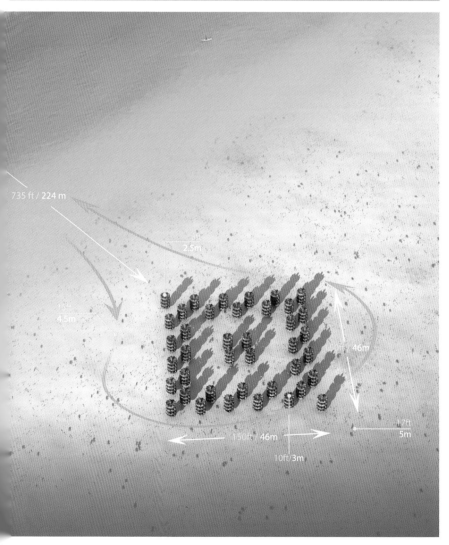

735 ft / 224 m

2.5m

4.5m

46m

150ft / 46m

17ft
5m

10ft/3m

Pompano Street Reef

Difficulty ● ○ ○
Current ● ○ ○
Depth ● ○ ○
Reef ★★★
Fauna ★★★

Destin

Pompano
Street Reef

Access 🚙 about 12 mins from downtown Destin
🏊 about 8 mins from shore

 Level Open Water

 Location
Destin, Okaloosa County
GPS 30°22.683'N, 86°25.138'W

Getting there

From downtown Destin, head east along US-98. After passing Henderson Beach State Park, turn right onto Matthew Boulevard. The road ends after 0.4 miles (0.65 kilometers). At the intersection, turn left onto Scenic Highway 98. Continue east along this road for 0.7 miles (1.1 kilometers) to reach the Pompano Public Beach Access located on the right, opposite Pompano Street. There is limited parking at this access point. The official address is 322 Pompano Street, Destin, Florida, 32541.

Access

There are no facilities or lifeguards on duty at this beach access point. A long boardwalk provides access to the beach from the road. The reef modules are located directly off shore from this boardwalk, starting 800 feet (240 meters) from the beach. There are no buoys in the water to mark the site, so divers and snorkelers should navigate to the reef using the yellow navigational poles located on shore.

To navigate using the poles, keep them in line, one in front of the other, as you swim out to the reef facing back to shore. If you can see both poles at the same time (meaning they are no longer one in front of the other) then you have drifted off course. It is important to keep the poles in line in order to reach the reef modules as it is easy to get pushed off course when navigating out to the site.

The surf can be high at times, so divers and snorkelers should be careful when entering and exiting the water. A "diver down" flag is required in the water for both divers and snorkelers at this site.

Description

Pompano Street Reef is one of four shore-accessible reefs deployed by Okaloosa County in the spring of 2021. It features 90 four-disc modules in the shape of a star surrounded by a circle, with a cluster of six reef modules at each corner of the site. The shallowest modules are embedded in the sandy seafloor at a depth of 16 feet (5 meters), while the deeper ones bottom out at closer to 22 feet (6.5 meters). All modules are at least 6 feet (2 meters) below the surface of the water to allow for safe navigation, while the tops of the deepest modules sit closer to 16 feet (5 meters) deep.

Divers and snorkelers are likely to see damselfish, blennies, snapper, sea bass, triggerfish, sheepshead and grouper here, along with the occasional octopus, sea turtle and stingray. Flounder are also commonly seen in the sand around the modules.

A close-up render of a set of four-tiered reef modules.

800ft / 244m

16ft
5m

107m

73m

22ft
6.5m

137

Crab Trap Destin Reef

Destin

Crab Trap
Destin Reef

Difficulty	● ○ ○
Current	● ○ ○
Depth	● ○ ○
Reef	★★☆
Fauna	★☆☆

Access 🚙 about 13 mins from downtown Destin
🏊 about 8 mins from shore

Level Open Water

Location
Destin, Okaloosa County
GPS 30°22.630'N, 86°24.482'W

Getting there
From downtown Destin, head east along US-98. After passing Henderson Beach State Park, turn right onto Matthew Boulevard. The road ends after 0.4 miles (0.65 kilometers). At the intersection, turn left onto Scenic Highway 98. Continue east along this road for 1.4 miles (2.25 kilometers) to reach the parking lot adjacent to the Crab Trap Destin. Park in the spaces to the east of the main restaurant for easier access to the beach and snorkel reef – there are plenty of spots available. The official address is 3500 Scenic Highway 98 East, Destin, Florida, 32541.

Access
There are no public restroom facilities here. A series of short boardwalks provides access to the beach from the parking lot. The reef modules are located directly off shore from the second boardwalk to the east of the restaurant patio. The modules are located 835 feet (253 meters) from the beach. There are no buoys in the water to mark the site, so divers and snorkelers will need to navigate out to the reef using the yellow navigational poles anchored to the westernmost boardwalk.

To navigate using the poles, keep them in line, one in front of the other, as you swim out to the reef facing back to shore. If you can see both poles at the same time (meaning they are no longer one in front of the other) then you have drifted off course. It is important to keep the poles in line in order to reach the reef.

The surf can be high at times, so divers and snorkelers should be careful when entering and exiting the water. A diver down flag is required by law for both divers and snorkelers who enter the water at this site.

Description
Crab Trap Destin Reef is one of four shore-accessible reefs deployed by Okaloosa County in the spring of 2019. It features 68 four-disc modules placed to create a pattern of four wavy lines that run parallel to shore. The shallowest modules are embedded in the sandy seafloor at a depth of 15 feet (4.5 meters), while the deeper ones bottom out at closer to 23 feet (7 meters). All modules are at least 6 feet (2 meters) below the surface of the water while the tops of the deepest modules sit closer to 16 feet (5 meters) deep. Divers and snorkelers are likely to see damselfish, blennies, sheepshead, snapper, triggerfish and grouper here, along with the occasional octopus and sea turtle. Stingrays and flounder are commonly seen on the sand around the reef modules.

SAFETY TIP ❶

Divers or snorkelers should always notify someone about their plans to venture into the water. If they are at the beach with a group and at least one member of the party intends on staying on land, there should be clear communication about the dive or snorkel plan, including how long the group plans on staying in the water. If no one in a group intends on staying ashore, divers should reach out to friends or a family member to let them know when and where they are diving along with a check-in time. That way the friend or family member can alert the local authorities if the diver or snorkeler misses their call, and can provide the emergency personnel with the relevant information about who, when and where. This is an important step for divers diving from shore without the support of a dive operator. Although the snorkel reefs are not located in particularly deep water, anything can happen and it is best to be prepared.

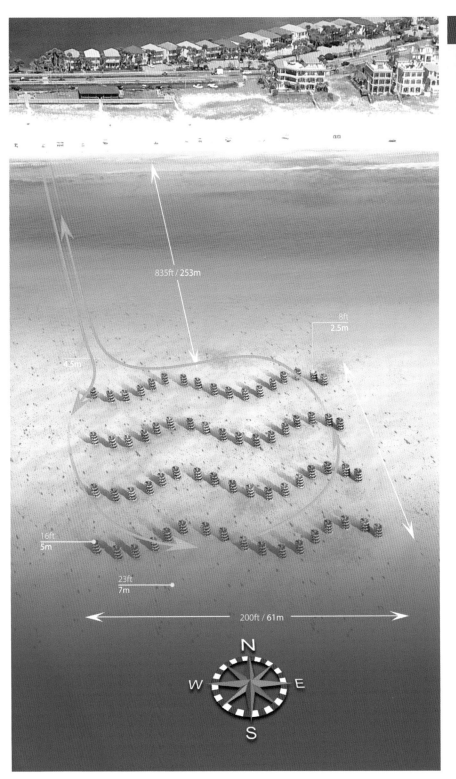

835ft / 253m

8ft
2.5m

4.5m

16ft
5m

23ft
7m

200ft / 61m

N

W E

S

OKALOOSA COUNTY

Zuess

Difficulty	● ● ○
Current	● ○ ○
Depth	● ● ●
Reef	★★★☆
Fauna	★★★☆

Destin · Zuess

Access 🚤 about 20.5mi (33.5km) southwest of Destin East Pass

🤿 **Level** Advanced

Location
Destin, Okaloosa County
GPS 30°09.422'N, 86°44.490'W

Getting there
Zuess is one of the westernmost sites off the coast of Okaloosa County. Given the distance from shore, it should only be visited by operators and private vessels with experience operating in the Gulf. There are no surface mooring buoys at this site, so operators typically tie in to the wreck or drop anchor in the sand nearby.

Access
This site is accessible to most divers but is perhaps better suited to advanced divers as the sandy seafloor reaches a maximum depth of 105 feet (32 meters). The wreck has a very low profile, meaning most of the dive will be spent close to this depth. The site is best reached via one of the dive shops operating out of Destin East Pass, although it is well within reach of Pensacola Pass.

Description
Zuess was a 105-foot (32-meter) towboat – a similar design but larger than the popular *Miss Louise* (page 178). Towboats are different from tugboats in that they push rather than pull barges, using the large bumpers that stick up from the bow. Built in Nashville, Tennessee by the Nashville Bridge Company 1943, *Zuess* was built for the Clark Super Gas Co. and named for the company's founder, Emory T. Clark. The Clark empire began with a single fill station in Wisconsin in 1932 and grew to include refineries in the states of Louisiana and Illinois, as well as some barges and associated towboats that plied the waters of the Mississippi. The *Emory T.* was one of those towboats.

It is not clear at what point she was renamed *Zuess*, or whether she remained within the Clark corporate empire for her entire career. Clark Super Gas evolved over time, acquiring other brands and expanding its scope until

it eventually was purchased by a Canadian company in 1992. It is possible that it was during this corporate transition that *Zuess* was made available to Okaloosa County for use as an artificial reef. She was ultimately sent to the bottom on June 29, 1992.

The wreck no longer features the superstructure that once graced the towboat. The wheelhouse and main cabins are gone, leaving just a large hole in the main deck and two upright push pads. The hull is largely buried in the sand, with the deck sitting just a few feet above the seabed near the bow and level with the sand near the stern. There is some space under the main deck near

SCIENTIFIC INSIGHT

Even low-profile structures, referred to as low rugosity by scientists, can be effective artificial reefs so long as they provide ample surface area on which organisms can settle and complex internal structure for fish to use as shelter. This is why barges make for good fish habitat, even if they may be less interesting for divers to explore. These wide, stable wrecks provide plenty of suitable habitat for decades before finally succumbing to the elements. And as long as fish find them interesting, there will always be something for divers to see.

Even without a large profile, *Zuess* still shelters a lot of marine life.

Alex Fogg – Destin-Fort Walton Beach©

the bow, but not enough to allow for penetration. The push pads are the tallest point of the wreck, reaching a depth of 92 feet (28 meters).

Despite the relative lack of upright structure on this wreck, there is plenty to explore. The artificial reef plays host to a variety of jack species, including almacos. Tomtates and vermilion snapper form dense schools around the wreck, while large mangrove and lane snapper cruise through the site, making this popular with spearfishing divers and hook-and-line fishers. Grouper are also known to frequent the site, particularly scamp grouper that sometimes hide in the space under the decking.

Zuess was added to the Florida Panhandle Shipwreck Trail in 2020.

Route

Due to the depth and low profile of the towboat, divers will need to carefully monitor their bottom time when exploring this artificial reef. The open nature of the site means divers do not need to plan a specific route, but most divers circumnavigate the wreck before spending time exploring the main deck and the narrow spaces beneath.

92ft
28m

Bow

35

62

33

39

106ft
32.5m

105ft / 32m

Other species commonly found at this site:

2   23   26   28   41   43   47   50   61

69   80   82   83   85

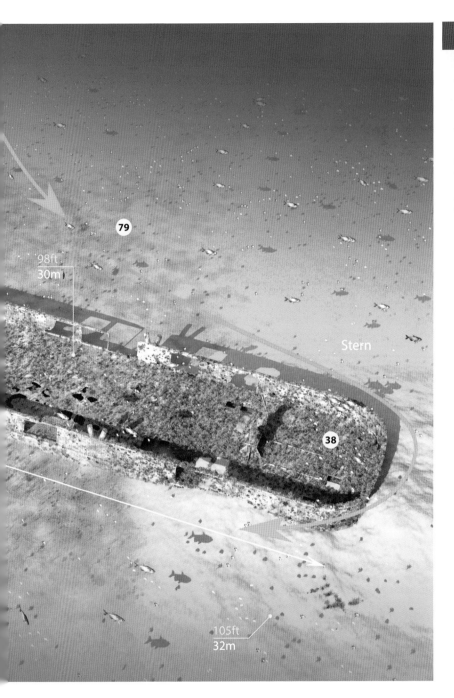

Name:	*Zuess*		Nashville, TN, 1943
Type:	Towboat	**Last owner:**	Clark's Super Gas Co.
Previous names:	*Emory T.*	**Sunk:**	June 29, 1992
Length:	105ft (32m)		
Tonnage:	223grt		
Construction:	Nashville Bridge Co.,		

Mohawk Chief

Destin

Mohawk Chief

Difficulty ● ● ●
Current ● ○ ○
Depth ● ● ●
Reef ★★☆
Fauna ★★☆

Access 🚤 about 20.5mi (33km) southwest of Destin East Pass

 Level Advanced

Location
Destin, Okaloosa County
GPS 30°08.807'N, 86°43.075'W

Getting there
Mohawk Chief is the central component of a hexagon-shaped artificial reef complex named Sand Dollar Reef. This site is one of the westernmost sites in Okaloosa County. Given the distance from shore, it should only be visited by operators and private vessels with experience operating in the Gulf. There are no surface mooring buoys at this site, so operators typically tie in to the wreck or drop anchor in the sand nearby.

Access
This site is only accessible to advanced divers due to its maximum depth of 126 feet (38.5 meters). The upper reaches of the wheelhouse top 107 feet (32.5 meters), which makes for some variability in depth profile but still a deep dive. The site is best reached via one of the dive shops operating out of Destin East Pass.

Description
Mohawk Chief was a 93-foot-long (28.5-meter) tugboat. She was originally built in 1941 in Beaumont, Texas for the Moran Towing Co., under the name *Sheila Moran*. She operated out of New York City where the company was located. Her name changed to the *Captain Harold* when the company leased her out, although she continued to operate out of New York. At the end of her lease in 1978, she was sold to the Ocean Transport Corporation of Vero Beach, Florida, and renamed *Mohawk Chief*. She operated as part of that company for more than three decades. By 2003, she was handed over to Okaloosa County for deployment as an artificial reef.

The county had her cleaned and prepped for deployment, including pumping her full of concrete before she was towed out into the Gulf and scuttled on June 23, 2003. She

was added to the popular Florida Panhandle Shipwreck Trail in 2020.

After sinking, she settled upright on the sandy seafloor, but sediment has built up around her so that her main deck is now just a few feet above the bottom. The wreck is relatively intact and sports a long, partially enclosed structure on the main deck along with a wheelhouse perched as a second level up by the bow.

A large hole cut out of the rear section of the main structure allows for easy access to the interior of the ship, as does a hole cut in the roof of the main level behind the wheelhouse. However, many of the doorways along the sides of the main level are partially obstructed

RELAX & RECHARGE

Nestled together off Harbor Boulevard in Destin are two establishments that generate plenty of positive reviews. **East Pass Coffee Co.** (529 Harbor Boulevard) serves up a great cup of Joe as well as acai bowls, smoothies, killer sandwiches and toast specials, like avocado toast and banana toast. Their breakfast sandwich served with hot pepper jelly is guaranteed to jump-start your day. Visit: **Eastpasscoffeeco.com**

Red Onion Organic Restaurant (also at 529 Harbor Boulevard) is just a few feet away, directly opposite East Pass Coffee. As the name suggests, they specialize in delicious and wholesome organic cuisine. Their gyro sandwiches and salads are raved about. Entrees include butter filet mignon, olive oil braised ribeye, and Swedish meatballs with cranberry sauce. They also serve a range of tasty tapas.
Visit: **Facebook.com/redonionsgyros**

by old fishing line, so divers choosing to penetrate the ship should be careful of potential entanglements.

The hull of the tug has mostly filled with sand toward the stern, but there is space between the main deck and the seabed looking forward toward the bow. This narrow space is accessible from the aft end of the partially enclosed structure. The roof of the wheelhouse is also relatively intact, which permits divers with good buoyancy control to enter the space. The starboard side of the wheelhouse has been completely removed, making it easy to access the space.

Plenty of large reef fish have colonized this artificial reef in part because of its depth and time spent underwater. The many fishing lines offer a testament to this site's popularity with local fishers. Divers are likely to see plenty of large snapper, including red and vermilion snapper, as well as a variety of grouper species including a goliath grouper that is often encountered in the wheelhouse. Atlantic spadefish typically form schools around the wreck, while whitespotted soapfish often perch on the side of the hull. Stingrays frequent the sands around the tug as well, so divers should occasionally look out into the space around the wreck.

Mohawk Chief remains upright despite many powerful storms over the years.

Virgil Zetterlind ©

88

107ft
32.5m

64

116ft
35.5m

Bow

126ft
38.5m

Route

Due to the depth of the tug, divers will need to carefully monitor their bottom time, particularly if they plan on exploring inside the main structure. A typical route will start at the stern, as the main deck there is the lowest point of the tug.

Divers can circle the tug and then head toward the bow, which is slightly shallower than the stern. The wheelhouse and the top of the main structure are good places to end the dive with their remaining bottom time.

114ft
34.5m

Stern

119ft
36.5m

40

39

63

126ft
38.5m

93ft / 28.5m

Name:	*Mohawk Chief*	**Construction:**	Bethlehem Steel,
Type:	Tugboat		Beaumont, TX, 1941
Previous names:	*Sheila Moran,*	**Last owner:**	Ocean Transport
	Captain Harold		Corporation
Length:	93ft (28.5m)	**Sunk:**	June 23, 2003
Tonnage:	133grt		

88

114ft
34.5m

40

122ft
37m

39

119ft
36.5m Stern

126ft
38.5m

107ft
32.5m

116ft
35.5m

Bow

126ft
38.5m

Other species commonly found
at this site:

5   12   15   20   33   35   41   42   52

60   69   83   86   90

Belize Queen

Difficulty	● ● ○
Current	● ○ ○
Depth	● ● ●
Reef	★ ★ ☆
Fauna	★ ★ ☆

Destin

Belize Queen

Access 🛥 about 18.5mi (30km) southwest of Destin East Pass

Level Advanced

Location
Destin, Okaloosa County
GPS 30°08.807'N, 86°40.402'W

Getting there
Belize Queen is located relatively far from shore, meaning it should only be visited by operators and private vessels with experience operating in the Gulf. There are no surface mooring buoys at this site, so operators typically tie in to the wreck or drop anchor in the sand nearby.

Access
With a maximum depth of 112 feet (34 meters), *Belize Queen* is better suited to advanced divers. The wreck has a relatively low profile, with the top of the wheelhouse reaching just 96 feet (29 meters) in depth. The site is best reached via one of the dive shops operating out of Destin East Pass.

Description
Belize Queen was an 85-foot-long (26-meter) tugboat deployed as an artificial reef by Okaloosa County in May 2001. The site is also officially known as the Bob Reay Reef, after an Okaloosa County resident who died in 2000 just before the ship was scuttled. *Belize Queen* is a popular site with many local divers and was added to Florida Panhandle Shipwreck Trail in 2020.

Not much is known about the history of the *Belize Queen* prior to her deployment as an artificial reef by the county. But after decades spent underwater, the tugboat has settled deep into the sandy seabed. Her stern is all but buried at this point, while her bow still rests about 12 feet (3.5 meters) above the seafloor. As a result, she has a pronounced upward tilt and looks like she is sinking into the sand. The wheelhouse and part of the main cabin remain upright, although the entire rear section has been lost, leaving a large open space facing the stern. There is also a hole in the rear deck that

overhangs the sand along its edges. There is a narrow space between the foredeck and the seabed that offers shelter to a variety of reef fish but represents a tight fit for divers.

This artificial reef hosts a variety of sea life. Schools of jacks patrol the water column above the wreck, including greater amberjacks and almaco jacks. Divers are likely to see porgies on this wreck, and blue angelfish are often seen patrolling the bow. Rock hinds are frequently spotted hiding in nooks and crannies of the hull while tomtates and snapper form large schools above the wheelhouse. Divers should take care as they explore under the main deck as invasive lionfish are commonly spotted on this site (See the Scientific Insight box on page 18). Divers poking around in the shadowy recesses of this wreck may also spot slipper lobsters on this wreck.

Route

The open nature of this site means that divers do not need to plan a specific route to explore the area. Most divers circumnavigate the wreck before spending time exploring the space behind the wheelhouse. Limited penetration is possible in the wheelhouse for those with experience in overhead environments.

Anita Kainath/ Shutterstock ©

Loggerhead sea turtles are occasionally seen around the *Belize Queen* and other artificial reefs.

RELAX & RECHARGE

Brotula's Seafood House & Steamer (210 Harbor Boulevard) is a locally owned and operated seafood restaurant with killer views over the Destin Harbor. The restaurant has gained a reputation for serving quality, fresh, locally sourced and sustainable seafood. The mouth-watering menu combines new culinary preparations with unique twists on Southern classics. Some of the most popular dishes include lobsters, oysters, snapper, grouper, and the steak and scampi. Brotula's also has a "you hook, we cook" option, so you can bring along your catch and let the chef decide how best to prepare it. Brotula's offers happy hour from 2 to 6pm every day, including half off many drinks and appetizers. Visit: **Brotulas.com**

96ft
29m

105ft
32m

Bow

100ft
30.5m

60

112ft
34m

102ft
31m

Stern

114ft
35m

80

29

L

90

3

Name:	*Belize Queen*	Last owner:	n/a
Type:	Tugboat	Sunk:	May 30, 2001
Previous names:	Bob Reay Reef		
Length:	85ft (26m)		
Tonnage:	110grt		
Construction:	n/a		

109ft
33m

80

114ft
35m

Stern

90

96ft
29m

Bow

100ft
30.5m

60

29

L

3

105ft
32m

112ft
34m

Other species commonly found
at this site:

C G J 4 16 33 38 42 50

63 69 81 83 85

Chepanoc

Destin

Chepanoc

Difficulty ● ● ○
Current ● ○ ○
Depth ● ● ●
Reef ★★☆
Fauna ★★☆

Access 🚤 about 18mi (29km) southwest of Destin East Pass

Level Advanced

Location

Destin, Okaloosa County
GPS 30°08.821′N, 86°37.625′W

Getting there

Chepanoc is located relatively far from shore, meaning it is generally only visited by operators and private vessels with experience operating in the Gulf. There are no surface mooring buoys at this site, so operators typically drop anchor in the sand nearby or tie in to the wreck.

Access

This site is accessible to advanced divers with enough experience to comfortably reach the sandy seafloor that sits between 106 and 108 feet (32.5 and 33 meters) in depth. The top of the wreck reaches as high as 83 feet (25.5 meters), meaning there are alternate depth profiles for divers looking to extend their bottom time. The site is best reached via one of the dive shops operating through Destin East Pass.

Description

Chepanoc was built in 1944 in Port Arthur, Texas,

Virgil Zetterlind ©

Powerful storms have led to the loss of the wall panels of *Chepanoc*'s wheelhouse.

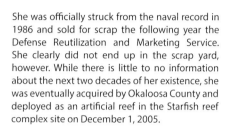

for the U.S. Navy. She was originally a large harbor tug and held the designation *YTB-381*, which stood for "yard tug big." She was placed into service with the Pacific Fleet for two years before being transferred to the Pacific Reserve Fleet. She was reactivated in 1957 and began service in Newport, Rhode Island, with a new designation of *YTM-381*, or district harbor tug medium. She operated out of the 1st Naval District and Naval Station in Newport, moving barges and large naval vessels in the waters around the naval station.

She was officially struck from the naval record in 1986 and sold for scrap the following year the Defense Reutilization and Marketing Service. She clearly did not end up in the scrap yard, however. While there is little to no information about the next two decades of her existence, she was eventually acquired by Okaloosa County and deployed as an artificial reef in the Starfish reef complex site on December 1, 2005.

Chepanoc took just over an hour to sink beneath the surface, settling upright on a sandy seabed. She now rests with a slight list to port, with her bow pointing roughly south. She is relatively intact, with the wheelhouse and superstructure still standing tall. Her funnel was removed prior to scuttling, and a large hole behind the wheelhouse permits limited penetration into the superstructure. Some of the walls of the deck level and the wheelhouse – particularly along the starboard side – have experienced some corrosion over time.

The wreck supports a variety of reef life. Jacks swarm the wreck, including almaco and greater amberjacks. Schools of Atlantic spadefish and vermilion snapper sometimes obscure the wreck, while angelfish and butterflyfish often cruise across the hull alone or in pairs. Divers should be sure to look out for the resident goliath grouper often seen hanging out in the wheelhouse. Large barracuda are usually swimming in the water column above the wreck, while bull sharks are spotted, from time to time, cruising the outskirts of the site.

Chepanoc is popular with spear and hook-and-line fishers, and fishing line can be seen draped and snagged across the stern section of the superstructure, which can pose an entanglement risk for divers. The open nature of the superstructure means that limited penetration is possible, weaving through the open doorways of the superstructure, while the large access point in the top of the main structure provides exit and entry.

Chepanoc was added to the Florida Panhandle Shipwreck Trail in 2020.

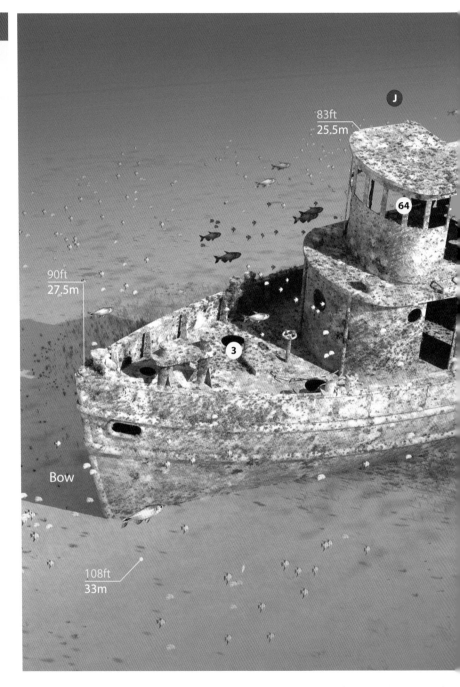

83ft
25.5m

J

64

90ft
27.5m

3

Bow

108ft
33m

Route

This site is deep, and with plenty to explore divers will need to monitor their bottom time carefully. Most divers begin at the stern of the wreck, which sits slightly deeper than the bow. Divers can circumnavigate the exterior of the wreck before entering through one of the open doorways in the superstructure. Beware of entanglement risks in this interior space and when exiting the doorways.

Divers can rise through the open ceiling if the doorways feel too tight, and then make their

80 85ft
26m

97ft
29.5m

40

Stern

106ft
32.5m

H

N
W
E
S

Name:	*Chepanoc*	Welding Works, Port Arthur,
Type:	Tugboat	TX, 1944
Previous names:	*YTB-381, YTM-381*	**Last owner:** n/a
Length:	129ft (39.3m)	**Sunk:** December 1, 2005
Tonnage:	325grt	
Construction:	Gulfport Boiling and	

85ft
26m

80

40

106ft
32.5m

.97ft
29.5m

Stern

way to the wheelhouse. If the goliath grouper is at the helm, consider giving the gentle giant a little space, as they can often feel threated when cornered. After checking out the inside of the wheelhouse, divers can grab a top-down view of the wreck as they ascend for their safety stop.

83ft
25.5m

90ft
27.5m

Bow

108ft
33m

Other species commonly found
at this site:

12   19   20   23   28   32   39   43   48

51   52   79   83   90

Thomas Heyward Liberty Ship

Difficulty	● ● ○
Current	● ○ ○
Depth	● ● ○
Reef	★★☆
Fauna	★★☆

Destin
Thomas Heyward Liberty Ship

Access 🚤 about 7.5mi (12km) southwest of Destin East Pass

Level Open Water

Location
Destin, Okaloosa County
GPS 30°18.375′N, 86°36.221′W

Getting there
Thomas Heyward, also known as the *Destin Liberty Ship*, is one of four Liberty Ships located in the waters off Northwest Florida – the others include *Joseph L. Meek* off Pensacola, *Joseph E. Brown* off Navarre and *Benjamin H. Grierson* off Panama City. The wreck sits closer to shore than many of the other artificial reefs in this area, so she is easier and quicker to reach by boat. She also sits just over 500 feet (150 meters) to the south of White Hill Ledge (page 168). There are no surface mooring buoys at this wreck, so operators typically tie in to the wreck or drop anchor in the sand nearby.

Access
Thomas Heyward is accessible to most divers as she sits upright on a sandy seafloor at a depth of around 86 feet (26 meters). Given that her hull sits open like a canoe, the wreck is also suitable for divers with limited wreck diving experience. *Destin Liberty Ship* is best reached via one of the dive shops operating out of Destin East Pass.

Description
Thomas Heyward (spelled *Hayward* in some records) was built during World War II in Mobile, Alabama. She was one of 2,711 Liberty Ships built to ferry supplies to Europe during the war. Liberty Ships were named after prominent Americans, and *Thomas Heyward*'s namesake was Thomas Heyward, Jr. Born in South Carolina in 1746, he was part of that state's delegation to the Continental Congress and was one of the signers of the Declaration of Independence.

Built in July 1942, *Thomas Heyward* was immediately put into service ferrying materials over to Europe. According to records, she survived striking a floating mine off the coast of Europe in 1946 after the war was over. She made

it back to port for repairs and was eventually laid up in the reserve fleet just a few years later. She was eventually purchased by the Florida Department of Natural Resources and deployed as an artificial reef on April 17, 1977.

Liberty Ships were massive vessels that measured 440 feet (134 meters) in length and had a beam of 57 feet (17.5 meters). Before being deployed as a reef, all of *Heyward*'s superstructure and upper decking were removed, leaving only the hull and a few interior bracing walls. Even so, she is the largest artificial reef in Okaloosa. The scale of the wreck is impressive, even though the actual structure itself is relatively simple. The wreck has split in two, with a small stern section lying separate and slightly out of alignment by 15 feet (4.5 meters) with the rest of the wreck. A portside section of hull near the bow collapsed at some point during the summer storm season in 2020. The rest of the hull is surprisingly intact, however, and divers swimming down the middle of the site may forget they are actually diving on a wreck rather than through a large canyon.

There are plenty of reef fish that can be spotted on the dive, both large and small. Almaco jacks and tomtates are common, along with reef and spotfin butterflyfish, and cocoa damselfish. Lucky divers may see a passing spotted eagle ray cruising down the middle of the wreck, or perhaps a patrolling sandbar shark. Nurse sharks are also a common sight here, resting in the gap between the hull and the sandy seafloor while even whale sharks and manta rays have made an appearance here during the summer and Fall. Spanish mackerels often swim through the water column above the wreck, which helps explain why this is a very popular site with fishers as well as divers.

Destin Liberty Ship was added to the Florida Panhandle Shipwreck Trail in 2020.

Route
Given the size of the site, divers may want to decide whether to focus on the bow or stern before entering the water, as there may not be enough bottom time to explore both sections

properly. A second dive at this site is often warranted.

With no upper decking, the site itself is easy enough to explore, with most divers spending their time exploring the interior space of the hull, rather than the outside. The middle section of the vessel has a large crack running across its beam that is interesting to explore, and divers will likely see the many bricks that were once part of the furnaces located midship that heated the boilers. There are a few swim-throughs possible in the

Spotfin butterflyfish on the hull of the *Destin Liberty Ship*.

David Bailey ©

DID YOU KNOW?

Liberty Ships were not exactly pretty, but their simple and functional design made them quick to build, which was vital for transporting supplies to Europe during World War II. Parts for these ships were mass-produced by manufacturers scattered around the U.S., and then welded together in as little as 42 days at designated shipyards. The record for construction time was set by *Robert E. Peary*, which was completed in less than five days by the Permanente Metals Corporation in Richmond, California. The Alabama Drydock and Shipbuilding Company launched 13 Liberty Ships in total, including *Thomas Heyward*, in just a six-month period in 1942. As many as 2,400 Liberty Ships survived the war and a large number were used for commercial cargo shipping purposes around the world. In the 1970s, the U.S. government started donating mothballed Liberty Ships for deployment as artificial reefs.

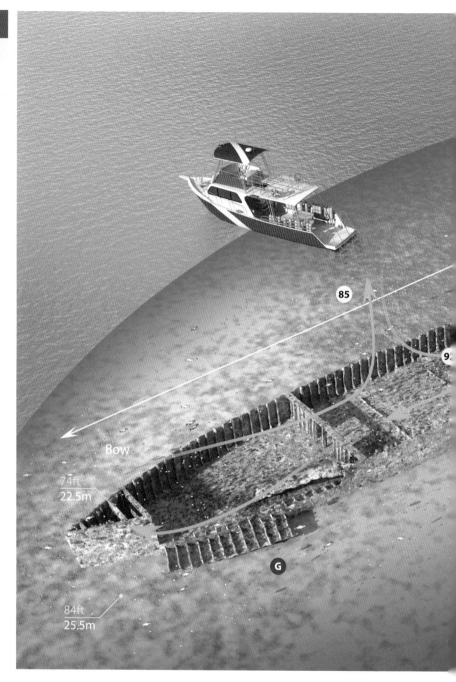

85

9

Bow

74ft
22.5m

G

84ft
25.5m

middle of the wreck and near the bow, where the
bulkheads still stand.

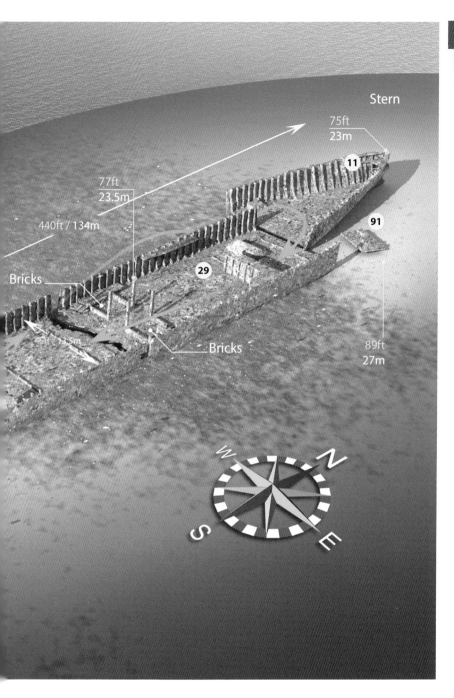

Stern

75ft
23m

77ft
23.5m

440ft / 134m

Bricks

45ft / 13.5m

89ft
27m

Bricks

THOMAS HEYWARD LIBERTY SHIP

Name:	*Thomas Heyward Liberty Ship*
Type:	Liberty Ship
Previous names:	n/a
Length:	440ft (134m)
Tonnage:	7,200grt
Construction:	Alabama Drydock &

Shipbuilding Co., Mobile,
AL, 1942

Last owner: Florida Department of
Natural Resources

Sunk: April 17, 1977

THOMAS HEYWARD LIBERTY SHIP

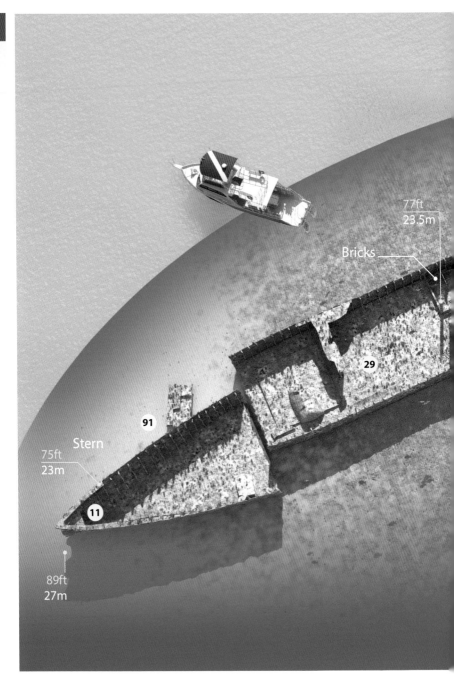

77ft
23.5m

Bricks

29

91

Stern

75ft
23m

11

89ft
27m

74ft
22.5m

Bow

84ft
25.5m

85

92

Bricks

Other species commonly found
at this site:

4   12   19   27   33   36   39   46   52

69   77   79   87   88

White Hill Ledge

Difficulty ● ○ ○
Current ● ○ ○
Depth ● ● ○
Reef ★★★☆
Fauna ★★★☆

Destin
White Hill
Ledge

Access 🚤 about 7.5mi (12km) southwest of Destin East Pass

Level Open Water

Location

Destin, Okaloosa County
GPS 30°18.503'N, 86°36.168'W

Getting there

White Hill Ledge is located a short distance southwest of Destin East Pass. This natural ledge site is easier to reach than many other dive spots as it is relatively close to the Destin East Pass. There are no surface mooring buoys to tie to, so operators typically drop anchor in the sand above or below the ledge, taking care not to contact or otherwise damage the ledge itself.

Access

This natural ledge is accessible to most divers although those with experience diving at depth will get more out of the site as the it ranges in depth from 80 to 87 feet (24.5 to 26.5 meters). The site is best reached via one of the dive shops operating out of Destin East Pass.

Description

White Hill Ledge (also called White Hill Reef or Whitehill Reef) is a natural limestone ledge that runs roughly east-west and offers between 5 and 7 feet (1.5 and 2 meters) of relief from the sandy seafloor. The ledge is heavily undercut along its length. In places, the ledge has broken off and formed boulders that stick out of the sand at random angles, creating additional complexity to the habitat. The site is bounded to the west by a split in the ledge into upper and lower sections. The upper ledge heads off in a west-northwest direction, while the lower one heads off in a west-southwest direction. To the east the ledge tapers off and is eventually swallowed by the sand. At any given time, more or less of the ledge may be visible depending on the impact of recent storms on sand deposits in the area.

The western half of the ledge is well defined with a sharp edge and a single row of fragments, while the eastern half is characterized by a wider swath of rocks and fragmented ledge which can make it harder to see where the actual ledge runs. A sharp S-curve in the middle of the site marks the half-way point of the explorable section of ledge, which stretches just over 530 feet (160 meters) in length.

Around 500 feet (150 meters) to the south of the ledge sits the wreck of the *Thomas Heyward Liberty Ship* (page 162). The two sites are rarely explored on the same dive given the distance that separates them, but they are commonly paired as a two-tank dive trip. The ledge is often visited first when there are too many vessels already anchored around the wreck. Given the Liberty Ship's proximity to the pass, it is popular with fishers as well as divers, and these sites are on a first-come-first-served basis.

The convenience of having the wreck close to the ledge does not just benefit dive planning. Together the two sites support a higher diversity of reef creatures than might be found if the two sites were separated. As a result, divers are likely to encounter quite a diverse array of reef fish, including spotted moray eels, toadfish, scorpionfish, angelfish, damselfish and even some octopus along the broken edge of the ledge. And thanks in part to the proximity of the artificial reef to the south, there are also many game fish at the site, including scamp, red and gag grouper, as well as red and mangrove snapper, and triggerfish. Sharks are also frequently seen on White Hill Ledge as well as plenty of lobsters.

Route

Divers typically descend to the ledge and gauge their position based on the depth of the seafloor. If the sand is around 80 feet (24.5 meters) deep, they should head south to find the ledge. If the seafloor is at 85 feet (26 meters) or deeper, they turn north to reach the ledge. Once at the ledge, divers can choose to head east or west, usually depending on the direction of the current if there is any present. The ledge is easy enough to follow and offers plenty of opportunity to explore under overhangs and in crevices for the wide diversity of reef life that can be found here.

SCIENTIFIC INSIGHT

Sponges have existed in Earth's oceans for at least 500 million years. They are one of the oldest types of animals on our planet and are very different from other life forms. For instance, sponge cells do not have specialized functions, meaning that each individual cell can do any and all jobs that any other sponge cell can do. This lack of specialization helps sponges regenerate from fragments. When violent storms break apart larger sponges, like some of the barrel sponges found on

White Hill Ledge, those pieces are spread across the reef where they can potentially take root and start growing again.

Giant barrel sponges can live as long as 2,000 years (maybe longer), and they can grow up to 6 feet (2 meters) across. So the next time you go diving and see a particularly large sponge, consider that it might have been around since the time of the Ancient Romans.

The natural ledges in Northwest Florida support large sponges and plenty of marine life like here on White Hill Ledge.

David Bailey ©

169

85ft
26m

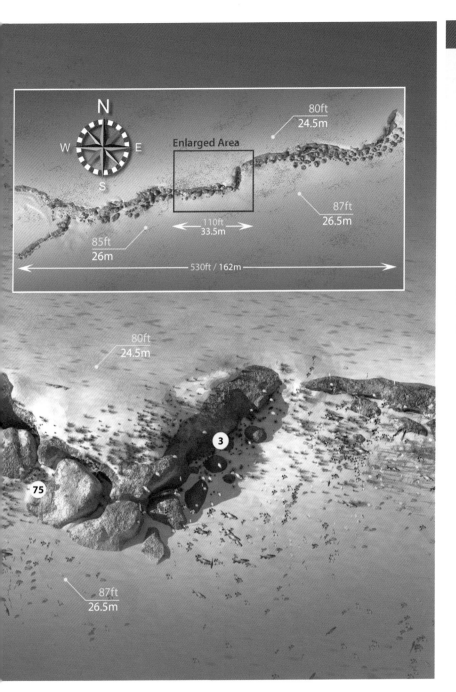

Other species commonly found at this site:

2   9   15   19   22   23   33   48   49

57   63   72   90   91

Mac's Reef

Difficulty	● ○ ○	
Current	● ○ ○	
Depth	● ● ○	
Reef	★★☆	
Fauna	★★☆	

Destin
Mac's Reef

Access 🚤 about 3mi (4.5km) southwest of Destin East Pass

Level Open Water

Location
Destin, Okaloosa County
GPS 30°21.395'N, 86°32.878'W

Getting there
Mac's Reef is located just southwest of Destin East Pass. The site is one of the closest artificial reefs to shore and is therefore just a short boat ride from the pass. There are no surface mooring buoys at the site,

so operators typically drop anchor in the sand near the artificial reef. Given its proximity to the pass, the site experiences a higher level of boat traffic compared to many of the other sites, so operators and divers must use caution when in the water.

Access
This site is accessible to all divers due to its open nature and shallow depth – the seabed sits at just 75 feet (23 meters). The site is best reached via one of the dive shops operating out of Destin East Pass.

Peter Leahy/Shutterstock ©

Spotted moray eels often hide under ledges and in rubble.

SCIENTIFIC INSIGHT

Artificial reefs have been used to modify the marine environment and attract marine life for thousands of years. In 250 BC, ancient Persians used ships to create artificial reefs to block pirates from accessing the Tigris River. These wrecks ended up attracting marine life and expanding local fishing grounds. In recent decades, humans have tested numerous structures and materials to determine what works best to attract fish and benthic organisms such as corals, sponges and other invertebrates. The worst materials are light and easily broken apart, such as PVC and plastic. Flexible materials such as car tires are not well suited for artificial reefs either, as they do not readily allow corals and sponges to grow on their surface. Cars in general, although metal, also make poor artificial reefs as their metal structure is designed to be light, which rusts and breaks down rapidly in salt water. Steel ships and concrete structures – like the culverts and targets of Mac's Reef – are generally recognized as making the best artificial reefs.

Description

The Charles H. McClenahan Memorial Reef is named after Charles "Mac" McClenahan, a former Department of Defense employee with 50 years

of service. Beginning in 1964, Mac spent 20 years of his 22-year stint at the Eglin Air Force Base as part of the Explosive Ordinance Disposal team. He then went on to spend 28 years in the Civil Service, specializing in guns and munitions. His main work focus was concrete structures and how best to defeat them. His work led to the destruction of an untold number of concrete targets over the years. The memorial reef, known colloquially as "Mac's Reef," is fittingly made up of old concrete targets from nearby Eglin Air Force Base, where he worked.

A total of 981.5 tons of concrete materials were deposited at Mac's Reef, located at the center of Okaloosa County's Fish Haven 13 permitted site. The deployment included targets that were dropped in a pile on November 7th, 2015, which now rises 12 feet (3.5 meters) above the sandy seabed.

The rest of the materials include concrete culverts using materials also provided by Eglin AFB. The culverts create complex habitat immediately to the south of the pile of targets, with many culverts settling on top, and to the sides, of the targets. Also, a 9/11 memorial was deployed to the site's northeast corner in September 2020, featuring steel and concrete pieces from the World Trade Center and the Pentagon.

The result is a veritable playground of complex habitat for a variety of reef creatures. Both the targets and the culverts vary in size, with some of the largest culverts measuring nearly 5 feet (1.5 meters) in diameter and large enough for divers to swim through. A few culverts stand upright, with their bases buried in the soft sand, but most lie on their sides or angled on top of one another. The pile of targets makes up the northern third of the site, while the culverts are concentrated in the southern two-thirds of the site. In all, the site stretches roughly 184 feet (56 meters) from north to south.

The site is a fun place for divers to explore thanks to the varied structure and the plentiful animal life. Tomtates are particularly abundant here, while divers are likely to see mackerel and barracuda in the water column above the jumbled reef, along

with greater amberjacks and cobia. Meanwhile, damselfish and angelfish are frequent visitors to the reef. There is plenty of sand in between the individual culverts, and flounder are plentiful at this site, although they can be hard to spot as they lie camouflaged in the soft sand. Divers should keep a

look out for southern stingrays as well, since these creatures generally stick to the periphery of the artificial reef.

Route

Divers should have plenty of bottom time to

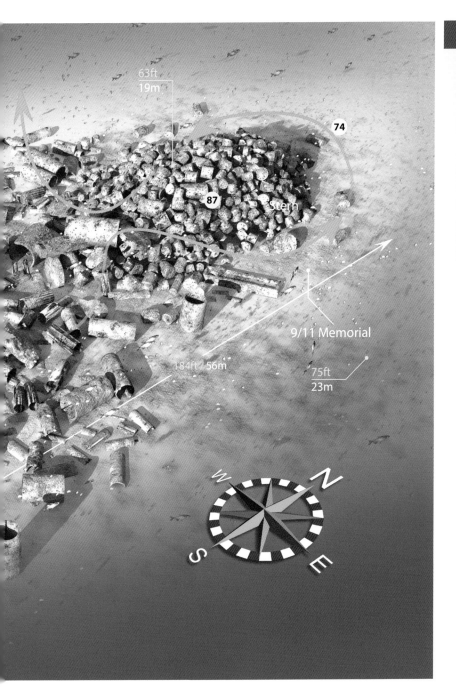

Other species commonly found
at this site:

J **K** **L** **4** **19** **20** **24** **27** **38**

48 **56** **75** **80** **91**

63ft
19m

87

74

71

75ft
23m

investigate Mac's Reef. The site is open, which means divers can choose whichever route they want to fully explore the area. They may want to consider splitting their bottom time in half between the culverts and the targets. The only real risk of not having a planned route is that divers may spend so much time exploring the many nooks and crannies in one part of the reef that they run out of time to explore the rest of it. While some of the culverts may be large enough to swim through, only divers with experience and excellent buoyancy control should attempt

67ft
20.5m

74ft
22.5m

64

67

this feat. Contact with the inside edges of the culverts reef risks damaging the reef life that has colonized those surfaces.

Miss Louise

Difficulty ● ○ ○
Current ● ○ ○
Depth ● ○ ○
Reef ★☆☆
Fauna ★★☆

Destin ●
Miss Louise

Access 🚤 about 5mi (8km) east
of Destin East Pass

Level Open Water

Location
Destin, Okaloosa County
GPS 30°22.285'N, 86°25.315'W

Getting there
Miss Louise is located just 0.65 miles (1 kilometer) off the beach, which makes it one of the closest wrecks to the Okaloosa shoreline. Even so, it remains out of range of shore divers and is best accessed via boat. There are no surface mooring buoys at this site, so operators typically tie in to the wreck or drop anchor in the sand nearby.

Access
This site is accessible to all divers and is often used as a training site for open water divers. It sits upright on a sandy seafloor at a depth of just 57 feet (17.5 meters). The site is best reached via one of the dive shops operating out of Destin East Pass.

Description
Miss Louise was a small towboat (or push tugboat) that likely started her career plying the waters of the Mississippi river. Towboats were the backbone of river commerce from the late 19th century onwards. To this day, towboats still operate in these waters, pushing and pulling barges filled with materials, and providing a vital link between commercial ports.

There are a few towboats named *Miss Louise* that match her general size and description built as far back as 1957 and as recently as 1971. Records for tugboats and towboats are difficult to find and even more difficult to confirm, making it hard to know for sure where this small vessel was built and where she operated. The best guess, based on the available records, places *Miss Louise* as being built in Nashville, Tennessee, by the Nashville Bridge Co. in 1957. She was originally named the *Lola H* and was built for the Tennessee Towing Co., according to the Mississippi transportation records of the time. Some records name the Barrett Line as

DID YOU KNOW? ❓

The Mississippi River has been a vital source of food and trade for centuries. Native Americans fished these waters in cottonwood dugouts and bark canoes. French Canadians used the river to connect their settlements from Canada to Louisiana on the shores of the Gulf of Mexico. By the time of the Louisiana Purchase in 1803, the most commonly used boat on the river was the long, cigar-shaped, keelboat, sometimes known as a poleboat. These powerless rafts could measure nearly 100 feet (30 meters) in length, and they were floated downstream with the current and worked back upstream using poles or a cordelle, which was a long heavy rope used to pull boats along the shore. Sometimes boatmen would even use overhanging tree branches to pull the boats upstream – a process known as bushwhacking. Under ideal conditions, this backbreaking work enabled boats to move upstream at a speed of about one mile per hour (1.6 kilometers per hour). A trip up stream from the coast to Minneapolis could take six months and typically involved grueling 15-hour days.

the original owner of the *Lola H*, however. The latter company was an important transportation company based in Cairo, Illinois, dating back to the late 1800s that operated a fleet of towboats in the Mississippi watershed.

Whatever the specifics of her past, *Miss Louise* was deployed as an artificial reef on March 19, 1997. The shallow site meant that a portion of her superstructure needed to be removed

before deployment. Storms and wave action took care of what was left, leaving nothing more than the main deck and the sturdy, upright bumpers that rise up 8 feet (2.5 meters) from the top of the bow.

The wreck does not offer much in the way of penetration opportunities, but it supports a wide range of fish and other reef creatures. Large schools of grunts, including tomtates,

A diver inspects the portside push pad on *Miss Louise*.

form over the wreck, often to the point of obscuring the wreck itself. Atlantic spadefish are commonly seen schooling in the waters above the wreck, while cocoa damselfish are usually close to the hull. The nooks and crannies of the wreck provide ample space for grouper to hide, including scamp and gag grouper, while batfish often rest on the sand and rubble just a few feet from the wreck itself. Lucky divers have even reported seeing large goliath grouper and sea turtles here, although the former are less common.

Miss Louise is one of the original members of the Florida Panhandle Shipwreck Trail.

Route

Given the small size and open nature of the site, there is little need for a specific route plan for this wreck. Most divers take their time exploring around the outside of the wreck before moving on to the central portions of the wreck, including the hold. There is plenty of bottom time to check out every nook and cranny of the site.

42ft
13m

63

52

Bow

33

N

E

W

S

71

57ft
17.5m

Other species commonly found at this site:

3   4   5   30   32   47   51   62   66

68   74   78   85   88

53ft
16m

77

65ft
17m

67

Stern

Name:	*Miss Louise*		TN, 1957
Type:	Towboat	**Last owner:**	Tennessee Towing Co
Previous names:	*Lola H*	**Sunk:**	March 19, 1997
Length:	67ft (20.5m)		
Tonnage:	135grt		
Construction:	Nashville Bridge Co. Nashville,		

Eglin LCM-8

Difficulty	● ○ ○	
Current	● ○ ○	
Depth	● ● ○	
Reef	★☆☆	
Fauna	★★☆	

Destin ●
Eglin LCM-8

Access 🛥 about 11mi (17.5km) southeast
of Destin East Pass

Level Advanced

Location
Destin, Okaloosa County
GPS 30°15.916'N, 86°23.159'W

Getting there
Eglin LCM-8 is located relatively close to shore compared to some of the deeper wrecks and is accessible via a short boat ride out of the pass. There are no surface mooring buoys at this site, so operators typically tie in to the wreck or drop anchor in the sand nearby.

Access
This site is accessible to advanced divers due to its depth. The low profile of the wreck means it sits quite close to the seabed, which is at 97 feet (29.5 meters). However, the open structure means it requires no particular experience with wrecks. The site is best reached via one of the dive shops operating out of Destin East Pass.

Description
Eglin LCM-8 was a 74-foot (22.5-meter) military landing craft. The LCMs (Landing Craft Mechanized), as a group, are sometimes referred to as a "Mike boats," and they were originally designed for deploying troops and equipment onto beaches during amphibious landings. There are many different types of LCM, but the basic design has remained the same for decades, consisting of raised lateral walls, a front drop-down gate and an open deck area for troops and equipment. The "8" in the name LCM-8 denotes the specific design of this model, which was originally for use in rivers during the Vietnam War. First deployed in 1959, these LCMs operated with either a three- or four-man crew. They were apparently very adaptable platforms that were used for everything from rescue missions to equipment transport.

Very little is known about the history of this particular LCM-8 craft or where and when she was built. Prior to her deployment as an artificial reef, she was in service at Tyndall Air Force Base. She was transferred to nearby Eglin AFB for use as an instrumentation platform. She was cleaned of all fluids and running gear in May 1996 and set aside until Okaloosa County could use her as an artificial reef. She was further cleaned of potential hazards in September 2000 and prepped for deployment before being inspected by the U.S. Coast Guard. The preparation included cutting holes in the unconnected bilge compartments so that the water would distribute evenly during scuttling. She was towed out to sea on November 29, 2000 and deployed as an artificial reef with the help of two large anchors.

She originally settled on her port side, but has since fallen back to an upright position, although she still has a noticeable list to port. About the only structure she had to begin with was a small wheelhouse that now sits as debris just off the port side and is in the process of sinking into the soft sand. There is an internal framework that still stands in the open hold of the boat where troops, trucks and other machinery would have been located, but the twisted metal represents more of an entanglement risk than a swim-through opportunity.

Eglin LCM-8 was intended to replenish the structure of the county's Fish Haven #6 site. Despite her low profile, the site supports a variety of reef fish, most noticeably red snapper, which makes the site popular with fishers. Vermilion snapper and tomtate grunts form dense schools that can sometimes obscure the shape of the wreck. Meanwhile, gag grouper and large porgy also frequent the site, along with schools of jacks, most notably greater amberjacks. Individual white-spotted soapfish can be found sheltering in the various nooks and crannies of the artificial reef, while blue angelfish often cruise through the site.

Route
Due to the depth of *LCM-8* and her low profile, divers will have little bottom time to explore the site. Fortunately, the relatively small size of the wreck makes it easy for divers to circumnavigate

SCIENTIFIC INSIGHT

Scientific research suggests that many marine fish species around the world form spawning aggregations at distinct locations, which are often areas where currents are strong, such as pinnacles, channels between reefs, and outer reef slopes. The presence of a current is an important factor as it helps take fish gametes (eggs and sperm) that are released into the water, away from the reef to increase their chances of survival.

Commercially important species are extremely vulnerable to over exploitation if these sites are targeted by fishers during spawning aggregations. Many grouper species are aggregate spawners, including the gag grouper that are commonly found at this site. For decades, fishers across the Caribbean have focused their efforts on known spawning sites during the time of year when spawning takes place. This has led to devastating declines in many grouper populations across the region.

Thankfully, these days more grouper spawning sites than ever before are being protected and it is hoped this action will help preserve these fish for future generations.

the structure. Such an open site does not require a specific route, but divers might consider circling the outside of the wreck first before checking out the main hold. The internal structure represents an entanglement risk, so divers should monitor their surroundings carefully if they want to approach the hull and investigate the bilge areas.

A diver hangs out over a wreck amid a school of reef fish.

Lureen Ferretti ©

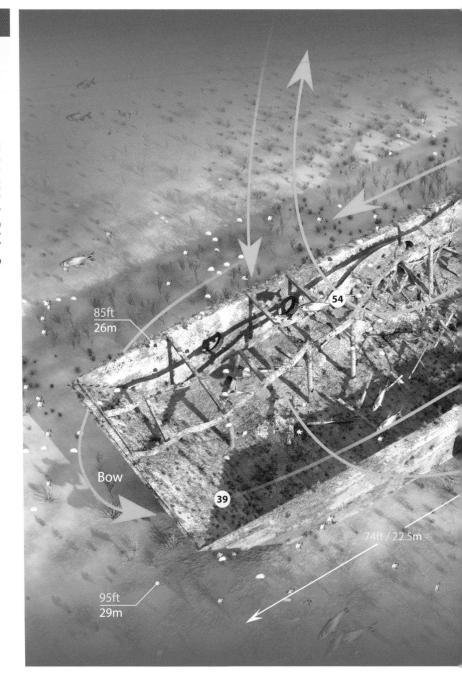

85ft
26m

54

Bow

39

74ft / 22.5m

95ft
29m

Other species commonly found at this site:

23   31   33   38   42   48   49   61   72

74   80   82   86   88

Name:	*Eglin LCM-8*	**Last owner:**	U.S. Air Force
Type:	Landing craft	**Sunk:**	November 29, 2000
Previous names:	n/a		
Length:	74ft (22.5m)		
Tonnage:	105grt		
Construction:	n/a		

Janet

Difficulty	● ● ○
Current	● ○ ○
Depth	● ● ○
Reef	★ ☆ ☆
Fauna	★ ★ ☆

Destin ○
Janet ●

Access 🚤 about 11mi (17.5km) southeast of Destin East Pass

Level Advanced

Location

Destin, Okaloosa County
GPS 30°15.839′N, 86°23.104′W

Getting there

Janet is a dive site that is relatively close to shore compared to some of the deeper artificial reefs and she sits just 500 feet (180 meters) southeast of nearby *Eglin LCM-8*. The site is accessible with a short boat ride out of Destin East Pass. There are no surface mooring buoys at this site, so operators typically tie in to the wreck or anchor in the sand nearby.

Access

This site is most accessible to advanced divers with experience at depth. Those with the qualifications to explore overhead environments may get more out of the site. The seabed is 97 feet (29.5 meters) deep, although the top of the wreck reaches a depth of 80 feet (24.5 meters), which means divers can keep to a slightly shallower profile if they wish. The site is best reached via one of the dive shops operating out of Destin East Pass.

Description

Janet was an 85-foot-long (30-meter) tugboat deployed as an artificial reef on October 1, 1997. Very little is known about the history of this vessel before she was scuttled. She was originally a standard model of tugboat that resembles many other artificial reefs in the region. These tugboats make excellent artificial reefs as they are often built with thick steel hulls necessary for their tough line of work. The thickness helps the steel survive well in the harsh saltwater environment.

Janet is in excellent condition given her time spent underwater. She sits upright on a sandy seabed, and her two-tiered superstructure reaches 17 feet (5 meters) above the sand. Her intact superstructure offers divers plenty of opportunities for limited penetration through both her wheelhouse and her main

superstructure level. The top of the main structure is open, allowing for easier exploration by divers with wreck experience. Slight corrosion of some walls and doorways is visible in the aft section of the wreck on the port side.

Along with the normal complement of schooling tomtates and vermilion snapper, divers are also likely to spot blue angelfish, cobia and grouper swimming around the wreck. Stingrays and toadfish are often found out in the sand that

A diver is surrounded by schooling fish off *Janet*'s stern.

RELAX & RECHARGE

The Destin family has a long and rich history in the Panhandle. Dewey Destin's great, great grandfather, Leonard Destin, founded the town in 1835. For over a century, he, his children and grandchildren helped build a thriving fishing industry on the Emerald Coast. Seafood stores grew from this industry and ultimately **Dewey Destin's Seafood Restaurants**, which are located in both Destin (at 9 Calhoun Avenue and 202 Harbor Boulevard) and nearby Navarre (8673 Navarre Parkway). They specialize in fast-casual dining – you order at a window and then relax outside with a drink while your fresh seafood is prepared. The restaurants serve multiple fried and grilled staples, including shrimp, mahi mahi, scallops, tuna, oysters and catfish. There are also rotating catch-of-the-day options that may include swordfish, grouper, triggerfish, tripletail and cobia among others. These are served as bronzed, blackened or in a honey teriyaki style. Visit: **Destinseafood.com**

surrounds the wreck, while barracuda tend to hang out above the wheelhouse. They often greet divers as they descend onto the wreck at the start of their dive, or see them off as they depart the wreck.

Route
Due to the depth of the seabed here, divers will not have a lot of bottom time if they spend too much time investigating the hull. Most routes circle the wreck at the main deck level before exploring the main structure and wheelhouse. The openings cut into this wreck allow divers with penetration experience to enter and exit in numerous places. The wheelhouse is relatively small, but has space for divers with good buoyancy control to enter and look through the windows toward the bow. With the

David Bailey ©

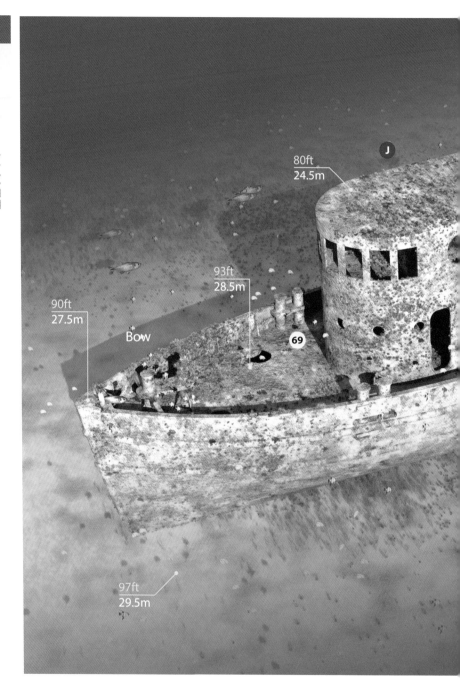

80ft
24.5m

J

93ft
28.5m

90ft
27.5m

Bow

69

97ft
29.5m

highest point of the wreck reaching just 80 feet
(24.5 meters), divers will want to manager their
limited bottom time wisely, as there is plenty to
explore on this wreck.

92ft
28m

Stern

88ft
27m

3

63

33

72

97ft
29.5m

N

E

S

W

Name:	*Janet*
Type:	Tugboat
Previous names:	n/a
Length:	85ft (30m)
Tonnage:	n/a
Construction:	n/a

Last owner:	n/a
Sunk:	October 1, 1997

92ft
28m

63

88ft
27m

Stern

97ft
29.5m

72

80ft
24.5m

90ft
27.5m

93ft
28.5m

Bow

97ft
29.5m

J

3

69

33

Other species commonly found
at this site:

2   5   6   11   38   48   49   56   61

79   81   83   86   88

Monica Lee

Difficulty ● ● ○
Current ● ○ ○
Depth ● ● ●
Reef ★★★☆
Fauna ★★★☆

Destin ○
Monica Lee

Access 🚤 about 18mi (29km) southwest of Destin East Pass

Level Advanced

Location
Destin, Okaloosa County
GPS 30°09.341'N, 86°22.223'W

Getting there
Monica Lee is located far enough from shore that she should only be visited by operators and private vessels with experience operating in the Gulf. There are no surface mooring buoys at this site, so operators typically tie in to the wreck or anchor in the sand nearby.

Access
This site is accessible to advanced divers due to its maximum depth of 117 feet (35.5 meters). Even the top of the wreck sits at a depth of 100 feet (30.5 meters), which means the site offers divers a relatively deep profile without much opportunity for extended bottom time. The site is best reached via one of the dive shops operating out of Destin East Pass.

Description
Monica Lee was a small, 49-foot (15-meter) tugboat deployed as an artificial reef on May 10, 2011. She currently anchors the center of an X-shaped artificial reef area known as Conch Reef. Pyramid-shaped artificial reef modules extend in lines out toward the northeast, northwest, southeast and southwest – although divers are unlikely to see the modules from the wreck itself as they are hundreds of feet away.

Originally built in 1955, *Monica Lee* started her career on the east coast of Florida with McCulley Marine Services, based out of Stuart, Florida – a company that does a lot of artificial reef work in the southeast Florida region. She was sold to Turn Key Marine Service in 2006 – a boating company located just east of Destin – and eventually acquired by Okaloosa County as an artificial reef.

Monica Lee currently sits upright on a sandy seafloor with a slight list to her port side. The depth of this site is what makes it accessible to

A diver explores *Monica Lee* a few years back when the chicken coops were still attached to her deck.

RELAX & RECHARGE

Burrito del Sol started as a Destin-based food truck in 2012. Only a year later, they opened permanent locations in Fort Walton Beach (201-B Miracle Strip Parkway) and Destin (517 Harbor Boulevard). The menu is packed with tasty Mexican favorites, such as burritos, tacos, quesadillas and nachos – all built to order. You can select from a range of meats, including chicken, ground beef, steak, shrimp and fish, or go for a vegetarian option like ginger marinated tempeh. All the seasonings, sauces, salsa and guacamole are homemade, and there are ever-changing and unique daily specials. Happy hour runs from 4pm to 6pm on weekdays, where certain shots and margaritas are $3 each. They also have daily drink specials. Visit: **Burritodelsol.com**

experienced divers only. The top of the wreck reaches rises to just 100 feet (30.5 meters) in depth. The wreck is relatively intact, although the forward wall of the wheelhouse has been torn away. Jagged metal from the window casings descend from the existing wheelhouse roof. The hanging metal makes accessing the wheelhouse difficult for all but the most experienced wreck divers. Fortunately access points to the tug's small interior are still present in the first level of the superstructure, and through the hole in the superstructure's roof.

There are plenty of crevices and recesses in the wreck to support marine life, and it has attracted the usual complement of schooling tomtates and snapper, including large red snapper. The artificial reef is also popular with barracuda, yellow jacks and greater amberjacks. Whitespotted soapfish, blue angelfish and several species of damselfish are also common on this site, closer in to the surface of the wreck.

Route

While the site is deep, the wreck is small enough that divers should have little trouble exploring the entire artificial reef. Most routes begin at the stern, and gradually circle the wreck. Divers with experience and good buoyancy control can penetrate the first level of the superstructure through the doors or the roof of the main level. The wheelhouse can be readily accessed via the large windows on either side of the upper level. However, divers should be aware of the risk posed by the damaged metal window frames in the forward area of the wheelhouse.

David Bailey ©

J

100ft
30.5m

106ft
32.5m

40

110ft
33.5m

Bow

117ft
35.5m

49ft / 15m

80

78

114ft
34.5m

Stern

111ft
34m

33

3

119ft
36m

Name:	*Monica Lee*		San Francisco, CA, 1955
Type:	Tugboat	Last owner:	Turn Key Marine Services
Previous names:	n/a	Sunk:	May 10, 2011
Length:	49ft (15m)		
Tonnage:	n/a		
Construction:	Maine Ironworks,		

114ft
34.5m

Stern

111ft
34m

119ft
36m

100ft
30.5m

110ft
33.5m

Bow

106ft
32.5m

J

40

117ft
35.5m

N
W
E
S

Other species commonly found at this site:

11   38   41   50   61   63   69   72   79

82   85   86   87   88

Other Okaloosa County sites

The following list represents other popular dive sites in Okaloosa County visited by local operators.

47 FH-16

GPS 30°20.890'N, 86°46.875'W

Difficulty	● ○ ○		
Current	● ○ ○		
Depth	● ● ○		
Reef	★☆☆		
Fauna	★☆☆		

This site features 395 tons of concrete material, including Jersey barriers and manhole covers, donated by Eglin Air Force Base and deployed by the county in 2017. These materials sit at a depth of 66 feet (20 meters) and offer 10 feet (3 meters) of relief from the sandy bottom.

48 Burgess Barge

GPS 30°09.247'N, 86°44.671'W

Difficulty	● ○ ○
Current	● ● ○
Depth	● ● ●
Reef	★☆☆
Fauna	★☆☆

Once a 120-foot (36.5-meter) lighter barge, *Burgess Barge* now sits at a depth of 125 feet (38 meters). This site is also sometimes referred to as 18's Teens Reef or simply Steel Barge. With just 6 feet (2 meters) of relief, this site has a deep average depth. The barge was deployed as an artificial reef back in 1979, which makes it one of the older "official" artificial reefs off shore of Okaloosa County. The vessel has become well-colonized with marine life.

51 FH-15

GPS 30°21.891'N, 86°42.374'W

Difficulty	● ○ ○
Current	● ○ ○
Depth	● ● ○
Reef	★☆☆
Fauna	★★☆

FH15 features 370 tons of concrete culverts, manhole covers, slabs and bridge beams donated by Eglin Air Force Base. It was deployed in 2017 with a max depth of 71 feet (21.5 meters) and 11 feet (3.5 meters) of relief from the sandy bottom.

52 Sea Barb

GPS 30°08.934'N, 86°40.593'W

Difficulty	● ● ○
Current	● ○ ○
Depth	● ● ●
Reef	★★☆
Fauna	★★☆

Sea Barb (also called *Odyssey*) was an 85-foot (26-meter) steel-hulled paddlewheeler used as an artificial reef in 2002. The vessel once plied the waters of the Mississippi River by some accounts. Currently, the wreck rests on a sandy seabed at a depth of 110 feet (33.5 meters).

55 FH-14

GPS 30°21.139'N, 86°36.878W

Difficulty	● ○ ○
Current	● ○ ○
Depth	● ● ○
Reef	★★☆
Fauna	★★☆

Smaller than the more popular Mac's Reef located to the east (see pg 172), FH14 features 590 tons of concrete targets from Eglin Air Force Base. Deployed in 2015 at a depth of 72 feet (22 meters), this debris sits in a north-south pile that acts as the center for reef clusters to the west, north and east. These clusters are connected by more than 500 feet (150 meters) of debris trails to aid navigation.

56 Angelina B.

GPS 30°07.387'N, 86°36.693'W

Difficulty	● ○ ○
Current	● ○ ○
Depth	● ● ○
Reef	★☆☆
Fauna	★★☆

One of the more compact tugboats deployed as an artificial reef in Okaloosa County, *Angelina B.* measures just 65 feet (20 meters) in length but offers up to 32 feet (10 meters) of relief. Originally owned by Brown Marine Services, a local barge and tug company that has since closed, the county deployed the tug as an artificial reef in 1999 at a depth of 135 feet (41 meters). Divers may spot a resident goliath grouper on the wreck, along with jacks, barracuda and even the occasional bull shark.

59 Barrel Barge

GPS 30°21.818'N, 86°36.083'W

Difficulty	●	○	○
Current	●	○	○
Depth	●	●	○
Reef	★	★	☆
Fauna	★	★	☆

A popular site with local divers, *Barrel Barge* was deployed by Okaloosa County as an artificial reef in 1992 along with large fuel tanks and the bed of a dump truck welded to the top of the barge. Hurricanes have since scattered the additions around the site, but it still offers 16 feet (5 meters) of relief above the sand, with a maximum depth of 72 feet (22 meters). Divers report seeing plenty of jacks, spadefish, snapper and flounder at this site.

60 Brown Barge (aka Fort Walton Barge)

GPS 30°21.537'N, 86°35.622'W

Difficulty	●	○	○
Current	●	○	○
Depth	●	●	○
Reef	★	☆	☆
Fauna	★	★	☆

One of the longest barges deployed as an artificial reef in Okaloosa County, the 200-foot (61-meter) *Brown Barge* has since broken into three sections. The wreck sits at a depth of 78 feet (24 meters) and provides just 10 to 12 feet (3 to 3.5 meters) of relief above the seabed.

61 Deborah

GPS 30°07.503'N, 86°35.403'W

Difficulty	●	●	○
Current	●	○	○
Depth	●	●	●
Reef	★	☆	☆
Fauna	★	★	☆

Originally a 135-foot-long (41-meter) tugboat, *Deborah* flipped over as she was being deployed as an artificial reef in 1999, ultimately settling upside down at a depth of 135 feet (41 meters). The small space beneath her overturned hull shelters plenty of grouper, snapper and grunts, while stingrays are common in the nearby sand.

63 Main Stack

GPS 30°20.809'N, 86°29.636'W

Difficulty	●	○	○
Current	●	○	○
Depth	●	●	○
Reef	★	☆	☆
Fauna	★	★	☆

Also called Destin Bridge Rubble, this site is one of the most popular in the area. It features sections of roadway and other concrete rubble from the old Destin Bridge at a depth of 65 feet (20 meters). The debris stretches across three sites called Main Stack, East Stack and North Stack. Divers explore the many overhangs and small ledges formed by the debris, and often spot sea bass, angelfish, grunts and snapper.

64 Eglin Barge (aka Air Force Barge or 100' Barge)

GPS 30°21.248'N, 86°29.580'W

Difficulty	●	○	○
Current	●	●	○
Depth	●	●	○
Reef	★	☆	☆
Fauna	★	☆	☆

This artificial reef was deployed in 1977 – officially the seventh deployment of the Okaloosa County artificial reef program. The site goes by various names, including *100' Barge*, *Eglin Barge* and *Air Force Barge*, all descriptive of the origin and size of the original vessel. The site offers just 4 feet (1 meter) of relief from the seabed at a depth of 68 feet (20.5 meters). A goliath grouper is reported to inhabit the bow area.

65 Phoenix Barge (aka Lost Barge)

GPS 30°17.890'N, 86°27.385'W

Difficulty ● ○ ○
Current ● ○ ○
Depth ● ● ○
Reef ★★☆
Fauna ★★☆

This 80-foot-long (24.5-meter) steel barge sits at a depth of 75 feet (22.5 meters). It offers only 8 feet (2.5 meters) of relief above the sandy seabed and is a popular site with spearfishers.

67 Tully

GPS 30°07.155'N, 86°26.074'W

Difficulty ● ● ●
Current ● ● ○
Depth ● ● ●
Reef ★★☆
Fauna ★★☆

This deep site features a push tug measuring 100 feet (31 meters) in length. The wreck sits on the seabed at approximately 135 feet (41 meters). She provides shelter for plenty of reef fish that hang out in and around the structure.

68 A.J.'s/Carey Ricks Memorial Reef

GPS 30°17.890'N, 86°27.385'W

Difficulty ● ○ ○
Current ● ○ ○
Depth ● ● ●
Reef ★★☆
Fauna ★★☆

This site features a 75-foot-long (22.5-meter) former restaurant boat that was stripped down to its metal frame before being deployed as an artificial reef in 2011 along with stacks of chicken transport units for complexity. Local restaurant AJ's Seafood and Oyster Bar sponsored the memorial to local fisherman Carey Ricks. The site is a popular fishing spot and has a max depth of 113 feet (34.5 meters).

69 Dylan

GPS 30°07.614'N, 86°23.469'W

Difficulty ● ● ○
Current ● ○ ○
Depth ● ● ●
Reef ★★☆
Fauna ★☆☆

This 61-foot (18.5-meter) steel-hulled sailboat was seized by U.S. Customs in 2019 after agents found 400 pounds of cocaine on board with a street value of $7.5 million USD. The county acquired the vessel and sank her as an artificial reef one year later. She sits at a depth of 119 feet (36.5 meters) with her shallowest point at 107 feet (32.6 meters). She was the first element of the reef known as the "boatyard site" featuring multiple wrecks near one another.

DID YOU KNOW?

Many of the artificial reefs in this region were funded through the Natural Resource Damage Assessment Early Restoration Phase III – Northwest Florida Artificial Reef Creation and Restoration Project (or NRDA for short). The project spanned all five coastal counties of Northwest Florida with a total cost of more than $10 million USD and involved deploying more than 3,000 prefabricated artificial reefs in 48 different permitted areas. The money for the project was set aside to offset the negative economic impacts from the BP oil spill in 2010. The project was one of the most expensive artificial reef construction projects in Florida.

Courtesy of ScubaTech of NW Florida ©

Sea Cobra brings her divers back to shore after visiting one of the many Okaloosa dive sites.

73 Baskins Barge

GPS 30°05.188'N, 86°21.331'W

Difficulty ● ● ○
Current ● ● ○
Depth ● ● ●
Reef ★★☆
Fauna ★★☆

Baskins was an 80-foot-long (24.5-meter) lighter barge deployed as an artificial reef in 1996 at a depth of 135 feet (41 meters). She was originally used to deploy the range towers that currently sit to the east of Apalachicola. The wreck tops out at minimum depth of 92 feet (28 meters) offering over 40 feet (12 meters) of relief Divers are likely to see amberjacks, grouper, snapper and spadefish.

74 Eglin LCM-1

GPS 30°09.705'N, 86°19.636'W

Difficulty ● ● ○
Current ● ● ○
Depth ● ● ●
Reef ★☆☆
Fauna ★☆☆

The second of two LCMs deployed in Okaloosa County, *Eglin LCM-1* is a 74-foot (22.5-meters) landing craft donated by Eglin Air Force Base in 1991. The wreck sits at a depth of 103 feet (31.5 meters) and has deteriorated more than *LCM-8,* which is located to the northwest (see page 182 for more information).

75 Prewitt

GPS 30°03.696'N, 86°18.472'W

Difficulty ● ● ●
Current ● ○ ○
Depth ● ● ●
Reef ★★☆
Fauna ★★☆

Built in 1944 for the U.S. Army, this 86-foot (26-meter) tugboat was used by the Army Corps of Engineers before being bought by a company based in New Orleans. She was eventually deployed as an artificial reef in June 1998 and now sits at a depth of 137 feet (42 meters).

WALTON COUNTY

While Walton County may lack a pass that provides access to the ocean, the county has still invested in four shore-accessible snorkel reefs and a dozen or more artificial reef sites farther offshore. One of these sites is Northwest Florida's only underwater museum. The shore-accessible reefs feature modules that mirror the design popular along the rest of the coast, namely a central pole anchored to the seabed with three or four concrete discs affixed to the top of the pole. These discs support colonizing marine life and provide structure and habitat for a variety of reef creatures. Many offshore sites include larger reef modules that help create more varied habitat and help support the dive and fishing industry. These sites carry the names of the parks that sit on the coastline adjacent to them.

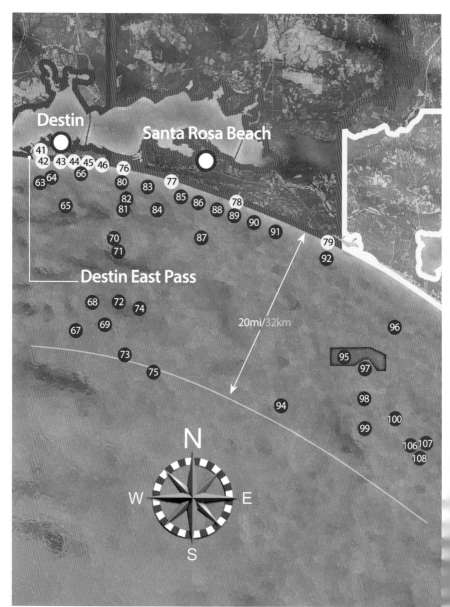

Walton County keeps an up-to-date list of all of its artificial reef sites online. To see if new reefs have been added since publication, please visit: **Swarareefs.org/reefs/**

Dive and snorkel sites

WALTON COUNTY

76	Dolphin Snorkel Reef		
77	Seahorse Snorkel Reef		
78	Turtle Snorkel Reef		
79	Grouper Snorkel Reef		
80	Miramar Beach Reef		
81	*Walton Hopper Barge*		
82	Miramar Frangista Reef		
83	Topsail Bluff Reef		
84	Fish Haven #1		
85	Fort Panic Reef		
86	Ed Walline Reef		
87	Fish Haven #2		
88	Blue Mountain		
89	Underwater Museum of Art		
90	Santa Clara Reef		
91	Deep Lake Reef		
92	Inlet Beach Reef		

A diver inspects the inside of the Swara Skull, one of the many sculptures of the Underwater Museum of Art.

Courtesy of UMA ©

Dolphin Snorkel Reef

Difficulty	● ○ ○
Current	● ○ ○
Depth	● ○ ○
Reef	★☆☆
Fauna	★★☆

Destin ○●
Dolphin Snorkel
Reef

Access 🚙 about 14 mins from downtown Destin
🏊 about 7 mins from shore

Level Open Water

Location
Miramar Beach, Walton County
GPS 30°22.521′N, 86°23.325′W

Getting there

From downtown Destin head east on US-98 along the coast for around 7 miles (11.5 kilometers). Just 0.6 miles (1 kilometer) after crossing into Walton County, turn right on Driftwood Road. After 0.5 miles (0.8 kilometers), Driftwood Road ends at the Scenic Gulf Drive and the water's edge. Turn right on Scenic Gulf Drive and then left into Miramar Regional Public Beach, where there is ample parking. The official address is 2396 Scenic Highway 98, Miramar Beach, Florida, 32550.

Access

This beach access has restroom facilities and several short boardwalks that lead from the parking lot to the beach adjacent to the site. The reef modules are located directly off shore from the yellow poles anchored in the sand just west of the buildings next to the parking lot. The reef modules themselves are embedded in the sand about 680 feet (207 meters) off the beach. There are no buoys in the water to mark the site, so divers and snorkelers will need to use the yellow navigation poles on the shore to locate the reef modules. A diver down flag is required by law for both divers and snorkelers at this site.

Description

This artificial reef complex was deployed in August 2017 and features 77 modules in the shape of a dolphin. The shallowest modules are anchored on the seabed at a depth of around 12 feet (3.5 meters), while the deeper ones bottom out at closer to 19 feet (6 meters). All modules are at least 6 feet (2 meters) below the surface of the water with the deepest modules rising to a depth of 12 feet (3.5 meters). Divers and snorkelers are likely to see damselfish, blennies, snapper, triggerfish and grouper here, along with the occasional octopus and sea turtle. Ironically, divers have even reported seeing dolphins here.

Public Beach Access

SAFETY TIP

The surf can sometimes be high at this site, so snorkelers and divers should be careful entering and exiting the water. The safest way to enter the water is to first ensure that both buddies are fully geared up and have completed their buddy check. Only then should they enter the water with air already in their BCDs and without fins attached. Once in the water, buddies should use each other for the support, if necessary, to attach their fins and push through the surf as quickly as possible. When exiting, divers should remember to keep their mask and regulator in place, their BCD inflated and remove their fins in the water so they can walk up the beach.

Yellow poles

685ft / 209m

200ft / 61m

340ft / 104m

12ft
3.5m

19ft
6m

Seahorse Snorkel Reef

Difficulty	● ○ ○	
Current	● ○ ○	
Depth	● ○ ○	
Reef	★★★	
Fauna	★★☆	

Destin
Seahorse
Snorkel Reef

Access 🚙 about 34 mins from downtown
Destin
🏊 about 7 mins from shore

Level Open Water

Location
Santa Rosa Beach, Walton County
GPS 30°21.350'N, 86°16.664'W

Getting there
From downtown Destin, head east on US-98 along the coast for around 13 miles (21 kilometers). With Topsail Hill Preserve State Park on your right, head southeast on West County Highway 30A. After 0.33 miles (0.5 kilometers) turn right into the state park entrance. Once in the park, there is a small parking lot serviced by the park tram that can take visitors down to the southern terminus of Pinecone Way, which is the closest point to the snorkel reef. Alternatively, visitors on bike can make their way directly to the turnaround at the southern end of Pinecone Way. The park's official address is 7525 W County Highway 30A, Santa Rosa Beach, Florida, 32459. There is a per vehicle fee to enter.

Access
There are restroom facilities near the start of the boardwalk and elsewhere in the park. The reef modules are located 870 feet (265 meters) east of the beach access boardwalk that connects Pinecone Way to the beach. Tall, yellow poles anchored in the sand mark the location of the reef and act as navigational aids for divers and snorkelers as they head out into the water. The reef modules themselves are located over 700 feet (215 meters) from the beach, and there are no buoys in the water to mark the site. The surf can be high at times, so divers and snorkelers should be careful when entering and exiting the water. A diver down flag is required for both divers and snorkelers while in the water.

Description
This reef complex was deployed in August 2017 and features 78 reef modules placed in the shape of a seahorse. The shallowest modules are anchored at a depth of around 13 feet (4 meters) on the sandy seabed, while the deeper ones bottom out at closer to 18 feet (5.5 meters). All modules are at least 6 feet (2 meters) below the

surface of the water with the deepest modules extending to a depth of about 12 feet (3.5 meters). Divers and snorkelers are likely to see damselfish, blennies, triggerfish and grouper here, along with the occasional octopus and sea turtle.

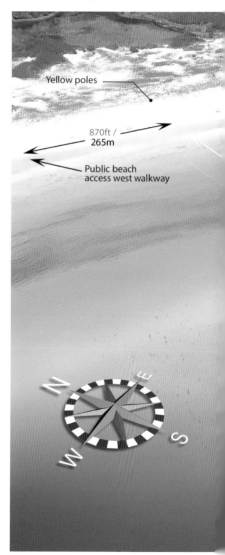

Yellow poles

870ft /
265m

Public beach
access west walkway

ECO TIP

Whenever possible, people should use boardwalks when crossing the sand dunes along Northwest Florida's barrier islands. Foot traffic in natural dunes can trample vegetation and cause erosion, which can become highly susceptible to blowouts. These events often occur during tropical storms, when strong tidal surges wash away parts of the weakened sand dune system. Such events can compromise roadways, neighborhoods, and wildlife habitat.

Vegetation, particularly dune grasses and shrubs, play a critical role in dune formation and stabilization. Wind blows dry sand inland from the beaches and it is when vegetation partially blocks the wind so the sand falls to the ground. Successful dune formation requires specific species of fast-growing, salt-tolerant vegetation that thrives in dry soils. Once the dune has formed, the plants' roots help stabilize the dune as it grows. Dunes are a critical part of the coastal ecosystem, but dunes need healthy vegetation to thrive. So, stay off the grass.

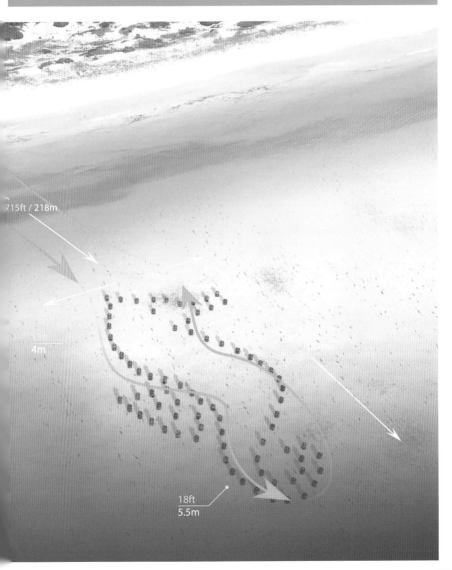

715ft / 218m

4m

18ft
5.5m

Turtle Snorkel Reef

Difficulty	● ○ ○	
Current	● ○ ○	
Depth	● ○ ○	
Reef	★★☆	
Fauna	★★☆	

Turtle Snorkel
Reef

Panama City

Access 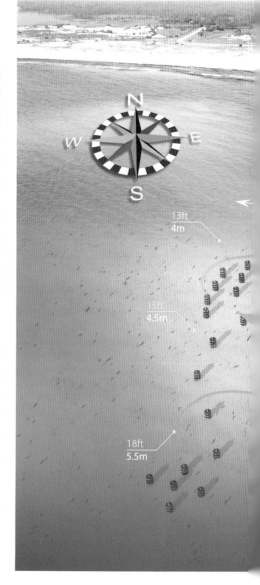 about 39 mins from downtown
Panama City
about 7 mins from shore

 Level Open Water

 Location
Santa Rosa Beach, Walton County
GPS 30°19.338′N, 86°09.491′W

Getting there

From Panama City, head west on US-98. After crossing the Hathaway Bridge to Panama City Beach, continue on US-98 for 28.3 miles (45.4 kilometers) until the intersection with County Road 283 South. Turn left and drive 1.7 miles (2.5 kilometers) south to the intersection with East County Highway 30A. Turn left and drive 0.6 miles (1 kilometer) east along 30A before turning right into Grayton Beach State Park. There is a fee to enter the park. After the fee station, follow the park's main road for 0.6 miles (1 kilometers) south toward the ocean. After reaching the beach, the road makes a sharp left turn and ends at a large parking lot where there is ample parking. The park's official address is 357 Main Park Road, Santa Rosa Beach, Florida, 32459.

Access

There are restroom facilities adjacent to the parking lot, and a boardwalk that snakes its way through the sand dunes to the beach. The reef modules are located just over 650 feet (198 meters) west of the beach access boardwalk. Tall yellow poles anchored in the sand mark the location of the reef and act as navigational aids for divers and snorkelers as they make their way out to the site. The reef modules themselves are located nearly 800 feet (240 meters) from the beach, and there are no buoys in the water to mark the site. The surf can be high at times, so divers and snorkelers should be careful when entering and exiting the water with their gear. A diver down flag is required by law for divers and snorkelers while in the water.

Description

The reef complex features 58 reef modules placed in the shape of a sea turtle. It was the first of the four Walton snorkel reefs to be installed, taking shape in 2015. The shallowest modules are anchored at a depth of around 13 feet (4 meters) on the sandy seabed, while the deeper ones bottom out at closer to 18 feet (5.5 meters). All modules are at least 6 feet (2 meters) below the surface of the water with the deepest modules reaching a depth of 12 feet (3.5 meters). Divers and snorkelers are likely to see damselfish, blennies, sea bass, snapper, triggerfish and grouper here, along with the occasional octopus and sea turtle. Stingrays and flounder are often resting on the sand near the modules.

Yellow poles

650ft / 198m

783ft / 238m

175ft / 53m

Public beach access west walkway

99m

Four modules

Three modules

Grouper Snorkel Reef

Difficulty ● ○ ○
Current ● ○ ○
Depth ● ○ ○
Reef ★☆☆
Fauna ★★☆

Grouper Snorkel ●○
Reef
Panama City

Access 🚐 about 24 mins from downtown
Panama City
🏊 about 10 mins from shore

Level Open Water

Location
Inlet Beach, Walton County
GPS 30°16.202'N, 86°00.352'W

Getting there
From Panama City, head west on US-98. After crossing the Hathaway Bridge to Panama City Beach, continue on US-98 for 16.2 miles (26 kilometers) to the border between Walton and Bay counties. Just 0.5 miles (0.8 kilometers) after the border, turn left onto South Orange Street. Follow South Orange Street for two blocks until it ends at West Park Place Avenue. This is the Inlet Beach Regional Access, which has ample parking. The park's official address is 438 South Orange Street Inlet Beach, Florida, 32461.

Access
Three boardwalks provide access to the beach from the parking lot adjacent to the site. There are restroom facilities located here. The reef modules are located 235 feet (71.5 meters) west of the central boardwalk that runs from the middle of the parking lot. Tall yellow poles located on the beach can act as navigational aids for divers and snorkelers as they make their way out to the site. The reef modules themselves are anchored in the seabed 970 feet (296 meters) from the beach, and there are no buoys in the water to mark the site. The surf can be high at times, so divers and snorkelers should be careful when entering and exiting the water. A "diver down" flag is required in the water for both divers and snorkelers at this site.

Description
Also called Cobia Snorkel Reef, or even simply the Fish Snorkel Reef, the Grouper Reef was deployed in August 2017, and features 95 reef modules placed in the shape of a fish with its head pointing away from shore. The shallowest modules form the tail and are anchored at a depth of around 12 feet (3.5 meters) on the sandy seabed, while the deeper modules bottom out at closer to 21 feet (6.5 meters). All modules are at least 6 feet (2 meters) below the surface of the water with

the deepest sitting at a depth of just over 12 feet (3.5 meters). Divers and snorkelers are likely to see damselfish, blennies, snapper, triggerfish and grouper here, along with the occasional octopus and sea turtle.

235ft / 71.5m
Yellow Poles

DID YOU KNOW?

While some artificial reefs do not require much precision (think bridge rubble strewn across acres of seabed) other reefs, such as the Grouper Snorkel Reef, require each reef module to be placed with a high level of precision in order for the reef to end up looking the way it is supposed to. Consider the influence of winds, waves and currents on a vessel. It is truly a feat of engineering to place 95 modules in such a specific pattern. So how was it done? This reef, along with the other three reefs that form the shape of a dolphin, a seahorse and a turtle, were installed with the help of complex computer systems and survey-grade GPS.

The vessel used to install these reefs, operated by Walter Marine, has a dynamic, computer controlled positioning system tied in to the ship's engines so that once at the deployment location, the vessel will keep itself in place automatically. What's more, the crane used to move the modules into position has a powerful GPS unit attached to the end of its boom, which allows a precise placement to within just a few feet.

Public beach access central walkway

970ft / 296m

160ft / 49m

360ft / 110m

12ft
3.5m

20ft
6m

Underwater Museum of Art

Difficulty ● ○ ○
Current ● ○ ○
Depth ● ○ ○
Reef ★★★
Fauna ★☆☆

Underwater ● ○
Museum of Art

Panama City

Access 🚤 about 20.5mi (30.5km) from Destin East Pass

🚤 about 28.5mi (46.5km) from St. Andrews Pass

Level Open Water

Location
Santa Rosa Beach, Walton County
GPS 30°18.671'N, 86°09.647'W

Getting there
The Underwater Museum of Art is located nearly a mile (1.3 kilometers) off shore from the beach at Grayton Beach State Park. As a result, it is only safely accessible by boat. The site is located between Destin East Pass and St. Andrews Pass, but is more commonly accessed from Panama City despite the longer distance because of the prevailing winds. Local operators are also developing an option to launch directly from nearby Grayton Beach.

Access
The site is accessible to divers of all experience levels. The sandy seafloor is at a depth of 59 feet (18 meters) putting it within reach of open water divers. The statues are situated between 15 and 20 feet (4.5 and 6 meters) apart, making it easy to navigate from one to the other.

Description
This site represents the first permanent underwater sculpture park in the U.S.. The initial deployment of seven statues took place in June 2018, with a second deployment in 2019 featuring an additional 10 sculptures. More sculptures are planned, which will add to the complexity of the habitat, as well as the artistic and cultural value of the site. The undertaking represents a partnership among three organizations: Visit South Walton, the South Walton Artificial Reef Association (SWARA) and the Cultural Arts Alliance of Walton County (CAA). Each sculpture is created by a separate artist and represents a theme or message chosen by the artist. These themes range from loving oneself to calling attention to ocean degradation to the joys of relaxing and socializing.

The statues themselves support some growth on their surfaces, and the habitat is home to a variety of reef species, including grunts and snapper. The invasive regal demoiselle has colonized some installations and are visible alongside other damselfish species. Divers may also encounter sea turtles and octopus, while sharks have been known to cruise through the museum.

Route
There is no particular route or order required to fully enjoy the sculptures of this expanding underwater museum. However, as additional sculptures are added, a star pattern radiating from the middle may be the easiest strategy to ensure divers get to experience all of the installations.

Starting from the center of the site the sculptures are as follows:

Swara Skull by Vince Tatum features a large, hollow skull measuring 8 feet (2.5 meters) in height.

The Grayt Pineapple by Rachel Herring is a thin metal structure that was flattened by Hurricane Michael in 2018.

Propeller in Motion by Marek Anthony features a tower of offset propeller shapes that conveys motion.

Concrete Rope Reef Spheres by Evelyn Tickle which will support the settlement of reef organisms.

JYC's Dream by Kevin Reilly is an homage to Jacques Yves Cousteau's "Aqualung."

Self Portrait by Justin Gaffrey features a stag built from a framework of welded steel bars.

X.MUTA by Vince Tatum features a large barrel sponge.

Depth of Decision by Gianna Stewart features multiple doorways representing a series of decisions.

I Found It! by husband-and-wife team Ingram Ober and Marisol Rendon features lost pirate treasure.

Anamorphous Octopus by Allison Wickey depicts an octopus when viewed from the front or back.

Let's Not Blow This by Kevin Reilly features a hand holding a dandelion globe showing the fragility of Earth.

Aspiration by Shohini Gosh features the outlined silhouette of a young girl's face.

To Replenish with Water by Beatriz Chachamovits features a small square of struggling corals.

Wave! by Benjamin Mefford features a hand built out of old limestone fenceposts from Kansas.

Flamingle by Rachel Herring features a series of columns topped by metal flamingos.

Love Thyself by Maxine Orange, Maurice Hunter, and Rick Goetchius features a woman looking in a mirror.

Saguaro by Ghazal Ghazi features an 8-foot (2.5-meter) depiction of the iconic cactus species.

The UMA's Depth of Decision sculpture was deployed in 2019.

48ft
14.5m

46ft
14m

70

58ft
17.5m

17

52ft
16m

51ft
15.5m

N

W

E

S

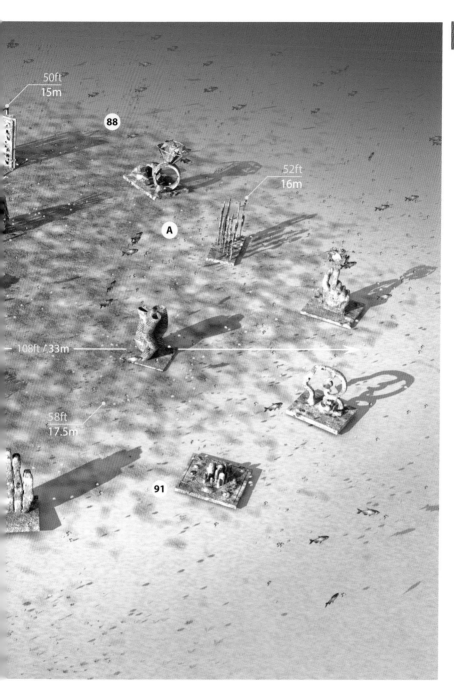

50ft
15m

88

52ft
16m

A

108ft / 33m

58ft
17.5m

91

Other species commonly found
at this site:

G **L** **2** **7** **13** **14** **18** **23** **27**

32 **46** **59** **65** **66** **78** **84**

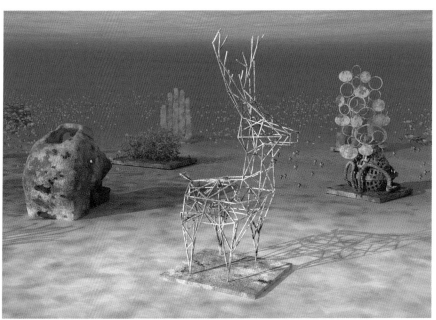

Other Walton County sites

80 Miramar Beach Fish/Dive Reef

GPS 30°21.874'N, 86°23.356'W

Difficulty ● ○ ○
Current ● ○ ○
Depth ● ○ ○
Reef ★☆☆
Fauna ★☆☆

Initially deployed in 2017, the Miramar Beach Reef features 98 tons of concrete in the form of 30 modules of varied design. The site provides 18 feet (5.5 meters) of relief off a sandy seabed that bottoms out at a depth of 62 feet (19 meters).

81 Walton Hopper Barge (aka Frangista)

GPS 30°19.686'N, 86°22.899'W

Difficulty ● ○ ○
Current ● ○ ○
Depth ● ● ○
Reef ★★☆
Fauna ★★☆

This steel hopper barge measures 195 feet (59.5 meters) in length and 35 feet (10.5 meters) in width. The county deployed it in 1999 along with 100 tons of steel ballast at a depth of 77 feet (23.5 meters).

82 Miramar Frangista Fish/Dive Reef

GPS 30°19.801'N, 86°22.829'W

Difficulty ● ○ ○
Current ● ○ ○
Depth ● ● ○
Reef ★☆☆
Fauna ★★☆

The county's original deployment in 2017 featured 121 tons of concrete in the form of 31 reef modules at a depth of 68 feet (20.5 meters). Since then, an additional 63 modules totaling 233 tons were deployed in 2019 in groups adjacent to the original site.

83 Topsail Bluff Fish/Dive Reef

GPS 30°21.373'N, 86°19.357'W

Difficulty ● ○ ○
Current ● ○ ○
Depth ● ○ ○
Reef ★☆☆
Fauna ★☆☆

The county's original deployment of 31 reef modules to Topsail Bluff took place in 2017 and included 101 tons of concrete at a depth of 61 feet (18.5 meters). Additional deployments in 2018 added another 100 tons in the form of 12 patch reefs located near the original group.

84 Fish Haven #1 Reef

GPS 30°19.323'N, 86°17.875'W

Difficulty ● ○ ○
Current ● ○ ○
Depth ● ● ○
Reef ★★☆
Fauna ★☆☆

Deployed in 2017, Fish Haven #1 Reef features 32 modules weighing 124 tons and offering 18 feet (5.5 meters) of relief off the sandy seafloor at a depth of 75 feet (23 meters).

85 Fort Panic Fish/Dive Reef

GPS 30°20.375'N, 86°15.361'W

Difficulty ● ○ ○
Current ● ○ ○
Depth ● ○ ○
Reef ★☆☆
Fauna ★☆☆

The county deployed 124 tons worth of reef modules to this site in 2017. The 32 modules sit at an average depth of 61 feet (18.5 meters) and provide a maximum relief of 18 feet (5.5 meters).

86 Ed Walline Fish/ Dive Reef

GPS 30°19.969'N, 86°13.856'W

Difficulty ● ○ ○
Current ● ○ ○
Depth ● ○ ○
Reef ★☆☆
Fauna ★★☆

Ed Walline Reef features 30 reef modules totaling 121 tons. The modules sit at an average depth of 59 feet (18 meters)..

87 Fish Haven #2 Reef

GPS 30°16.112'N, 86°13.870'W

Difficulty ● ○ ○
Current ● ○ ○
Depth ● ● ○
Reef ★☆☆
Fauna ★☆☆

Fish Haven #2 is one of the deeper artificial reefs off Walton County, and the farthest from shore. It features 30 modules deployed at an average depth of 89 feet (27 meters).

88 Blue Mountain Fish/Dive Reef

GPS 30°19.370'N, 86°12.051'W

Difficulty ● ○ ○
Current ● ○ ○
Depth ● ● ○
Reef ★☆☆
Fauna ★☆☆

Blue Mountain Reef was deployed in 2017 at a depth of 55 feet (17 meters). It features 30 artificial reef modules totaling 121 tons.

90 Santa Clara Fish/ Dive Reef

GPS 30°18.074'N, 86°07.348'W

Difficulty ● ○ ○
Current ● ○ ○
Depth ● ○ ○
Reef ★☆☆
Fauna ★★☆

Santa Clara Reef features 121 tons of concrete deployed in 2017 in the form of 30 modules, with another 44 modules deployed in 2020. The average depth of the site is 55 feet (17 meters), with relief of approximately 18 feet (5.5 meters).

91 Deer Lake Fish/ Dive Reef

GPS 30°17.381'N, 86°04.855'W

Difficulty ● ○ ○
Current ● ○ ○
Depth ● ○ ○
Reef ★☆☆
Fauna ★★☆

The county deployed 124 tons of reef modules at a depth of 57 feet (17.5 meters) in 2017. The Deer Lake Reef features 31 modules and provides approximately 18 feet (5.5 meters) of relief. .

92 Inlet Beach Fish/ Dive Reef

GPS 30°15.675'N, 86°00.860'W

Difficulty ● ○ ○
Current ● ○ ○
Depth ● ○ ○
Reef ★☆☆
Fauna ★★☆

This site, which was deployed in 2017, features 31 modules at a depth of 58 feet (17.5 meters). In total, there are 124 tons of concrete artificial reef habitat at this site.

BAY COUNTY

Bay County hosts one of Northwest Florida's major population centers with the combined Panama City and Panama City Beach, as well as Mexico Beach to the southeast. The county is also home to St. Andrews Pass, which provides easy access to the Gulf of Mexico for operators in this area. Many dive centers and charter boats are based in Bay County, and the region has invested heavily in artificial reefs over the years.

Bay County's efforts have gone a long way toward putting the region on the proverbial divers' map, with six of the 12 original members of the Florida Panhandle Shipwreck Trail. The county's artificial reefs range from reef modules to bridge spans to tugboats, and even a hovercraft. Bay County also boasts one of the most popular shore dives in the region in the form of St. Andrews Jetty.

In the pages that follow, you will find detailed information for the jetty at St. Andrews along with 10 of the most popular wrecks off the coast of Panama City. We have also included the historically significant, yet often overlooked, wreck of the *Empire Mica* that sits farther from shore than most of the region's other wrecks and is positioned south of Franklin County. Information about additional Bay County sites beyond the dozen we feature in these pages, can be found starting on page 288, including many of the popular sites off the city of Mexico Beach and near Cape San Blas.

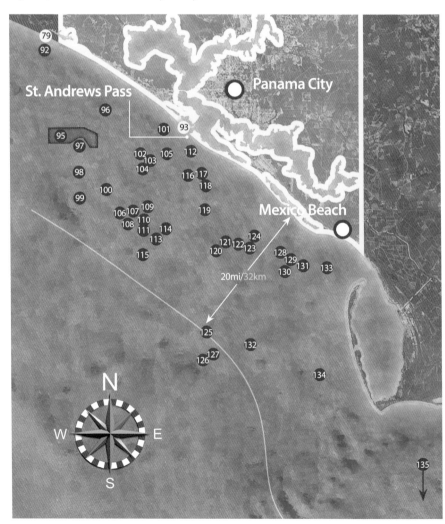

Bay County keeps an up-to-date list of all of its artificial reef sites online. To see if new reefs have been added since publication, please visit: **Rebrand.ly/BayCoReefs**
For a list of reefs off Mexico Beach, please visit: **Mbara.org/mexico-beach-artificial-reefs.cfm**

Dive and snorkel sites

BAY COUNTY

93	St. Andrews Jetty		
94	*Grey Ghost*		
95	NRDA Grant Reefs		
96	Hathaway Spans (6,5)		
97	*Tarpon*		
98	*Commander*		
99	Hathaway Spans (10,9,8,7)		
100	Stage 1		
101	Stage 2		
102	Hathaway Span 14		
103	*Jeff-A Hovercraft*		
104	*Black Bart*		
105	*Chickasaw*		
106	*Accokeek*		
107	DuPont Spans (1,2)		
108	*FAMI Tugs*		
109	Mac's Reef		
110	*El Dorado*		
111	DuPont Span 3		
112	*DAN Safety Barge*		
113	Hathaway Spans (4,3A)		
114	*Chippewa*		
115	*BJ Putnam*		
116	Hathaway Span (2,1,12)		
117	*Strength*		
118	*Red Sea*		
119	*Benjamin H Grierson Liberty Ship*		
120	*Sherman Tug*		
121	MB-251		
122	St. Joe Community Foundation Reef 2		
123	MB-248		
124	MB-256		
125	*Shady Lady*		
126	18-Mile Bridge (aka Hathaway Span 11)		
127	Courtney Knight Gaines Reef		
128	Tennessee Chuck McKibbonville Reef		
129	Mexico Beach 2002 Grant Reef		
130	Fish America Foundation Reef		
131	Garfield Wilson Reef		
132	*OAR BBSWC Barge*		
133	*Vamar*		
134	Air Force Tower		
135	*Empire Mica*		

St. Andrews Jetty

Difficulty ● ○ ○
Current ● ● ○
Depth ● ○ ○
Reef ★★☆
Fauna ★★★

Panama City
St. Andrews Jetty

Access 🚗 about 22 mins from downtown Panama City
🏊 about 1 min from shore

Level Open Water

Location
Panama City, Bay County
GPS 30°07.512'N, 85°44.019'W

Getting there
From Panama City, head west on US-98. Keep to the left while crossing the Hathaway Bridge to Panama City Beach. Once across, stay in either of the two left lanes and turn left at the traffic lights to head south along Thomas Drive. After 3 miles (5 kilometers), Thomas Drive crosses a narrow section of the Grand Lagoon. Another 0.6 miles (1 kilometer) past the water crossing, Thomas Drive splits at an intersection, continuing both left and right parallel to the coast. Turn left to head southeast and continue for another 0.6 miles (1 kilometer) until St. Andrews State Park. There is a fee to enter the park.

The jetties are at the far end of the park from the entrance. The park road is a large circle, so continue past the fee station and follow the road as it curves around to the east and then eventually curves back around south to run parallel to the St. Andrews Pass. The parking lot for the jetty is about 1 mile (1.6 kilometers) from the fee station. There is ample parking next to the jetty access points. The park's official address is 4607 State Park Lane, Panama City, Florida, 32408.

Access
There are restroom facilities adjacent to the parking lot, as well as picnic tables, pavilions and showers for rinsing off after a dive or swim. Multiple boardwalks provide access to both the

beach that faces the Gulf as well as the beach bordering the shallow lagoon adjacent to the pass itself – referred to by locals as the Kiddie Pool. Most divers stage their equipment in one of the pavilions at the southeast corner of the parking lot, since that is the shortest walk to access the lagoon.

The jetty runs roughly in a straight line stretching from the northeast to the southwest, extending out from the beach around 750 feet (229 meters) into the Gulf, depending on how much sand has accumulated along the shore. There are two access points along the jetty wall separating the channel from the Kiddie Pool that allow divers to cross over to the channel side of the jetty, while the Gulf side of the jetty is easily accessed from the beach. Divers and snorkelers require a surface marker buoy while in the water unless they remain in the Kiddie Pool. The best time to dive the jetty is at high slack tide, when the current is low and the visibility is typically at its best.

SAFETY TIP

Divers should avoid venturing out into the middle of the channel – there is rarely anything to see here and the boat traffic poses a significant threat to divers.

Description

St. Andrews Jetty is the most popular shore dive in the Panama City area, known for its high biodiversity and simple beach access. It supports a variety of reef life including damselfish, sergeant majors, butterflyfish, grouper, snapper and angelfish. Divers also regularly report seeing octopus among the rocks of the jetty, along with other cryptic species such as seahorses and batfish. At the interface between the rocks and sand, divers often encounter stingrays and flounder, while spotted eagle rays frequently cruise through the channel itself. As with many sites in Northwest Florida, invasive lionfish are also present at this site, as well as sand perch, hogfish and sheepshead.

The channel is shallow next to the jetty as it borders the Kiddie Pool but gets deep quickly as it heads out toward the Gulf. The channel bottoms out at a maximum depth of around

Courtesy of Red Alert Diving ©

Divers from Red Alert Dive Center enter the water from the beach on the Gulf side of the St. Andrews jetty.

75 feet (23 meters) adjacent to the wide beach that separates the Kiddie Pool from the Gulf. The channel shallows up somewhat as it approaches the end of the jetty, eventually topping out at a depth of 45 feet (13.5 meters).

The Gulf side of the jetty is much shallower than the channel side, with an area of deeper water often running between the jetty and the sandbar that sits just off the beach, to the northwest of the jetty. Depths can change at this site as sand either accumulates or is carried away by the currents of the Gulf. After a big storm, the jetties sometimes need to be rebuilt and the sand replenished. For instance, the outer bands of Hurricane Sally in 2020 removed much of the sand from the beach, effectively merging the Kiddie Pool with the Gulf of Mexico for a brief period. As such, it is worth confirming the conditions at the jetty with a local dive shop before heading to the park.

Route

There are many possible routes to dive St. Andrews Jetty. Divers typically make their way through the Kiddie Pool to one of the two gaps in the jetty wall that separates the Kiddie Pool from the channel. From there, most divers swim along the jetty toward the Gulf, keeping the wall to their right. Depending on bottom time and current, divers can choose to remain in the channel on their return route, keeping the jetty wall to their left and finishing their dive back in the Kiddie Pool, which bottoms out at just 9 feet (2.5 meters). Alternatively, divers can head out past the end of the jetty and return to shore along the Gulf side of the jetty, ending their dive on the open beach area.

The reverse of this dive plan is also possible, with divers beginning and ending their dive on the open beach or beginning on the beach and

ST. ANDREWS JETTY

Gulf Side

5ft
1.5m

10ft
3m

12

84

45ft
13.5m

68

60ft
18.5m

Channel Side

70ft
21.5m

Restricted area
Boat Channel

entering the channel in order to exit at the Kiddie Pool. Yet another potential route involves divers heading in shore along the channel toward the Grand Lagoon and away from the Gulf. The jetty is shallower here but still offers plenty to see. The diversity of route options and the size of the site is just another reason why St. Andrews Jetty is so popular with local divers who keep diving here time and time again.

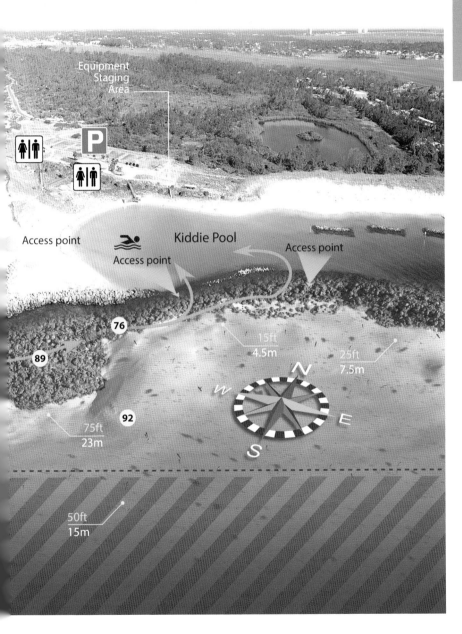

Equipment Staging Area

Access point

Kiddie Pool

Access point

Access point

76

89

15ft 4.5m

25ft 7.5m

92

75ft 23m

50ft 15m

Other species commonly found at this site:

I **L** **3** **18** **19** **24** **29** **33** **38**

46 **57** **62** **63** **71** **73** **74** **78** **88**

225

SS Tarpon

Difficulty	● ● ○
Current	● ○ ○
Depth	● ● ○
Reef	★★★☆
Fauna	★★★

Panama City
SS Tarpon

Access 🚤 about 13mi (20km) west
from St. Andrews Pass

Level Advanced

Location
Panama City, Bay County
GPS 30°05.701'N, 85°56.564'W

Getting there
The wreck of *SS Tarpon* is located just 9 miles (14.5 kilometers) from shore but it is a littler farther from the nearest suitable access point, which is St. Andrews Pass. It is one of the most northwesterly sites visited by dive centers operating out of Panama City and Panama City Beach. There is no permanent mooring buoy on *Tarpon*. Indeed the site was actually lost for a number of years as the wreck moved from its original location under the influence of multiple storms over the years. Operators typically anchor in the sand next to the wreck.

Access
Given its depth, *Tarpon* is primarily accessible to advanced divers. The wreck sits at a depth of 96 feet (29 meters) and tops out at just 85 feet (26 meters) in a few places. It is an open site, however, meaning that divers do not require wreck experience to properly explore it and there are no penetration opportunities. Visibility is usually good on *Tarpon*, although it can vary depending on weather conditions and currents.

Description
Tarpon was a twin-screw steamship constructed in Delaware in 1887. She was originally christened *Naugatuck* and was used to carry cargo and passengers between Connecticut and New York

in addition to serving as an icebreaker on the Housatonic River. After just two years in New England, she returned south and was based in the Tampa Bay, Florida area. In 1891, she was lengthened by 30 feet (9 meters) and renamed *SS Tarpon*.

In 1902, she was sold to the Pensacola, St. Andrews & Gulf Steamship Company and placed under the command of Captain Willis Green Barrow. For the next 35 years, *Tarpon* sailed weekly from Mobile, Alabama, to Carrabelle, Florida, stopping off at Pensacola, Panama City and Apalachicola. The ship provided a vital service for these coastal communities, carrying passengers and supplies at a time when few paved roads and bridges existed on land. *Tarpon* was the only vessel regularly servicing this route, and under Captain Barrow she gained a reputation for reliability and dependability. Incredibly, by 1922, after two decades of service, *Tarpon* had only missed one trip due to weather.

On August 30, 1937, *Tarpon* was docked in Mobile, Alabama, and taking on goods for her 1,735th trip along the coast. Captain Barrow, who was now 81 years of age and still captain of the *Tarpon*, was overseeing the loading. He was undoubtedly one of the most experienced captains in Florida but had also started to gain a reputation for being stuck in his ways. Barrow had resisted new technologies, such as ship-to-shore radios, which might have improved safety onboard his ship. He also ignored new international regulations that mandated ships be marked with a hull loading line, known as a Plimsoll line. This feature, which is still used on modern-day ships, indicates the water level on the outside of the hull and is used to determine

DID YOU KNOW?

After the *Tarpon*'s sinking, the survivors were left clinging to floating debris in the water for hours. As the weather cleared, one of the ship's oilers, Adley Baker, spotted land and decided to swim toward it in order to raise the alarm. It took Baker 25 hours to swim the distance, finally staggering ashore near Phillips Inlet, just west of Panama City. His actions undoubtedly saved many of his fellow crew members.

how much cargo can be placed onboard without a vessel getting overloaded. Despite repeated warnings from ship inspectors, Captain Barrow had refused to implement this feature on *Tarpon*, instead trusting his years of experience.

As a result, *Tarpon* was dangerously overloaded for her final voyage with 200 tons of cargo and 31 passengers and crew. The ship reached Pensacola without incident, but was loaded with yet more goods at that port, putting her freeboard (the distance between the waterline and her uppermost watertight deck) at less than 5 inches (13 centimeters). Calm weather had been forecasted for that night. But the wind began to pick up as the ship headed out into the Gulf, and she began to take on water. By 2am the pumps were unable to keep up with the water entering the hull, and Tarpon began listing to port. Cargo was jettisoned and the ship was temporarily stabilized. But by dawn, the wind had reached gale-force levels, and *Tarpon* began to list again, this time to starboard. The ship was turned toward shore, but she never made it. *Tarpon* sank approximately 9 miles (14.5 kilometers) southwest of Panama City with the loss of 18 people, including Captain Barrow.

All that remains of *Tarpon* is a debris field. However, the outline of the ship is still clearly visible and numerous iron hull plates are located along the perimeter of the ship. *Tarpon* lies on a seabed consisting of sand and rock, facing roughly due west, parallel to shore, at a depth of approximately 95 feet (29 meters).

The wreck site is fairly complex, with several large structures rising above the seabed. The main boiler is located just north of the starboard side of the ship and is the largest feature, rising close to 10 feet (3 meters) above the bottom. This section of the wreck supports the largest density and diversity of fish, including scrawled filefish, burrfish, spotfin butterflyfish, and several species of grouper, namely gag, scamp and black sea bass. The occasional lobster can be found hiding beneath overhanging pieces of wreckage, along with cryptic frogfish.

The boiler was originally mounted on supports that are still visible in the center of the site. The boiler became detached and was pushed off the main structure by currents and wave action at some point in the past and now lies closer to the middle of the ship off the starboard site. To the stern of these boiler mounts lie sections of the main engine and the auxiliary boilers, also known as donkey boilers, which were often used to power the ship's crane during the loading and unloading of cargo.

Frogfish are often found at *Tarpon* and other, natural-bottom sites in the region.

SS TARPON

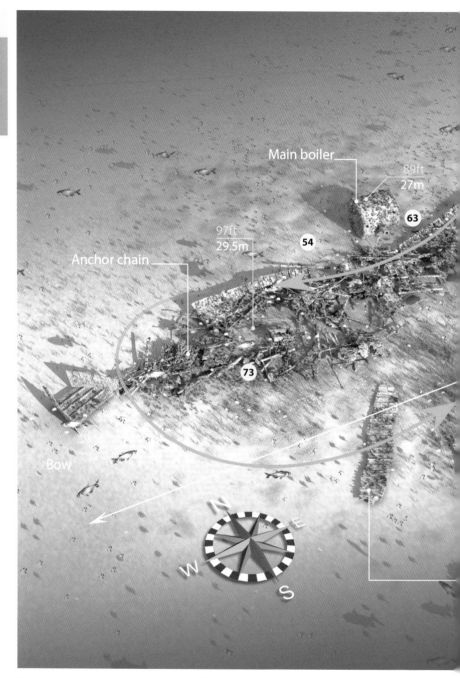

Main boiler

89ft
27m

63

97ft
29.5m

54

Anchor chain

73

Bow

Tarpon had twin screws, and sections of the propeller shafts, separated at their flange points, can be found in the stern area of the ship. In the bow of the ship, divers may identify the anchor windlass and a pile of rusted anchor chain that has become fused into a single piece of twisted metal, covered in sponge and encrusting coralline algae. *Tarpon*'s superstructure was made of wood and has largely disintegrated over the years. However, several areas of wooden decking remain visible throughout the site.

Engine mounts

Propeller drive shafts

80

85ft
26m

Stern

12

Donkey boilers

Engine

58

Plaque

96ft
29m

220ft / 67m

Hull plates

Name:	SS Tarpon	Tonnage:	449grt
Type:	Freighter and Passenger Carrier	Construction:	Pusey & Jones shipbuilders, Wilmington DE, 1887
Previous names:	Naugatuck	Last owner:	Pensacola, St. Andrews & Gulf Steamship Company
Length:	130ft (40m) original length; 160ft (49m) after rebuild	Sunk:	September 1, 1937

85ft
26m

80

94ft
28.5m

Stern

96ft
29m

12

Route

The route used to explore *Tarpon* depends on the mooring location. Most divers move throughout the site trying to identify the various features of the ship. The main boiler supports a high density and diversity of reef fish that pass in and out of the various openings on its structure, and is well worth spending some time exploring. Divers should also take the occasional glance upward at the water column above the wreck, as large amberjacks, barracuda and sharks frequently visit this site.

54

73

89ft
27m

58

97ft
29.5m

Bow

63

Other species commonly found
at this site:

G   **4**   **9**   **15**   **17**   **25**   **28**   **44**   **52**

53   **60**   **65**   **72**   **73**   **82**   **87**   **90**   **91**

Jeff-A Hovercraft

Difficulty ● ○ ○
Current ● ○ ○
Depth ● ● ○
Reef ★☆☆
Fauna ★★☆

Panama City
Jeff-A Hovercraft

Access 🚤 about 6mi (9km) southwest
of St. Andrews Pass

Level Open Water

Location

Panama City, Bay County
GPS 30°04.260'N, 85°48.702'W

Getting there

The wreck of the *Jeff-A Hovercraft* is located
southwest of St. Andrews Pass near Panama City.
The best way to reach the wreck is through a
dive center operating out of this pass. There is no
permanent mooring buoy on the *Hovercraft,* so
operators typically anchor in the sand nearby or
tie in to the wreck itself.

Access

The wreck is accessible to most divers due to
its relative shallowness and its open nature. The
seabed at this site is approximately 75 feet (23
meters) deep. Visibility is usually good on the
wreck, although it can vary depending on the
weather and the strength of the currents.

Description

The *Jeff-A Hovercraft* was a prototype Amphibious
Assault Landing Craft (AALC) designed for the U.S.
Navy in 1979. Hovercraft were first developed in
the 1950s by British inventor Sir Christopher
Cockerell. By 1970, the basic concept had been

DID YOU KNOW? ❓

As designs were improved and refined
over the 1960s, it looked like commercial
hovercraft travel was set to become the
way of the future. The massive SR-N4,
Mountbatten-class hovercraft was launched
in the United Kingdom in 1968, and was
capable of carrying up to 254 passengers
and 30 cars across the English Channel to
France. Increasingly larger models were
developed, culminating in the Mark III, which
was launched in 1976 and could carry up to
418 passengers and 60 cars. These hovercraft
could travel at 83 knots, equivalent to

nearly 100 miles per hour (154 km/h) and
make the 22-mile (35-kilometer) crossing
in approximately 30 minutes – about one
quarter of the time taken by cross-channel
ferries at the time. It was no wonder these
vessels were known as the Concordes of
the seas. But the hovercraft design was also
dogged by huge maintenance and running
costs. The four 19-foot (6-meter) propellers
that powered the SR-N4 each used one ton
of fuel per hour. With rising fuel prices and
the opening of the channel tunnel in 1994,
the financial viability of hovercraft travel was
starting to sink. The last SR-N4 was taken out
of service in 2000.

refined and even commercialized. The U.S. military recognized the potential uses of hovercraft in warfare and commissioned two companies to work on designs that could be used for moving troops and military equipment across challenging terrain.

Aerojet General Corporation, based in Sacramento, California, developed one prototype, codenamed *Jeff-A*. A second prototype, codenamed *Jeff-B*, was designed in parallel by Bell Aerospace, based in New Orleans, Louisiana. The *Jeff-B* design was ultimately chosen for further development and became the basis for the hovercraft used by the U.S. Navy today, known as Landing Craft Air Cushions (LCAC).

The *Jeff-A* design was later modified for Arctic use and was deployed in Prudhoe Bay, Alaska, in the 1980s to support offshore oil drilling in areas where sea ice would cause a hazard to conventional ships.

JEFF-A HOVERCRAFT

Lureen Ferretti ©

Toadfish are often hard to spot as they settle into recesses in reefs and wrecks with just their heads showing.

The *Jeff-A Hovercraft* was sunk as part of the Florida Artificial Reef program in 1995. Despite the fact that she weighs over 160 tons, she was clearly not designed to sink and actually took two days to settle to the bottom. *Jeff-A Hovercraft* now rests at about 75 feet (23 meters) on a sand and rubble bottom with the top of the structure reaching approximately 65 feet (20 meters).

Jeff-A Hovercraft is made of aluminum and has little marine growth covering its surface, but it still attracts plenty of marine fish and crustaceans. Her hatches were removed prior to sinking, so divers can explore the inside of the craft. Her skirt was also left in place, which makes for an interesting place for marine organisms to hide.

Route

The route used to explore the *Jeff-A Hovercraft* often involves making an initial pass around the outside of the structure. Divers can still identify the former locations of the propellers that once powered the hovercraft from each of its four corners. From there, many divers choose to swim through the central staging area, before exploring the open hatches that lead to the hovercraft's interior on each side of the vessel. It should be noted, however, that these spaces are quite confined and are therefore better suited to experienced divers.

233

JEFF-A HOVERCRAFT

65ft
20m

72ft
22m

67ft
20.5m

78

63

Bow

67

74ft
22.5m

Other species commonly found at this site:

K **2** **3** **26** **29** **32** **34** **40** **52**

53 **69** **72**

JEFF-A HOVERCRAFT

Name:	*Jeff-A Hovercraft*
Type:	Prototype Amphibious Assault Landing Craft
Previous names:	n/a
Length:	96ft (29m)
Tonnage:	n/a

Construction:	Aerojet General Corporation, Sacramento, CA, 1977
Last owner:	U.S. Navy
Sunk:	August 1995

Black Bart

Difficulty	● ● ○
Current	● ○ ○
Depth	● ● ○
Reef	★☆☆
Fauna	★☆☆

Panama City
Black Bart

Access 🚤 about 7mi (11km) southwest
of St. Andrews Pass

Level Open Water

Location

Panama City, Bay County
GPS 30°03.634'N, 85°49.417'W

Getting there

Black Bart is one of the many wrecks deployed in the nearshore region dedicated to artificial reefs just a short boat ride from the pass. There are no surface mooring buoys attached to this wreck, so operators typically tie in to the wreck or anchor on the nearby sand.

Access

The wreck is accessible to most divers because of its relative shallowness – the seafloor is 78 feet (24 meters) in this area and the shallowest point of the wreck tops out at 45 feet (14 meters) deep. The open plan of the wreck also makes it suitable for divers with limited wreck experience. The site is best reached via one of the dive shops operating out of Panama City and Panama City Beach, and it is often used as a second dive after visiting one of the deeper sites located farther off shore

Description

Black Bart was originally a 180-foot (55-meter) platform supply vessel built in 1977 in Louisiana for Texas-based Gulf Fleet Marine. It was given the creative name of *Gulf Fleet No.28* and used to resupply the offshore oilfield platforms in the Gulf. In 1991, she was given the slightly more romantic name of *Vulcano del Golfo*, and then renamed again sometime after that, this time as *Mary J*. Somewhere along the way as she changed names and ownership, she also switched careers to become a fishing vessel. Eventually she was acquired by Bay County and deployed as an artificial reef in July 1993.

She was given the name *Black Bart* before she was scuttled, in memory of Captain Charles "Bart" Bartholomew. He was director of ocean engineering for the U.S. Navy and supervisor of its salvage and diving operations. Captain Bart had previously headed the Navy Experimental

Diving Unit at Panama City and led numerous high profile salvage operations, including the space shuttle Challenger and the Exxon Valdez in Alaska. He died in November 1990 at age 50 during a deep recertification dive near Panama City.

Black Bart is a popular dive site with many locals and visitors. She sits upright on a sandy seafloor with plenty of levels to explore. Her main deck sits at a depth of 70 feet (21 meters) while her bow reaches up to 61 feet (18.5). Her wheelhouse is no longer enclosed, courtesy of Hurricane Michael in

SCIENTIFIC INSIGHT

During the 1990s, coastal freighters were popular targets for artificial reef programs. They were readily available thanks to the drug war of the '80s and '90s that led authorities to seize boats caught smuggling drugs into the U.S. The thick steel hulls and large open holds of these freighters provided habitat for reef fish and plenty of areas for divers to explore. But the underwater environment is unforgiving, however, and the open cargo holds of these vessels often collapse into debris fields. Today, artificial reef programs aim to secure more robust vessels as artificial reefs. *Black Bart* represents an excellent example of a sturdier vessel that can provide many decades' worth of complex habitat for marine life and divers.

Virgil Zetterlind ©

Black Bart's large wheelhouse before its roof was torn off and deposited near her starboard bow.

2018. The currents from the powerful storm ripped the roof off the superstructure and deposited it on the seabed just off the starboard side.

But the loss of the roof has only removed one of the many swim-through and penetration opportunities on this wreck for divers with appropriate experience. The large holds in the main deck are open and intact, as are the forward compartments at both the main deck and bow deck levels. Stairs lead from the compartment on the first level up into the open wheelhouse for those adventurous enough to investigate. In

general, the wreck has held up very well to the elements over the many decades she has spent underwater.

Divers are likely to see plenty of reef fish around *Black Bart*. In addition to the blue runners, greater amberjacks and Atlantic spadefish that are often seen schooling above the wreck, divers frequently report seeing grey triggerfish, blue angelfish and Queen angelfish. Whitespotted soapfish, cocoa damselfish and spotfin butterflyfish tend to stick close to the structure, while large barracuda hover in the currents above the wreck. Divers

57ft
17.5m
J

65ft
20m

61ft
18.5m

67

Bow

78ft
24m

who venture into the holds or the compartments are also likely to see schools of grunts sheltering there, particularly tomtates.

Route

The open nature of the wreck makes it easy for divers to choose a route that works best for them and for their planned depth profile. Divers commonly descend to the bow and head along the main deck toward the stern. There is usually enough time for divers to fully explore the main deck and deep holds toward the stern before

Name:	Black Bart	**Construction:**	Halter Marine, Lockport, LA, 1977
Type:	Platform Supply Vessel	**Last owner:**	n/a
Previous names:	Gulf Fleet #28, Vulcano del Golfo, Mary J	**Sunk:**	July 27, 1993
Length:	180ft (55m)		
Tonnage:	183grt		

BLACK BART

71ft
21.5m

82

64ft
19.5m

70ft
21m

78

79ft
24m

Stern

moving shallower on the wreck and regaining bottom time. Those with penetration experience can investigate the forward compartments on both the main deck and bow deck levels, including the head and galley areas with toilet and appliances still intact. From there, divers can ascend to check out the now-exposed wheelhouse to finish off their dive.

Other species commonly found
at this site:

9   27   28   42   45   52   54   62   64

69   79   86

Accokeek

Difficulty ● ● ○
Current ● ○ ○
Depth ● ● ○
Reef ★☆☆
Fauna ★★☆

Panama City ○
Accokeek ●

Access 🚤 about 12.7mi (20.5km)
southwest of St. Andrews Pass

Level Open Water

Location
Panama City, Bay County
GPS 29°58.475'N, 85°51.915'W

Getting there
Accokeek is one of many artificial reefs deployed in a large area that sits off shore from the pass. These offshore sites are all roughly 10 to 15 miles (16 to 24 kilometers) from the pass, and thus readily accessible to operators and private vessels with experience operating in the Gulf. There are no surface mooring buoys to tie to, so operators typically tie in to the wreck or anchor in the sand nearby.

Access
This site is accessible to most divers. The highest point of the wreck reaches a depth of 57 feet (17.5 meters) while the seabed sits at 100 feet (30.5 meters). The site is best reached via one of the dive shops operating out of Panama City and Panama City Beach.

Description
Accokeek was originally an auxiliary ocean tugboat built for the U.S. Navy in Orange, Texas. She was commissioned in October 1944 with the name *USS ATA-181* and her first major tour of service was in the Pacific Fleet. She played an active role in the assault and occupation of Okinawa in the spring and summer of 1945, where her primary role involved towing damaged warships to safety and then on to Allied bases for repairs. She earned one battle star for her wartime service.

The ship remained in the western Pacific after the end of World War II in support of the occupation, but she crossed back through the Panama Canal in 1946 to serve in the Atlantic fleet. Renamed *Accokeek* in July 1948, she provided submarine and cruiser support for multiple decades along the U.S. Eastern Seaboard. Her operations took her as far north as Labrador, Canada, into the Great Lakes and frequently down to the

Caribbean. She was decommissioned and placed into the naval reserve fleet in 1972, after which she was transferred to the Naval Diving and Salvage Training Center at Naval Coastal Systems Center in Panama City, Florida.

She was first scuttled in February 1987 as part of a training exercise but was refloated. She was re-sunk and refloated multiple times over the next 13 years as part of a Navy salvage and ordinance training program. *Accokeek* finally went to the bottom for the last time in July 2000, when she was deployed as an artificial reef off the coast of Panama City.

The wreck is in remarkably good condition for her many decades spent underwater. Aside from

RELAX & RECHARGE

Capt. Anderson's Restaurant is a Panama City Beach favorite that has been serving incredible seafood since 1953. There is a wide selection of fish dishes available, including salmon, grouper, pompano, snapper, tuna and mahi mahi; the lobster tails, stuffed jumbo shrimp and Johnny's Greek salad are particularly popular. Do not worry if you have trouble making up your mind, you can simply opt for the lot by ordering the Seafood Platter, which includes lobster, shrimp, scallops, fish and crab! There is a gluten-free menu, a children's menu and a wide range of steaks and burgers for land lovers. For those that live far away, Capt. Anderson's also has a "Captain's Classics" cookbook, now in its fifth edition, so diners can recreate the dishes they love in the comfort of their own homes. While it is the food that draws many people to this spot, it is interesting to check out the enormous bronze propeller located in front of the restaurant that was salvaged from the *Empire Mica* in the 1980s. Visit: **Captandersons.com**

some holes in the main deck and the wheelhouse, most of her structure is intact. However, the funnel has collapsed into the wreck, limiting access and penetration opportunities in this area.

Divers can explore her three levels – main deck, upper deck and wheelhouse – keeping an eye open for the many species of fish that are often seen around the wreck. In particular, divers are likely to see grunts sheltering in the interior, while blue angelfish and cocoa damselfish forage along the deck. Above the wreck, divers are nearly guaranteed to see Atlantic spadefish, amberjacks, snapper and large barracuda, while rainbow and blue runners frequent the water column higher up. Goliath grouper have also been spotted at this site.

Route
A typical route involves divers descending to the main deck near the stern, which is at a maximum depth of 85 feet (26 meters). From there, they can circle the stern, checking out the rudder and propeller that are still intact on the wreck. Divers can then swim under the overhang of the upper deck, exiting the swim-through to make their

The wheelhouse of the *Accokeek* remains in good condition despite decades spent underwater.

Barry Shively ©

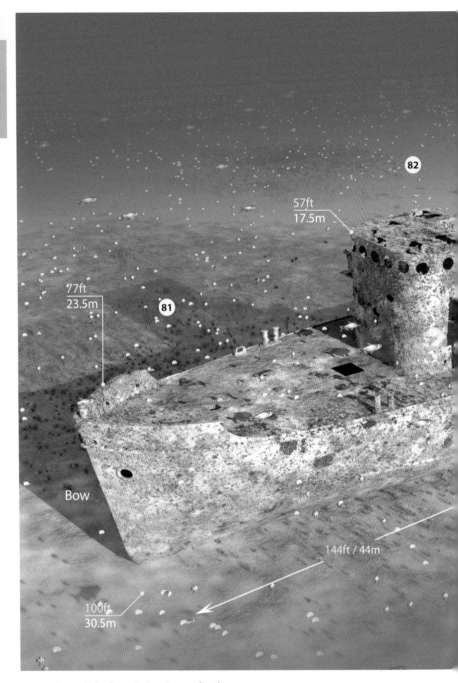

82

57ft
17.5m

77ft
23.5m

81

Bow

144ft / 44m

100ft
30.5m

way up toward the bow. Swimming under the wheelhouse, divers can explore the space below the bridge, before entering the wheelhouse itself. As open and accessible as this wreck is, however, only divers with experience in overhead environments should enter the wheelhouse or explore the many swim-throughs.

80

88

Stern

85ft
26m

J 81ft
24.5m

3

100ft
30.5m

Name:	*Accokeek*		Orange, TX, 1944
Type:	Auxiliary ocean tugboat	**Last owner:**	Naval Diving and Salvage
Previous names:	*ATA-181*		Training Center at Naval
Length:	144ft (44m)		Coastal Systems Center
Tonnage:	600grt	**Sunk:**	July 9, 2000
Construction:	Levingston Shipbuilding Co.,		

80

81ft
24.5m

88

Stern

85ft
26m

3

100ft
30.5m

57ft
17.5m

81

77ft
23.5m

J

82

Bow

100ft
30.5m

Other species commonly found at this site:

1   **5**   **6**   **11**   **19**   **23**   **25**   **35**   **43**

49   **51**   **62**   **78**   **85**

FAMI Tugs

Difficulty ● ● ○
Current ● ○ ○
Depth ● ● ○
Reef ★☆☆
Fauna ★★☆

Panama City ○
●
FAMI Tugs

Access 🚤 about 12.7mi (20.5km) southwest of St. Andrews Pass

Level Open Water

Location
Panama City, Bay County
GPS 29°58.137'N, 85°51.257'W

Getting there
The *FAMI Tugs* is actually a double-wreck site that is one of the many sets of artificial reefs deployed in a large area located roughly 10 to 15 miles (16 to 24 kilometers) off shore from the pass. These sites are readily accessible to operators and private vessels with experience operating in the Gulf. There are no surface mooring buoys at this site, so operators typically tie in to the wrecks or anchor in the sand nearby.

Access
The two tugboats at this site are stacked one on top of the other, making for an interesting and complex site. The highest point of the top wreck reaches up to 74 feet (22.5 meters), while the seabed sits at 102 feet (31 meters) at its lowest point, making this site better suited to experienced divers. The *FAMI Tugs* are best reached via one of the dive shops operating out of Panama City and Panama City Beach.

Description
The *FAMI Tugs* is a pair of tugboats deployed as artificial reefs with funding help from the Florida Aquatic and Marine Institute, Inc (hence the name FAMI). They are often referred to as the "Twin Tugs" or the "Two Tugs" by local operators and divers. The tugboats were reportedly U.S. Navy surplus tugs that were part of a fleet of four tugs abandoned when a local company went bankrupt. They are smaller than most of the nearby wrecks at just 85 feet (26 meters) and 95 feet (29 meters) in length, but they make up for their smaller size with the unique feature of being stacked one on top of the other.

Originally deployed in a bow-to-bow formation and attached with a 30-foot (9-meter) tether, a powerful storm ended up lifting one tug and placing it at an angle, on top of the other. The

bottom tug is just a hull with a relatively intact main deck featuring multiple holes that grant limited access to the hold. The midsection of the bottom tug is slowly getting crushed by the keel of the upper tug. The latter still has an intact superstructure with a wheelhouse and main structure that remain both open and accessible to divers with experience in overhead environments. Both tugboats currently sit with a list to their respective starboard sides but are otherwise upright. The sandy seabed bottoms out at 102 feet (31 meter) at its lowest point – just off the bow of the bottom tug.

The time spent underwater has helped these tugs become well colonized with algae and sponges. There are many reef creatures at this site, including large barracuda and amberjacks. Divers will likely see grey triggerfish and Atlantic spadefish around the wheelhouse and above the wrecks. Blue angelfish, spotfin butterflyfish, banded butterflyfish and sharpnose puffers are frequently spotted in and around the structure, along with numerous grunt and damselfish species. Some divers have even reported seeing sandbar sharks patrolling the perimeter of the site during their dive.

Route

The two wrecks provide an interesting structure for divers to explore. The lack of superstructure on the bottom tug does little to diminish the nooks and crannies available for divers to investigate. Most dive routes begin by circumnavigating the

David Bailey ©

Townsend angelfish are common on reefs in the area, believed to be a hybrid of Queen and blue angelfish.

SCIENTIFIC INSIGHT

It may seem highly unusual for a storm to physically move shipwrecks such as the *FAMI Tugs*, which are underwater at depths of over 100 feet (30 meters). And yet, this exact event has been documented numerous times in the past. In North Carolina, the wreck of the *SPAR* was moved about 200 feet (61 meters) by Hurricane Irene in 2011. In the Florida Keys, the former *USS Spiegel Grove* – a massive 510-foot (160-meter) ship at a depth of 130 feet (39.5 meters) – was flipped upright by Hurricane Dennis as the storm passed 200 miles (322 kilometers) to the west of the wreck in 2005. More recently in Southern Florida, Hurricane Irma picked up a large tugboat called the *Okinawa*, which was deployed at a depth of 70 feet (21 meters), and moved it more than 200 feet (61 meters) across the seabed. The same storm also caused major structural changes to other wrecks in the area, such as *Captain Dan*, *Rodeo 25* and *Ancient Mariner*. You can read more about these wrecks and the events of Hurricane Irma in Reef Smart's Fort Lauderdale guidebook.

Visit: **Reefsmartguides.com**

249

FAMI TUGS

86ft
26m

88

82ft
25m

80

Stern

G

88ft
27m

Bow

102ft
31m

entire site and exploring the intersection of the
two tugs. From there, many divers opt to focus
on the upper tugboat, which offers more areas
for exploration given the intact superstructure.
Most routes conclude with a full inspection of the
wheelhouse before ascending.

FAMI TUGS

Name:	*FAMI Tugs*	Last owner:	A Panama City-based company
Type:	Tugboats	Sunk:	July 10-11, 2003
Previous names:	n/a		
Length:	85ft (26m) and 95ft (29m)		
Tonnage:	n/a		
Construction:	n/a		

74ft
22.5m

J

84ft
25.5m

Bow

54

90ft
27.5m

28

Stern

99ft
30m

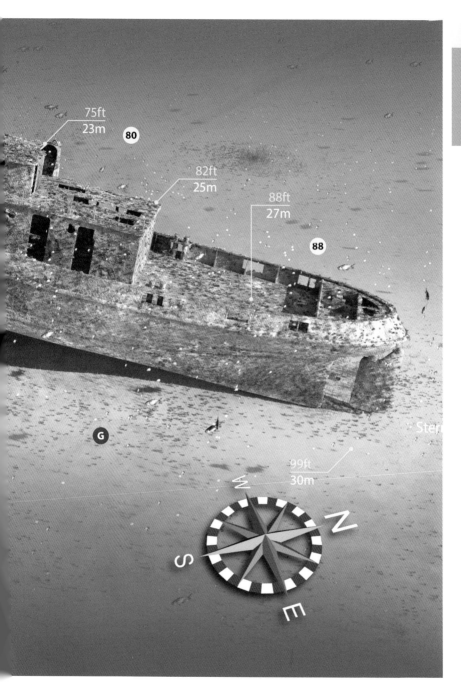

75ft
23m

80

82ft
25m

88ft
27m

88

G

Ster

99ft
30m

Other species commonly found at this site:

3   4   7   9   12   13   30   33   55

59   67   77   78   79

El Dorado

Panama City ○
El Dorado •

Difficulty	●	●	○
Current	●	○	○
Depth	●	●	●
Reef	★	☆	☆
Fauna	★	☆	☆

Access 🚤 about 12mi (19.5km) southwest of St. Andrews Pass

Level Advanced

Location

Panama City, Bay County
GPS 29°58.568'N, 85°50.487'W

Getting there

El Dorado is one of the many artificial reefs deployed in a large area that sits off shore from St. Andrews Pass. These offshore sites are all roughly 10 to 15 miles (16 to 24 kilometers) from the pass, and thus readily accessible to operators and private vessels with experience operating in the Gulf. There are no surface mooring buoys at the site, so operators typically tie in to the wreck or anchor in the sand nearby.

Access

El Dorado tops out at a depth of 83 feet (25.5 meters) at the tip of her bow. Her collapsed structure offers limited dive profiles, while much of the debris from her stern sits only slightly shallower than the seabed, which is 103 feet (31.5 meters) deep. As such, this site accessible only to advanced divers. The site is best reached via one of the dive shops operating out of Panama City and Panama City Beach.

Description

El Dorado's fate seems inextricably tied to extreme weather events in the Gulf of Mexico. The 157-foot (48-meter) vessel was originally a luxury yacht registered in Boston, Massachusetts. Back in 2004, Hurricane Ivan broke her free of her moorings in Panama City Beach and carried her for 6 miles (9.5 kilometers) until she ran aground in marshland in West Bay. There she sat for nearly five years before a local salvager by the name of Lee Ingram refloated her and brought her back to the dock in 2009.

He was unable to entice potential buyers to purchase the stripped-down former luxury cruiser, and so he decided he would fix her up himself. To his misfortune, she was ripped from her moorings once again – this time by Hurricane Michael in 2018. The powerful storm tossed her onto a nearby sandbar just behind the Florida State University campus. Later that same year, a local with a sense of humor painted a large Christmas tree on the derelict's upper deck, along with the words "Happy Holidays," to the delight of drivers crossing the Hathaway Bridge each day.

Faced with the prospect of investing more money to salvage the vessel a second time, Ingram opted to donate it to the community as an artificial reef in partnership with the Florida Fish and Wildlife Conservation Commission (FWC) and Bay County. After she was cleaned, the already-stripped vessel had holes cut in her hull to permit greater access for divers and fish. She was then towed out into the Gulf where she was scuttled and sent to the bottom on May 3, 2019 – just 150 feet (45.5 meters) north of DuPont Span #3 (see page 260).

Unfortunately, she still was not safe from the weather on the bottom of the Gulf. Strong spring storms in 2020 pancaked her stern and caused her bow and wheelhouse to tilt backwards. The complex interior space of the wreck has collapsed leaving only the bow pointing up at an angle to the surface.

Although the diving community lost an interesting and complex wreck to explore, the marine life does not appear to have taken much notice to the change. The wreck still shelters a number of snapper and grunt species, including mangrove, red and vermilion snapper. Porgies are regularly seen here, as are jacks, particularly almacos and bar jacks. Wrasse and damselfish have colonized the debris while Atlantic spadefish form small schools near the wheelhouse.

Route

El Dorado no longer provides much opportunity for penetration. Moreover, as the wreck continues to settle, it may be dangerous for divers to attempt to explore the interior of the bow and the forward spaces. Post collapse, most recommended routes now stick to exterior options. Divers can start by circumnavigating the upright bow section before spending some time exploring the debris

RELAX & RECHARGE

Schooners (5121 Gulf Drive), in Panama City Beach, bills itself as "the last local beach club." This establishment could not be better located – the beach-side steps literally disappear into the sand with an unobscured view of the setting sun. It is paradise!

Every night, rain or shine, Schooners fires off the old cannon at sunset to celebrate another beautiful day on the beach. You can welcome in the evening's entertainment, which usually involves local bands, with a "canon blast" cocktail, consisting of rum and peach or passion fruit, topped with a 151 floater. The drinks menu is packed full of cocktails and includes nearly 40 domestic and craft beers. The cuisine is fresh and simple, and includes a range of salads and sandwiches, a 10oz Schooner burger, and delicious entrees like jerk chicken, shrimp and grits, fresh Gulf grouper, and seared ahi tuna.
Visit: **Schooners.com**

Even collapsed wrecks can create ample habitat for schools of fish such as these grunts.

Lureen Ferretti ©

255

99ft
30m

Stern

3

88

40

38

103ft
31.5m

field that has spread out behind the wreck. Divers can shallow up gradually, checking out the top of the wheelhouse and the upraised bow as they gain back some bottom time from their dive computers.

88ft
27m

80

33

Bow

83ft
25.5m

31.5m

Name:	*El Dorado*	Last owner:	Lee Ingram, local salvager
Type:	Luxury yacht	Sunk:	May 3, 2019
Previous names:	n/a		
Length:	157ft (48m)		
Tonnage:	216grt		
Construction:	n/a		

257

88ft
27m

80

85ft
25.5m

33

Bow

103ft
31.5m

157ft / 48m

99ft
30m

Stern

88

3

40

38

150ft / 45.5m
to Dupont Span *3

N
E
W
S

Other species commonly found
at this site:

14   20   21   28   36   39   48   60   63

69   78   81

DuPont Span #3

Panama City
DuPont Span #3

Difficulty	●	●	○
Current	●	○	○
Depth	●	●	●
Reef	★	☆	☆
Fauna	★	★	☆

Access 🚤 about 12mi (19.5km) southwest of St. Andrews Pass

Level Open Water

Location

Panama City, Bay County
GPS 29°58.518'N, 85°50.499'W

Getting there

The DuPont Span #3 is part of a group of artificial reefs deployed farther from shore yet still easily accessible from the pass. There are no surface mooring buoys at this site, so operators typically tie in to the structure or anchor in the nearby sand.

Access

The seafloor beneath the bridge bottoms out at 102 feet (31 meters) while the roadway sits slightly above at a depth of 100 feet (30.5 meters). As such, this site is more suitable to experienced divers with an Advanced certification. However, the bridge beams that form the support trusses for the 180-foot (55-meter) span top out at a depth of 69 feet (21 meters). This means that a portion of this site is within reach of less experienced divers. The site is best reached via one of the dive shops operating out of Panama City and Panama City Beach.

Description

DuPont Span #3 was originally a section of bridge that connected Panama City to Tyndall Air Force Base via U.S. Route 98. The bridge was built in 1927 following a design known as a Parker Through Truss, which was typical of that period. The bridge was known as DuPont Bridge – hence the name of the site – but it also went by Tyndall Bridge and Old East Bay Bridge, after the body of water it crossed. The bridge was replaced in 2008, and three of the spans were deployed as artificial reefs in the latter part of that same year. Dupont Span #3 was the last to be sunk with an official deployment date of December 19, 2008. The other two spans were dropped nearby in late October and earlier in December, but those two spans have deteriorated more noticeably than this span, which remains upright and relatively intact. This third span is also more popular as it rests just

150 feet (45.5 meters) south of the *El Dorado* – although the two sites are rarely explored on the same dive.

The truss structure of the bridge is heavily encrusted with soft corals, sponges and macroalgae. The only parts of the bridge that shifted during the deployment were a few sections of the concrete roadway toward the eastern end of the span. The shifted panels allow divers to look into the space under the roadway, but there is not enough room to truly explore under here given that these structural elements have sunk into the soft seabed.

While DuPont Span #3 is interesting enough to explore, it is the reef life this structure attracts that divers are most drawn to. Schools of grunts, particularly tomtates, are common throughout the site and jacks and snapper are often spotted cruising between the trusses. Grey triggerfish, Atlantic spadefish and barracuda are also regular visitors to this site.

The roadway itself sports a field of soft corals, which provide shelter for smaller species, including damselfish, blennies and butterflyfish. Queen and French angelfish can be seen patrolling the bridgeway – generally in pairs – while whitespotted soapfish watch cautiously from the railings.

Route

A common route involves circling the outside of the span and then passing through the middle of the roadway beneath the many trusses. Divers can shallow-up slightly to gain back time on their computers by taking a second tour of the span from within the truss structure of the bridge.

This site is popular with hook-and-line fishers, as indicated by the number of lead weights and monofilament fishing line that can be seen hanging between the structural trusses of the span. Divers should consider these entanglement risks as they explore the site, along with the old anchor ropes that drape down from the cross beams.

Lureen Ferretti ©

The DuPont Bridge Spans are almost entirely overgrown in sponges and other reef life.

ECO TIP 🌐

Abandoned monofilament line and fishing hooks pose a real threat to marine life and divers. Some divers advocate removing fishing line whenever it is encountered, particularly nylon monofilament which can take as long as 500 years to degrade. However, in some cases, removing line can disturb corals and sponges that have colonized a wreck or reef. If you encounter line or other fishing gear, carefully assess whether removing it would do more damage than leaving it.

261

DUPONT SPAN #3

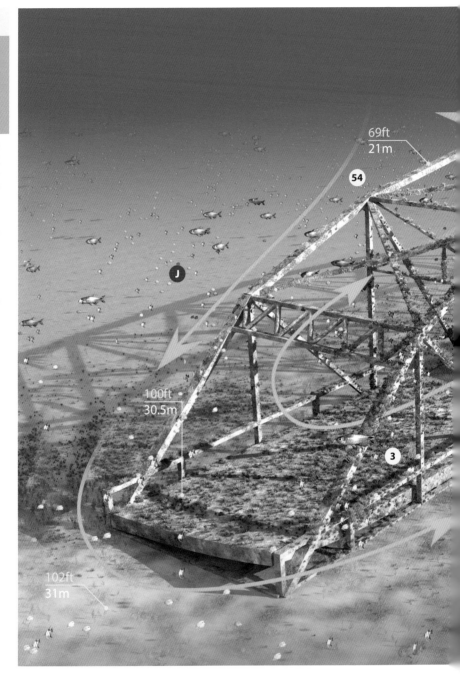

69ft
21m

54

J

100ft
30.5m

3

102ft
31m

DUPONT SPAN #3

80ft
24.5m

12

69

38

102ft
31m

Other species commonly found at this site:

L 4 8 9 10 19 33 36 45

61 64 67 79 88

Chippewa

Difficulty ● ● ○
Current ● ○ ○
Depth ● ● ○
Reef ★★☆
Fauna ★★☆

Panama City ○
Chippewa ●

Access 🚤 about 11.5mi (18.5km) southwest of St. Andrews Pass

Level Open Water

Location
Panama City, Bay County
GPS 29°57.676'N, 85°48.464'W

Getting there
Chippewa is one of the many offshore artificial reefs deployed in a group about 10 to 12 miles (16 to 19.5 kilometers) southwest of the St. Andrews Pass. There are no surface mooring buoys at this site so operators typically tie in to the wreck itself or anchor in the sand nearby.

Access
The wreck is accessible to most divers, but at a maximum depth of just over 100 feet (30.5 meters), it is better suited to experienced divers. The most interesting parts of the wreck to explore are located shallower, however, and are accessible to open water divers. The site is best reached via one of the dive shops operating out of Panama City and Panama City Beach.

Description
Chippewa was originally built as a Navajo-class fleet ocean tug in 1943 in Charleston, South Carolina. Her classification was originally *AT-69* before being reclassified as *ATF-69* in 1944. The entire line of ships was eventually renamed the Cherokee class of tugs. They were a new breed of ocean-going tugboats capable of long-haul towing and salvage operations thanks to their length, wide beam and large fuel-carrying capacity.

According to various reports, *Chippewa* operated in the Atlantic and the Caribbean. During her brief naval career, she ventured as far east as Casablanca, where she laid buoys during the war, south to Trinidad and north to Newfoundland, Canada. She was decommissioned in 1947 and laid up in the reserve fleet in Texas. In January 1989, she was given to the Navy Experimental Dive Unit in Panama City. Used in an explosives training project, she was eventually sunk as an artificial reef in February 1990.

At over 200 feet (65 meters) in length, she is one of the larger naval tugs deployed as an artificial reef in Northwest Florida. Her many decades spent underwater have not been kind to her. There is extensive damage to her walls and most of the structure of the wheelhouse has gone. Even so, there is still plenty to explore, and the debris field has in many ways enriched the habitat for reef creatures. Her hull remains largely intact, although she lies with a strong list to port. A large crack exists in the deck and hull near the stern, which is yet another sign of the wear and tear that the ocean environment can have on vessels deployed as artificial reefs. The large tower that once stood high in the center of the ship, now lies on the sandy seafloor just off her port side.

Divers are almost guaranteed to see Atlantic spadefish schooling around the wreck, while grunts, including tomtates, school in the shadowy interior. Whitespotted soapfish and cocoa damselfish can be seen closer into the wreck itself, while barracuda, jacks and snapper patrol the waters above. The many nooks and crannies in the wreck make it a popular site with spearfishers as well as a regular hangout for a large goliath grouper.

Route
Divers often begin their exploration of the wreck by circling the outside near the seabed and the deck level. The portside main deck is almost at the level of the seabed given the wreck's notable list to port. There are limited penetration opportunities given the deterioration of the wreck. There are also plenty of entanglement risks, so divers should proceed with extreme caution if they plan to enter the structure.

Debris from the funnel and wheelhouse lies on top of the main structure, providing places for reef creatures to hide and for curious divers to explore. Most divers conclude their visit with a tour of the upper levels of the wreck.

DID YOU KNOW?

The red and white diver down flag that is standard in North America was created by a Northwest Floridian in 1956. Navy veteran Denzel James Dockery came up with the flag while in Michigan, but he gained Northwest Florida roots when he and his family bought the land in Ponce de Leon that would eventually become Vortex Spring (see page 296). The diver down flag was first adopted by the state of Michigan to help warn boat traffic that there are divers in the water, but it received its biggest support when Ted Nixon, a sales rep. for U.S. Divers, saw the flag for sale in Dockery's Michigan shop, and offered to sell it around the nation. Eventually the U.S. Federal government and most states came to recognize the flag and it is now used around the world.

A goliath grouper is often spotted hanging out in *Chippewa*'s interior.

Lureen Ferretti ©

Stern

83ft
26m

88

19

54

33

100ft
30.5m

N

W   E

S

75ft
23m

J

Bow

69

205ft / 62.5m

100ft
30.5m

Name:	*Chippewa*		& Drydock Company, SC, 1942
Type:	Navajo-class tugboat	**Last owner:**	Navy Experimental Dive Unit
Previous names:	n/a	**Sunk:**	February 8, 1990
Length:	205ft (62.5m)		
Tonnage:	1,240grt		
Construction:	Charleston Shipbuilding		

75ft
23m

J

69

33

Bow

100ft
30.5m

83ft
26m

88

Stern

54

19

100ft
30.5m

Other species commonly found
at this site:

11   16   24   28   34   36   40   49   55

61   64   67   72   85

Strength

Difficulty ● ○ ○
Current ● ○ ○
Depth ● ● ○
Reef ★☆☆
Fauna ★★☆

Panama City ○
Strength

Access 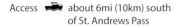 about 6mi (10km) south
of St. Andrews Pass

 Level Open Water

Location
Panama City, Bay County
GPS 30°01.938′N, 85°42.516′W

Getting there
Strength is one of the many artificial reefs deployed in a group that provides nearshore dive sites that are readily accessible from the St. Andrews Pass. There are no surface mooring buoys at this site, so operators typically tie in to the detached bow or anchor in the sand nearby.

Access
The wreck is accessible to most divers due to its relative shallowness and its open nature – the seafloor ranges from 70 feet (21.5 meters) to just 76 feet (23 meters) in depth. The wreck itself sits in a slight hollow in the seafloor, which consists of fine sediments that can influence visibility at times. Depending on currents and ocean conditions, visibility can be very low at the base of the wreck and near the seafloor, while it usually remains decent on the main deck and above. The site is best reached via one of the dive shops operating out of Panama City and Panama City Beach.

Description
Strength was originally a 185-foot (56.5-meter) Admirable-class U.S. Navy minesweeper with hull classification AM-309. Built in 1944 for the U.S. Navy, she was launched in Seattle, Washington, and after a brief training exercise went directly to the Pacific to help the Allied war effort. She played a key role in clearing mines ahead of the Allied beach landings on multiple Pacific islands under Japanese occupation, including Iwo Jima and Okinawa. She was attacked by Japanese planes during her efforts and even torpedoed by a submarine. She survived the war and earned three battle stars for her service. After the war, she was brought back to Texas and placed in reserve, where she sat in storage for over 20 years.

In 1967, she was removed from the mothball fleet for use in training exercises by Navy salvage divers based in Washington, D.C. and then in Panama City after that. She was scuttled and resurfaced multiple times before being sent to the bottom for the last time in 1987 as an artificial reef.

Although she originally settled on her side, hurricane Opal pushed her upright in 1995. Today, she remains largely upright, but her decades spent underwater have led to the separation of the bow section from the main structure of the ship, which rests on its port side. Her superstructure has largely collapsed as well, with pieces still visible just off the port side.

Despite her deteriorating physical condition, *Strength* provides divers with plenty to explore and remains a favorite among locals and visitors. There are swim-throughs beneath sections of the upper structure that still stand upright on the main deck, although hanging wires and debris create entanglement risks here. The main deck has subsided, which has limited penetration opportunities into the hold of the wreck, but there are still plenty of nooks and crannies to explore.

Divers are likely to encounter bait balls on this wreck, which can be dense enough to completely obscure one's view at times. Jacks and snapper are often plentiful above the wreck, likely attracted by the bait balls. Damselfish and angelfish are often seen on the wreck itself, while gag grouper can be found hiding in the nooks and crannies. Schools of Atlantic spadefish are often in the water column above the wreck.

Route
The shallowness of this site means there is plenty of bottom time for divers to explore the entire wreck, including the detached bow section and the larger stern section. The wreck no longer offers much profile, as it tops out at just 52 feet (16 meters), but there are still enough holes, overhangs and recesses on this wreck to make for an entertaining dive, particularly for divers under training.

STRENGTH

Lureen Ferretti ©

As wrecks degrade over time, their interiors often develop entanglement risks and require caution when exploring.

One potential route is for divers to drop down onto the bow section, circling it first before continuing on to explore the rest of the wreck. The debris-filled space between the bow and stern sections is relatively sheltered, and provides ample places for reef creatures to hide, although no real opportunities for penetration remain. From there, divers can opt to fully circle the stern, before focusing on the sections of superstructure that remain standing on the main deck. Divers should watch out for potential entanglements in the narrow swim-throughs in this area. Most divers finish up their dive exploring the main deck.

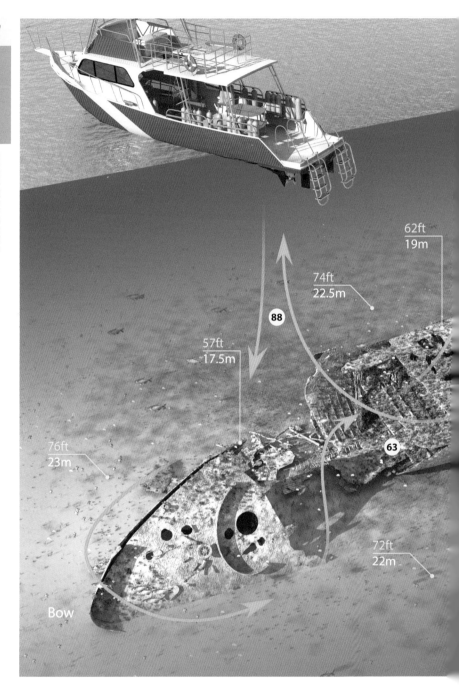

62ft
19m

74ft
22.5m

88

57ft
17.5m

76ft
23m

63

72ft
22m

Bow

52ft
16m

80

65ft
20m

Stern

69

1

40

70ft
21.5m

Name:	*Strength*			Seattle, WA, 1944
Type:	Minesweeper		**Last owner:**	U.S. Navy
Previous names:	n/a		**Sunk:**	May 15, 1987
Length:	185ft (56.5m)			
Tonnage:	945grt			
Construction:	Associated Shipbuilders,			

72ft
22m

80

52ft
16m

69

65ft
20m

Stern

1

70ft
21.5m

57ft
17.5m

76ft
23m

Bow

88

62ft
19m

40

63

74ft
22.5m

Other species commonly found
at this site:

I **J** **L** **3** **8** **20** **32** **33** **34**

39 **56** **62** **78** **84**

Red Sea

Difficulty	● ● ○
Current	● ○ ○
Depth	● ● ○
Reef	★★★☆
Fauna	★★★☆

Panama City
Red Sea

Access 🚤 about 7.5mi (12km) south
of St. Andrews Pass

Level Open Water

Location
Panama City, Bay County
GPS 30°00.963'N, 85°42.013'W

Getting there
Red Sea is one of the many artificial reefs deployed in a group, which are readily accessible from the St. Andrews Pass. There are no surface mooring buoys at this site, so operators typically tie in to the wreck itself or anchor in the sand nearby.

Access
Red Sea is accessible to most divers due to its relative shallowness and open nature. The seafloor is 76 feet (23 meters) deep and the top of the wreck is at 47 feet (14.5 meters). The site is best reached via one of the dive shops operating out of Panama City and Panama City Beach.

Description
Red Sea is a 125-foot-long (38-meter) tugboat originally built for the Panama Canal Commission in 1943. She began her career maneuvering the crane barges used to dredge and maintain the canal, as well as helping steer large ocean-going freighters and cargo ships into and out of the narrow confines of the canal's locks. Originally named *San Pablo*, she was part of the Panama Canal's fleet of tugs for nearly 50 years before being sold and renamed *San Pablo I* in 1990. She changed ownership and name twice more before moving from Panama to the U.S., where she ended up in Florida under the name *Red Sea*. She was sunk as an artificial reef on June 24, 2009 – part of a combined effort by state, local and private interests to deploy a new artificial reef in the waters of Bay County.

The wreck is relatively intact, sitting upright on sand. The top of her wheelhouse now sits upside down on the seabed just off her port side. Meanwhile, the large funnel that once dominated the midship area of the wreck has collapsed into the room below it. The resulting debris has made penetration into this interior space impossible,

Cobia and other fish are often seen patrolling the water surrounding a wreck.

although there are still penetration opportunities elsewhere on the ship for divers with appropriate experience.

While *Red Sea* has begun to show her years underwater, she remains a very popular dive site given her size and accessibility. She has also attracted a great deal of reef life over the years since her deployment as an artificial reef. Divers are likely to see large numbers of snapper and jacks here, which are attracted to the large bait fish that are known to form large schools on the wreck. Divers are also likely to find several

RELAX & RECHARGE

Patches Pub, located at 4723 Thomas Drive, Panama City Beach, is just the other side of St. Andrews State Park from Amazons surf site and the St. Andrews Jetty dive and snorkel site. This popular sports bar has a large covered outdoor terrace that hosts live music nightly. Patches has garnered a whole slew of Best of the Bay Awards over the years,

including best pizza, chicken wings and burger, of which there are a range of options, including Big Bills Bleu, with bleu cheese, and Patches Signature, which has provel cheese, bacon and an egg on top. There are vegetarian options, a kids' menu, and a selection of home-made desserts available. Happy hour runs from 3 to 6pm every day – all day on Thursdays. Visit: **Patchespub.com**

Kaschibo/Shutterstock ©

damselfish species, including cocoa damselfish, beaugregories and sergeant majors sheltering closer to the hull. Whitespotted soapfish are also a common sight here, as are blue and Queen angelfish. Schools of tomtates and other grunts are often spotted in the wreck's shadowy interiors.

Route

The shallowness of this site means there is plenty of bottom time for divers to explore the entire wreck. And with the top of the wreck reaching 47 feet (14.5 meters), there is always the option for divers to shallow their depth profile in order to

gain back some bottom time if they do not wish to drop as deep as the seabed.

Divers most commonly start by circling the outside of the wreck before making their way to the main deck. While the aft portion of the main deck structure is largely inaccessible due to the collapsed funnel, it is still possible to penetrate the wreck toward the bow. Divers can gradually shallow up until they finish their dive at the roofless wheelhouse and greet the barracuda that are often seen on this part of the wreck.

47ft
14.5m

80

53ft
16m

52

Bow

76ft
23m

57ft
17.5m

88

52ft
16m

38

19

33

Stern

N

E

W

S

125ft / 38m

Name:	*Red Sea*	**Construction:**	Speddon Shipbuilding
Type:	Tugboat		Company, Baltimore,
Previous names:	*San Pablo,*		MD, 1943
	San Pablo I, Aquilon	**Last owner:**	n/a
Length:	125ft (38m)	**Sunk:**	June 24, 2009
Tonnage:	391grt		

279

80

52ft
16m

88

57ft
17.5m

33

19

Stern

47ft
14.5m

53ft
16m

Bow

52

38

76ft
23m

Other species commonly found
at this site:

4   15   18   28   31   39   51   65   67

69   74   77   82   87

SS Empire Mica

Difficulty	● ● ●
Current	● ● ○
Depth	● ● ●
Reef	★★★☆
Fauna	★★★★

Apalachicola
SS Empire Mica ●

Access 🚤 about 35mi (56km) southwest of Apalachicola

Level Advanced

Location
Apalachicola, Franklin County
GPS 29°18.728′N, 85°21.139′W

Getting there
SS Empire Mica is located southwest of Apalachicola Bay, which is just east of Cape San Blas. It is about 43 miles (69 kilometers) south of Mexico Beach and even farther south from Panama City, which means that dive shops do not regularly visit this site. Given the distance from shore, it should only be visited by operators and private vessels with experience operating in the Gulf. There are no surface mooring buoys at this site, so operators typically drop anchor in the sand near the wreck.

Access
This site is more suited to advanced divers with enough experience to comfortably reach the wreck and sandy seafloor, which sits at approximately 105 feet (32 meters) in depth. The highest points on the wreck – the steamship's three giant boilers – reach as high as 87 feet (26.5 meters), which makes this dive relatively deep in terms of average depth. Currents can be moderate to strong at this site.

Description
SS Empire Mica was a 479-foot (146-meter) British tanker built in Middlesbrough, England. She transported fuel oil during the Second World War and was torpedoed and sunk by a

German U-Boat on June 29, 1942, only one year after her launch.

Empire Mica was loaded with 11,200 tons of kerosene aviation fuel in Baytown, Texas, which was bound for Britain to aid the Royal Air Force in the European war effort. The ship's captain had received instructions to seek a sheltered anchorage site at night in order to avoid attack by German U-Boats. However, the bays along the northwest Florida coast were not deep enough to accommodate the fully loaded ship, so there was little choice but to push on through the night toward Key West, which was the next scheduled stop before crossing the Atlantic Ocean.

Unfortunately, Empire Mica never reached her destination. Just after midnight, her crew spotted the conning tower of a German U-boat – it was later learned to be U-67 – off the port side of the ship. It was a calm and clear night with a full moon, and the unescorted ship was easy prey for the submarine. The U-boat launched two torpedoes, and both struck the heavily laden freighter. One hit the stern, where the engine room was located, while the second struck closer to the bridge. The torpedoes ignited the kerosene that the ship was carrying, and she erupted into a fireball, the glow of which could be seen on shore nearly 30 miles (50 kilometers) away. Many of the of the ship's crew were killed in the initial explosion, others died in the water or in their lifeboats as they were consumed by fire. In the end only one lifeboat containing 14 crew members escaped the inferno. Empire Mica continued to burn for

RELAX & RECHARGE

Oyster City Brewing Company is the place to visit for "damn good beer" in Apalachicola, as their website professes. This dock-side brew pub has been serving a wide selection of craft beers since 2014. Whatever your preference, from IPAs and pilsners, to fruit beers and stouts, Oyster City Brewing Company has you covered. Some of the options are truly unique, like the Peanut Butter Porter and the Mango Pale Ale. The selection is wide and constantly rotating at the brewery's tasting room, located at 17 Avenue D in Apalachicola, which is open from noon to 7pm on most days, and 8pm on Friday and Saturday. Visit: **Oystercity.beer**

A diver swims in between *Empire Mica*'s massive boilers, which dominate the site.

Bob Cox ©

24 hours before finally sinking to the bottom in its current location, due south of Cape San Blas, along with 33 of her crew.

After the catastrophic explosion and prolonged fire caused by the impact of two torpedoes, *Empire Mica* was already badly damaged when she sank to the bottom. But after more than eight decades, numerous hurricanes, at least one salvage operation, and some wreck-clearing attempts by the U.S. Coast Guard, the *Empire Mica* today consists largely of twisted steel beams and hull plates. The wreck site is essentially a complex debris field in the shape of the former ship, which stretches approximately 500 feet (152 meters) in length. The wreckage has numerous structures that provide shelter for large reef creatures, such as lobsters, nurse sharks, grouper and moray eels. Above the wreck, divers may spot large barracuda, amberjacks and sharks. While any penetration opportunities have long since collapsed, there is still plenty of structure to explore. However, divers should be aware that there is significant risk of entanglement from overhanging debris, and should proceed with caution when descending close to the wreck.

Route

Empire Mica is a large, deep and incredibly complex site with the potential for strong currents. Most divers will need to visit the wreck numerous times to fully explore the site. The stern area of the wreck, where the three large boilers sit elevated relative to the rest of

479ft / 146m

90ft
27.5m

100ft
30.5m

91

Bow

105ft
32m

the debris, is generally considered the most interesting part of the wreck to explore. These large structures rise over 20 feet (6 meters) off the seabed and attract a lot of schooling fish, including grunts and snapper. Divers may also be able to identify the rudder and propeller shaft amid the wreckage of the stern. The primary propeller was salvaged many years ago and is now located at Capt. Anderson's Restaurant in Panama City Beach (see Relax & Recharge box on page 243). However, the spare propeller is still located in a recessed section at the center of the ship. This solid cast bronze structure, which weighs 16 tons and is about 18 feet (5.5 meters)

SS EMPIRE MICA

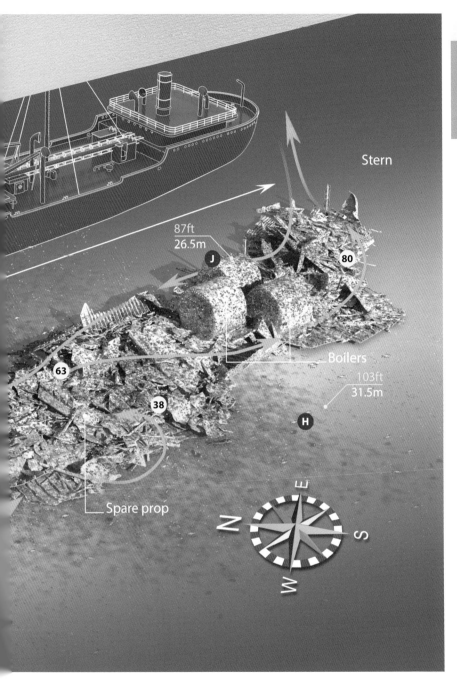

Stern

87ft
26.5m

J

80

Boilers

103ft
31.5m

63

38

H

Spare prop

Name:	*SS Empire Mica*		Ltd., Middlesbrough, UK, 1941
Type:	Tanker	Last owner:	British Ministry of War
Previous names:	n/a		Transport (MOWT)
Length:	479ft (146m)	Sunk:	June 29, 1942
Tonnage:	8,032grt		
Construction:	Furness Shipbuilding Co.		

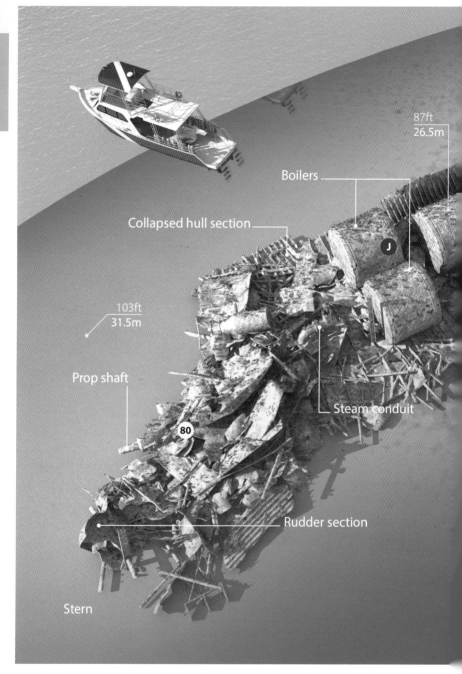

87ft
26.5m

Boilers

Collapsed hull section

J

103ft
31.5m

Prop shaft

Steam conduit

80

Rudder section

Stern

across, is definitely worth visiting during any dive on the *Empire Mica*.

Plenty of large fish species can be found on *Empire Mica*, but many individuals are familiar with spearfishing divers and tend to keep their distance. Divers should keep an eye out for

sharks during their ascent and safety stops – it is not uncommon to see multiple species here, including sandbar, lemon and bull sharks.

Spare prop

91

63

38

Bow

105ft
32m

Intact hull section

H

Other species commonly found
at this site:

C F G 3 4 5 8 10 12

15 21 40 54 67 81 82 85 90

Other Bay County sites

The following list represents other popular dive sites in Bay County frequently visited by local operators.

94 Grey Ghost

GPS 30°02.829'N, 86°05.556'W

Difficulty ● ● ○
Current ● ● ○
Depth ● ● ●
Reef ★★☆
Fauna ★★☆

Grey Ghost was originally a 105-foot (32-meter) U.S. Navy tugboat (also spelled *Gray Ghost*) scuttled quite a distance off shore in 1978. One of the earliest wrecks deployed as an artificial reef to the area, she currently sits at a depth of 110 feet (33.5 meters) near some interesting natural bottom habitat.

95 NRDA Grant Reefs

GPS (NRDA-3) 30°06.582'N, 85°59.511'W
(NRDA-4) 30°06.419'N, 85°59.683'W
(NRDA-6) 30°06.030'N, 85°58.224'W
(NRDA-7) 30°06.056'N, 85°58.065'W
(NRDA-5) 30°06.200'N, 85°56.994'W
(NRDA-8) 30°05.935'N, 85°55.648'W
(NRDA-9) 30°05.796'N, 85°55.522'W
(NRDA-10) 30°05.425'N, 85°54.268'W
(NRDA-1A) 30°05.320'N, 85°54.186'W
(NRDA-11) 30°05.250'N, 85°54.269'W
(NRDA-13) 30°05.100'N, 85°54.101'W
(NRDA-2A) 30°05.040'N, 85°54.172'W
(NRDA4-12) 30°04.990'N, 85°54.266'W

Difficulty ● ● ○
Current ● ○ ○
Depth ● ● ○
Reef ★★☆
Fauna ★★☆

This series of artificial reefs features over 205 reef modules totaling nearly 980 tons. They were deployed in 2020 as part of the National Resources Damage Assessment (NRDA) Restoration Program and were placed in clusters at 13 permitted locations. The sites quickly became popular with spearfishers and divers because of the marine life they support. They are all found at a depth of around 90 feet (27.5 meters).

96 Hathaway Bridge Spans #5 and 6

GPS (#6) 30°08.924'N, 85°53.273'W
(#5) 30°09.847'N, 85°53.813'W

Difficulty ● ○ ○
Current ● ○ ○
Depth ● ● ○
Reef ★☆☆
Fauna ★☆☆

These bridge spans were from the old Hathaway Bridge that once connected Panama City to Panama City Beach. Spans 5 and 6 are in shallower water (around 73 feet or 22.5 meters) than most of the other spans and have largely collapsed after the strong currents generated by Hurricane Michael in 2018.

98 Commander

GPS 30°03.235'N, 85°56.782'W

Difficulty ● ● ○
Current ● ○ ○
Depth ● ● ○
Reef ★★☆
Fauna ★★☆

Originally a 65-foot-long (20-meter) steel-hulled tugboat, this wreck sank by accident, allegedly as a result of fire. It now sits upright on a sandy seafloor at a depth 95 feet (30 meters).

99 Hathaway Bridge Spans #7, 8, 9, 10

GPS (#10) 30°01.463'N, 85°57.750'W
(#9) 30°00.525'N, 85°56.989'W
(#8) 29°59.879'N, 85°56.904'W
(#7) 29°59.141'N, 85°57.020'W

Difficulty ● ● ○
Current ● ○ ○
Depth ● ● ●
Reef ★☆☆
Fauna ★★☆

These bridge spans were from the old Hathaway Bridge that once connected Panama City to Panama City Beach. Spans 10, 9, 8 and 7 sit at a depth of around 113 feet (34.5 meters), which has helped protect these spans and kept them in decent condition compared to the other Hathaway spans.

 100 # Stage 1

GPS 30°00.768'N, 85°54.103'W

Difficulty ● ● ○
Current ● ○ ○
Depth ● ● ●
Reef ★★☆
Fauna ★★★

This deep site was once a Naval platform that was demolished in 1984. It is currently a mass of steel pipes and support structures that hosts a lot of reef creatures thanks to its large size and depth. The site is anchored on the sandy seabed at a depth of 105 feet (32 meters).

101 # Stage 2

GPS 30°07.244'N, 85°46.477'W

Difficulty ● ● ○
Current ● ○ ○
Depth ● ● ○
Reef ★★☆
Fauna ★★☆

This former Naval platform was first installed in 1957 before being demolished using explosives in August 1984. The violent end to its operating career is visible in the twisted jumble of steel pipes and support structures. The site makes excellent fish habitat, but it is a challenging reef to navigate. The depth ranges from 60 to 70 feet (18.5 to 21.5 meters) and is best visited at high tide for better visibility given its proximity to the pass.

102 # Hathaway Bridge Span #14

GPS 30°04.291'N, 85°48.876'W

Difficulty ● ● ○
Current ● ○ ○
Depth ● ● ○
Reef ★★☆
Fauna ★☆☆

This bridge span was from the old Hathaway Bridge that once connected Panama City to Panama City Beach. Span 14 is one of a set of spans deployed among the inshore artificial reefs closer to the pass in relatively shallower water (around 73 feet or 22.5 meters). Span 14 has largely collapsed after the strong currents generated by Hurricane Michael in 2018.

105 # Chickasaw

GPS 30°04.924'N, 85°46.763'W

Difficulty ● ● ○
Current ● ○ ○
Depth ● ● ○
Reef ★☆☆
Fauna ★★☆

Chickasaw was originally a 102-foot-long (31-meter) steam tugboat built in 1908 for the Army Corps of Engineers. She was scuttled to form an artificial reef in 1970, just a few miles outside of the pass at a depth of around 70 feet (21.5 meters).

107 # DuPont Bridge Spans #1 and 2

GPS (#1) 29°58.913'N, 85°51.117'W
(#2) 29°58.506'N, 85°50.863'W

Difficulty ● ● ○
Current ● ○ ○
Depth ● ● ○
Reef ★★☆
Fauna ★☆☆

These two spans match the DuPont Span #3 described on page 260. Spans #1 and #2 were deployed around the same time but have fallen over and deteriorated more than Span #3. They sit at a depth of 90 feet (27.5 meters).

109 Mac's Reef

GPS 29°58.926'N, 85°50.347'W

Difficulty	●	●	○
Current	●	○	○
Depth	●	●	○
Reef	★	☆	☆
Fauna	★	★	☆

This Navy work barge (2154) was used in training exercises by Navy salvage teams at the local base. It was deployed as an artificial reef in 2007 at a depth of 97 feet (30 meters). The site is named after Richard "Mac" McCullen, a local diver who died a few years before the reef was deployed.

112 DAN Safety Barge

GPS 30°04.830'N, 85°43.853'W

Difficulty	●	○	○
Current	●	○	○
Depth	●	○	○
Reef	★	☆	☆
Fauna	★	☆	☆

Located just south of the pass at a depth of 60 feet (18 meters), this small barge is a low-profile artificial reef that provides decent habitat for reef creatures in a relatively accessible spot close to the pass.

113 Hathaway Bridge Spans #3A and 4

GPS (#4) 29°56.690'N, 85°49.780'W
(#3A) 29°56.682'N, 85°49.115'W

Difficulty	●	●	○
Current	●	○	○
Depth	●	●	●
Reef	★	☆	☆
Fauna	★	★	☆

These bridge spans were from the old Hathaway Bridge that once connected Panama City to Panama City Beach. Spans 3A and 4 sit at a depth of around 100 feet (30.5 meters). Their depth has helped keep them in decent condition compared to the shallower Hathaway spans.

115 BJ Putnam

GPS 29°55.812'N, 85°50.093'W

Difficulty	●	●	○
Current	●	○	○
Depth	●	●	●
Reef	★	★	☆
Fauna	★	★	☆

Originally an oilfield supply boat that was converted to a fish processor, this 180-foot (55-meter) vessel was renamed *BJ Putnam* in honor of local charter captain, businessman and community leader. She was deployed as an artificial reef in November 1993 and sits at a depth of 106 feet (32.5 meters).

116 Hathaway Bridge Spans #1, 2 and 12

GPS (#1) 30°02.690'N, 85°43.745'W
(#2) 30°02.197'N, 85°43.707'W
(#12) 30°02.081'N, 85°43.893'W

Difficulty	●	●	○
Current	●	○	○
Depth	●	●	○
Reef	★	☆	☆
Fauna	★	☆	☆

These bridge spans are from the old Hathaway Bridge that once connected Panama City to Panama City Beach. Spans 1, 2 and 12 are clustered within the group of inshore artificial reefs that sit close to the pass and in relatively shallow water (around 73 feet or 22.5 meters). These spans have largely collapsed after the strong currents generated by Hurricane Michael in 2018.

119 Benjamin H Grierson Liberty Ship

GPS 29°59.095'N, 85°42.395'W

Difficulty	●	○	○
Current	●	○	○
Depth	●	●	○
Reef	★	☆	☆
Fauna	★	★	☆

The *Benjamin H Grierson Liberty Ship* was one of four Liberty Ships deployed as artificial reefs across Northwest Florida in the 1970s. She was named after a music teacher turned cavalry general in the Union Army made famous by a daring raid into Mississippi. The wreck is an empty, 440-foot-long (134-meter) hull that sits at a depth of 72 feet (22 meters).

120 Sherman Tug

GPS 29°55.410'N, 85°40.200'W

Difficulty	●	○	○
Current	●	○	○
Depth	●	●	○
Reef	★	★	☆
Fauna	★	★	☆

Sherman Tug was an 80-foot-long (24.5-meter) tugboat deployed as an artificial reef in May 1996. She sits at a depth of 80 feet (24.5 meters).

121 MB-251

GPS 29°55.075'N, 85°40.467'W

Difficulty	●	○	○
Current	●	○	○
Depth	●	●	○
Reef	★	★	☆
Fauna	★	☆	☆

MB-251 is an artificial reef that features 118 tons of reef modules. The site was deployed in May 2019 and has a depth of approximately 77 feet (23.5 meters).

122 St. Joe Community Foundation Reef 2

GPS 29°55.096'N, 85°39.120'W

Difficulty	●	○	○
Current	●	○	○
Depth	●	●	○
Reef	★	★	☆
Fauna	★	☆	☆

This artificial reef features 219 tons of reef modules deployed in July 2020 with a depth of approximately 80 feet (24.5 meters).

123 MB-248

29°55.105'N, 85°38.055'W

Difficulty	●	○	○
Current	●	○	○
Depth	●	●	○
Reef	★	★	☆
Fauna	★	☆	☆

MB-248 is an artificial reef consisting of 130 tons of reef modules deployed in April 2018. The modules form a north-south line that stretches 760 feet (230 meters) in length at an average depth of 78 feet (24 meters).

124 MB-256

GPS 29°55.460'N, 85°37.667'W

Difficulty	●	○	○
Current	●	○	○
Depth	●	●	○
Reef	★	★	☆
Fauna	★	☆	☆

MB-256 is an artificial reef consisting of more than 50 tons of reef modules deployed in May 2020 at a depth of 78 feet (24 meters).

125 Shady Lady (Duke Energy Reef)

GPS 29°47.145'N, 85°42.029'W

Difficulty	●	●	○
Current	●	○	○
Depth	●	●	○
Reef	★	☆	☆
Fauna	★	★	☆

Deployed in March 2007 as an artificial reef, *Shady Lady* was originally a 110-foot-long (33.5-meter) steel-hulled shrimp boat. The wreck now lies on her side at a maximum depth of 95 feet (29 meters).

126 18-Mile Bridge (Hathaway Span #11)

GPS 29°44.378'N, 85°41.854'W

Difficulty	●	●	○
Current	●	○	○
Depth	●	●	●
Reef	★	☆	☆
Fauna	★	★	☆

This site features a span from the old Hathaway Bridge that once connected Panama City to Panama City Beach. The bridge was also called 18-Mile Bridge, hence the name for this site. Span 11 was deployed in May 1988 and sits on the seabed at a depth of 107 feet (32.5 meters). Despite the depth, this span has deteriorated somewhat after several decades underwater.

127 Courtney Knight Gaines Reef

GPS 29°44.546'N, 85°41.660'W

Difficulty	●	●	○
Current	●	○	○
Depth	●	●	●
Reef	★	★	☆
Fauna	★	★	☆

This memorial reef sits over 20 miles (32 kilometers) off shore. It features 63 tons of limestone and concrete reef modules deployed April 2018 at a depth of 101 feet (31 meters). An additional set of artificial reefs was deployed here in May 2019.

128 Tennessee Chuck McKibbonville Reef

GPS 29°54.810'N, 85°33.054'W

Difficulty	●	○	○
Current	●	○	○
Depth	●	●	○
Reef	★	★	☆
Fauna	★	☆	☆

Deployed in May 2020, this reef features more than 75 tons of limestone and concrete reef modules at a depth of 65 feet (20 meters).

129 Mexico Beach 2002 Grant Reef

GPS 29°54.022'N, 85°32.499'W

Difficulty	●	○	○
Current	●	○	○
Depth	●	●	○
Reef	★	★	☆
Fauna	★	☆	☆

Deployed at a depth of 66 feet (20 meters), this artificial reef features 100 reef balls sitting close to one another on a sandy seafloor.

130 Fish America Foundation Reef

GPS 29°53.628'N, 85°32.634'W

Difficulty	●	○	○
Current	●	○	○
Depth	●	●	○
Reef	★	★	☆
Fauna	★	★	☆

Deployed in February 2003, this reef features 100 reef balls totaling 200 tons. The site has an average depth of around 65 feet (20 meters). The deployment was funded by a grant from the Fish America Foundation.

131 Garfield Wilson Reef

GPS 29°53.688'N, 85°31.260'W

Difficulty	●	○	○
Current	●	○	○
Depth	●	○	○
Reef	★	☆	☆
Fauna	★	☆	☆

Named after a former President of the Mexico Beach Artificial Reef Association (MBARA) from 1999 through 2001, the Garfield Wilson Reef features 512 tons of concrete culverts donated by the Sikes Concrete Company of Panama City. The reef was deployed in June 2001 at a depth of 51 feet (15.5 meters).

132 OAR BBSWC Barge

GPS 29°46.093'N, 85°36.716'W

Difficulty ● ○ ○
Current ● ○ ○
Depth ● ● ○
Reef ★★☆
Fauna ★★☆

This 100-foot-long (30.5-meter) steel barge was deployed as an artificial reef in June 2007 at a depth of 89 feet (27 meters). The barge was sunk along with concrete culverts and boxes, and the deployment was funded primarily by the Organization for Artificial Reefs (OAR).

133 Vamar

GPS 29°53.957'N, 85°27.803'W

Difficulty ● ○ ○
Current ● ○ ○
Depth ● ○ ○
Reef ★★☆
Fauna ★★☆

Also called the Lumber Ship, *Vamar* was originally a gunboat built in 1919 in the United Kingdom and made famous by her role in the American expedition to Antarctica in 1928. Later in her career, she was converted into a freighter, which sank in 1942 loaded with lumber destined for Cuba. The wreck lies in just 25 feet (7.5 meters) of water off the coast of Mexico Beach. She is one of three Florida Underwater Archaeological Preserves in Northwest Florida and an original member of the Florida Panhandle Shipwreck Trail.

134 Air Force Tower

GPS 29°43.479'N, 85°28.514'W

Difficulty ● ○ ○
Current ● ○ ○
Depth ● ○ ○
Reef ★★☆
Fauna ★★☆

This wreckage is believed to be a section of an Air Combat Maneuvering Instrumentation (ACMI) Tower that fell off a transport barge in rough seas in 1993. The tower now lies on its side at a depth of around 65 feet (20 meters). It rises to within 20 feet (6 meters) of the surface.

The artificial reefs of Northwest Florida support a variety of marine life for divers to observe.

Bob Cox ©

SPRINGS

Florida plays host to many freshwater springs that exist courtesy of the unique geology found in the state's northern areas. Slightly acidic rainwater slowly erodes underground layers of soluble rock, such as limestone and dolomite, forming caverns, caves and tunnels that fill with fresh water. These springs, as they are often referred to in Florida, consistently discharge large volumes of freshwater that feed the state's rivers and lakes. In fact, some of the larger springs discharge hundreds of millions of gallons of water each day, equivalent to an Olympic sized swimming pool every few minutes.

Florida's springs are confined to the northern part of the state and the eastern part of Northwest Florida. By some accounts, there are as many as 700 freshwater springs scattered across the state. Many of these springs can be dived or snorkeled, providing the opportunity to explore a unique ecosystem that remains a steady 68°F to 72°F (20°C to 22.2°C) throughout the year.

There are two main freshwater springs available to divers in Northwest Florida: Vortex Spring and Morrison Springs. Many dive operators schedule regular trips to these springs during the winter or when the weather restricts diving in the Gulf. Some operators conduct open water training classes at these springs.

Dive and snorkel sites

DID YOU KNOW? ❓

There is another diveable spring in Northwest Florida called Cypress Spring. This large, clear spring was very popular with snorkelers and divers in the past, although its popularity has waned due to accessibility issues. The land surrounding the spring was bought up by a bottled-water company that proceeded to bar access to the spring from land. Fortunately, Florida has strong laws governing public access to its waterways, and so divers can still access the spring by boat, as long as they do not go ashore. The Big Pine Lane Boat Launch in Vernon, Florida, is located just a mile down the river from the spring. A canoe or kayak is needed to access the spring because sections of the river are too shallow to navigate by powered boats. But divers can put their gear in a boat, paddle up the river and safely (not to mention legally) dive to their heart's content.

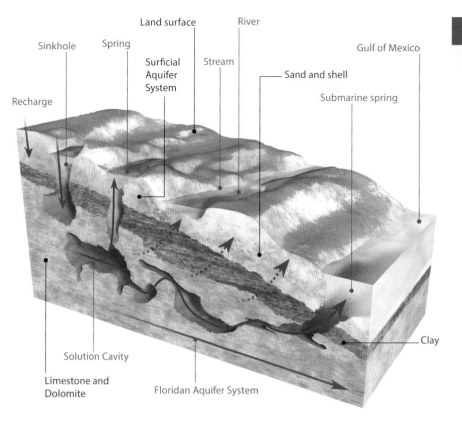

Sinkhole

Spring

Land surface

River

Recharge

Surficial Aquifer System

Stream

Sand and shell

Gulf of Mexico

Submarine spring

Solution Cavity

Limestone and Dolomite

Floridan Aquifer System

Clay

Divers enjoy exploring the clear waters of Florida springs throughout the year.

Valerijs Novickis/Shutterstock ©

Vortex Spring
Panama City

Access 🚐 about 85 mins from Pensacola
🚐 about 69 mins from Destin
🚐 about 75 mins from Panama City

Level n/a

Location

Ponce de Leon, Holmes County
GPS 30°46.243'N, 85°56.903'W

Getting there

Vortex Spring is located just a few miles north of I-10. From Pensacola, take I-10 east until exit 96. Head north on FL-81 for 3.7 miles (6 kilometers) before turning right onto Vortex Springs Lane. Follow that road to the end to reach the spring. From Destin, head north toward the I-10 before heading east toward exit 96 and following the directions outlined above. From Panama City, head west along Highway 98 before turning north onto FL-79 at Gulf Highlands in Walton County. Head north on FL-79 for 15.4 miles (25 kilometers) before turning left on FL-20. Head west along FL-20 for 5.5 miles (9.1 kilometers) before turning right onto FL-81. Follow FL-81 north until it crosses I-10, then follow the directions detailed above. There is ample parking at Vortex Spring. The official address for the site is 1517 Vortex Springs Lane, Ponce De Leon, Florida 32455.

Access

Vortex Spring is owned by a private organization, Vortex Spring Adventures, which is one of the largest dive resorts in Florida. Visitors can dive, snorkel, swim and engage in plenty of other recreational activities at this site for a fee payable at the dive shop, which is on the left as you enter the property. The site includes, a campground, restrooms and picnic areas. Access is on a first-come, first-served basis. The spring can get crowded during holiday weekends. For more information on the site, visit: **Vortexspring.com**

Dive shop

Spring head

Cave

Private residence

Description

Vortex Spring provides access to a complex network of underground caves and caverns linked by narrow passageways that extend over 1,600 feet (488 meters) in total length. The open basin of the spring allows for easy access with steps leading into the water and low platforms with space for diving classes to assemble. There are additional platforms underwater for divers to practice skills, as well as an artificial cavern system and a sunken sailboat.

The spring is open to the surface inside the main basin, which bottoms out at a depth of around 58 feet (17.5 meters), making it accessible to open water divers. The bottom of the basin has a cave opening that provides access to the network of caverns that extend underground to a depth of more than 150 feet (45.5 meters). Access to the deep caverns is strictly limited to divers with cave certifications, and a locked gate blocks the route just over 300 feet (91.5 meters) into the cavern system at a depth of 110 feet (33.5 meters).

A rope system and lighting helps non-cave-certified divers explore the caverns that lead to the gate, but these areas should only be accessed by advanced divers with experience in overhead environments. Divers will find freshwater fish in the spring, including catfish, carp, bass and bluegill. Freshwater eels live in the caverns.

Artificial cavern

Swim area

P

Morrison Springs
Panama City

Access 🚙 about 84 mins from Pensacola
🚙 about 67 mins from Destin
🚙 about 67 mins from Panama City

Level n/a

Location
Ponce de Leon, Walton County
GPS 30°39.459'N, 85°54.290'W

Getting there

Morrison Springs is located in the aptly named Morrison Springs County Park in Walton County. The park is located just a few miles south of I-10. From Pensacola, head east on I-10 to exit 96. Head south on FL-81 for 3.7 miles (6 kilometers) before turning left onto Route 181. Continue along Route 181 for 1.6 miles (2.5 kilometers) before turning right onto Morrison Springs Road, which ends at the park. From Destin, head north toward the I-10 before heading east toward exit 96 and following the directions outlined above. From Panama City, head west along Highway 98 before turning north onto FL-79 at Gulf Highlands in Walton County. Head north on FL-79 for 15.4 miles (25 kilometers) before turning left on FL-20. Head west along FL-20 for 5.5 miles (9.1 kilometers) before turning right onto FL-81. Follow FL-81 north for 5 miles (8 kilometers) before turning right onto Route 181. Then follow the directions detailed above. There is ample parking at the county park. The official address is 874 Morrison Springs Road, Ponce De Leon, Florida, 32455.

Access

There are restroom facilities at the county park, along with covered picnic tables and boardwalks that provide easy access to the spring. The main access point for divers is the sandy beach immediately adjacent to the parking lot. Divers can easily enter

P

Boat ramp

the water here or can make their way along the boardwalk and stride jump off the floating dock that extends farther out into the water. A boat ramp just to the south of this access point is used by fishing boats, which have the right to fish in the area. As such, divers should use diver-down flags while in the water, and surface with caution. Visibility is greatly influenced by the nearby Choctawhatchee River, and when the river is running high (above 5 feet or 1.5 meters) visibility can drop quickly.

Description

The open basin at Morrison Springs bottoms out at a depth of around 20 feet (6 meters), with a platform anchored near the bottom that is often used by divers to practice underwater skills. A funnel-shaped opening in the middle of the basin provides access to an underwater cave that bottoms out between 45 and 50 feet (13.5 and 15 meters). Only divers with cave diving experience should enter the cavern, although it is not nearly as extensive as the system found in nearby Vortex Spring.

Many divers also enjoy exploring the shallow water near the edges of the basin, looking for fish and other creatures that hide among the roots of the large cypress trees that surround the spring. Divers can see spotted and largemouth bass, bluegill, catfish, carp, mullet and sunfish, among other freshwater species.

Species

Identifying coral reef organisms is an enjoyable part of any underwater adventure. Not only can you appreciate the diversity and wonder that surrounds you on a reef, but you will be better able to understand the story that is unfolding right before your eyes.

For example, you will know where and when to look for certain species, as well as what they eat, who eats them, how big they get and how long they live. But more specifically, you will understand certain behaviors that can be observed on coral reefs, such as why damselfish attack larger creatures or which creatures form symbiotic relationships and why.

Many times, behaviors are an integral part of the identification process. In some cases, understanding how a particular fish behaves,

SAFETY TIP ❶

The section on dangerous species that follows is intended to provide the information you need to recognize the handful of species that can cause injury. These species should not be considered "active threats," but rather organisms that have the potential to cause harm. Most injuries occur because the organism in question has felt threatened and because a diver or snorkeler has not recognized the warning signs. By engaging in safe and conscientious diving and snorkeling practices, and by keeping in mind a few key safety tips, you can avoid having your experience ruined by an unpleasant sting or bite.

A pair of juvenile spotted drums swim through a shipwreck.

such as whether it is active during the night or day or whether it is an ambush predator or active forager, can be more useful in determining its identity than its color or shape.

Many reef organisms may appear very similar at first glance, and the wide diversity of species on coral reefs can appear to be a chaotic jumble. But by combining an understanding of animal behavior with some basic identification information, you can start to tease apart that puzzle and experience the wonder of the coral reef.

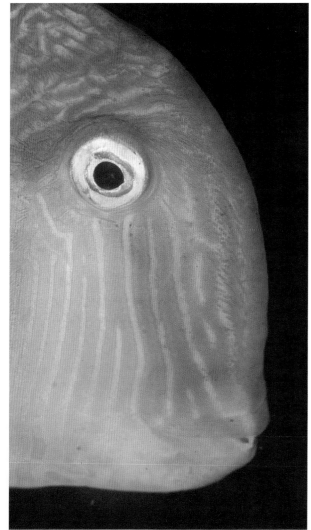

Antonio Martin/Shutterstock ©

Pearly razorfish are found at a number of sites in Northwest Florida.

NORTHWEST FLORIDA SPECIES

The information provided in this guide represents the most up-to-date science available at the time of publication. It covers some of the most common reef species you will find during your time in the waters off Northwest Florida. However, it should be noted that ecologists continue to discover new information about species, their behaviors and their interactions. Later editions of this book may contain modifications that reflect new knowledge.

The following pages are divided into three sections that feature information about sea turtles, which have a rather unique life history; dangerous species, including details on the kind of threat they pose and how to treat injuries caused by them; and finally, a general species section that helps you identify and learn about the most common species found at the dive and snorkel sites featured in this guide.

Jono Gaza/Shutterstock ©

301

Sea turtle identification

GREEN TURTLE
CHELONIA MYDAS

Maximum size: 4ft (1.4m)
Longevity: Up to 75 years
Habitat: Seagrass beds, reefs
Diet: Jellyfish and crustaceans when young;
algae and seagrass as adults
Sightings: Common

A

Behavior: Green turtles can be found grazing on vegetation in shallow water or cruising the reef. Most green turtles migrate short distances along the coast to reach nesting beaches, but some may migrate up to 1,300 miles (2,100 kilometers) to reach nesting beaches.
Predators (adults): Tiger sharks, orcas (killer whales)

HAWKSBILL SEA TURTLE
ERETMOCHELYS IMBRICATA

Maximum size: 3ft (0.9m)
Longevity: Up to 50 years
Habitat: Reefs
Diet: Sponges, tunicates, squid, shrimp
Sightings: Common

B

Behavior: Hawksbills can be found feeding throughout the day or resting with their bodies wedged into reef cracks and crevices. Some hawksbills do not migrate at all, while others migrate over thousands of miles.
Predators (adults): Tiger sharks, orcas (killer whales)

SEA TURTLE CONSERVATION STATUS: ENDANGERED

All species of sea turtles are endangered and many human activities contribute to their decline.
- Turtles are hunted in many parts of the world, targeting their meat and eggs for food, and their shells to make jewelry, eyeglass frames and curios. Many others drown in fishing nets intended for shrimp or fish, or are struck and killed by passing boats.
- Turtles eat and choke on plastic and other trash, while pollution increases the frequency of turtle disease.
- Coastal development is rapidly reducing the number of active nesting beaches.

ECO TIP

Sea turtles need our help to survive and thrive alongside our coastal communities. Consider the following tips:

LIGHTS OUT
Turn out lights visible from the beach to avoid disorienting nesting turtles and hatchlings.

DON'T LITTER
Plastic cups, bags and other trash can kill turtles when they mistake them for food.

DON'T DISTURB
Turtles you see on the beach or in the water, whether nesting, feeding or hatching, should be left alone and observed from a distance – without flashlights.

PLEASE DON'T FEED
Human food can make sea turtles sick and can leave them vulnerable to capture.

VOLUNTEER
Support your local turtle conservation programs, including participating in beach cleanups.

LOGGERHEAD SEA TURTLE
CARETTA CARETTA

Maximum size: 3.5ft (1.1m)
Longevity: Up to 60 years
Habitat: Reefs and open ocean
Diet: Crabs, shrimp, jellyfish, vegetation
Sightings: Common
Behavior: Loggerheads are occasionally found in the open ocean, but regularly move inshore to feed on reef invertebrates. Loggerhead sea turtles can migrate for thousands of miles to reach new feeding grounds before returning to the same nesting beaches.
Predators (adults): Tiger sharks, orcas (killer whales)

C

LEATHERBACK TURTLE
DERMOCHELYS CORIACEA

Maximum size: Up to 10ft (3m)
Longevity: Up to 80 years
Habitat: Open ocean
Diet: Jellyfish and tunicates
Sightings: Rare
Behavior: Leatherbacks feed in deep water during the day and at the surface at night, following the daily migratory patterns of their favorite food: jellyfish. During the mating season, leatherbacks may migrate up to 3,000 miles (4,800 kilometers) from their feeding grounds to their nesting beaches.
Predators (adults): Tiger sharks, orcas (killer whales)

D

KEMP'S RIDLEY SEA TURTLE
LEPIDOCHELYS KEMPII

Maximum size: Up to 2ft (0.7m)
Longevity: Up to 50 years
Habitat: Nearshore, shallower water
Diet: Crabs, shellfish, jellyfish and small fish
Sightings: Rare
Behavior: Kemp's ridleys are the smallest of the Florida sea turtles, and the only one that nests primarily during the day – 95 percent of their nesting activity takes place in Mexico. They practice mass nesting, where thousands of females come ashore at the same time to lay eggs. Individuals inhabit shallow, coastal waters, using their large, triangular crushing beak to feed on their favorite food: crabs.
Predators (adults): Tiger sharks, orcas (killer whales)

E

Sea turtle ecology

Nesting

Females generally crawl onto the beach at night (or during the day in the case of Kemp's ridleys) and dig a shallow nest. They lay up to 200 small white eggs before covering the nest and returning to the sea. The eggs incubate for 45 to 70 days, depending on the species.

Mating

Most sea turtles reproduce in the warm summer months except for the leatherback, whose mating season spans fall and winter. Many species migrate great distances to return to the their customary nesting beach. Courtship and mating occur in the shallow waters off shore.

Pete Niesen/Shutterstock ©

Adulthood

In adulthood, some sea turtle species return to coastal waters where coral reefs and nearshore waters provide plenty of food and protection from predators.

Gail Johnson/Shutterstock ©

UWPhotog/Shutterstock ©

2A

2B

Hatching

3

At hatching, hundreds of tiny turtles dig their way out of the nest and head toward the moonlight reflecting off the sea. As many as 90 percent are eaten by predators as eggs or as hatchlings within the first few hours of their lives.

Juvenile stage

Young turtles drift through the open ocean for years, often associating with floating sargassum (seaweed) mats. They feed on plankton and small jellyfish. Little is known about this stage of their lives.

Dangerous species

BLACKTIP SHARK
CARCHARHINUS LIMBATUS

Maximum size: 6.5ft (2m), 154lb (70kg)
Longevity: 12 years
Typical depth: 3–213ft (1–65m)
Behavior: Blacktip sharks are common throughout Florida on coral reefs and also in low-salinity environments such as estuaries and mangroves. They have black tips on their fins when young, but these markings may fade with age. Blacktip sharks sometimes form large schools and they feed mainly on fish, but may also eat marine molluscs, crustaceans, smaller shark species, rays and skates.
Predators: Larger shark species, such as tiger and great white sharks

WARNING: Although attacks on humans by blacktip sharks are very rare, they have been known to cause injury if they feel threatened or cornered. Warning signs of an attack include head swings, exaggerated swimming, back arching and lowered pectoral fins. Attacks usually result in biting or raking with the teeth, which can cause deep lacerations. The severity of shark bites often depends on the species that bites. There have been numerous documented attacks on human by blacktip sharks, but most result in only minor injury.

TREATMENT: Exit the water as soon as possible. Rinse the bite with soap and water, and apply pressure to control bleeding. Shark attacks often result in shock, so keep the patient warm, calm and shaded. Elevate the feet unless that may cause additional injury. Do not provide anything to eat or drink. Seek medical attention as soon as possible, since even minor bites require cleaning and suturing.

SANDBAR SHARK
CARCHARHINUS PLUMBEUS

Maximum size: 8.2ft (2.5m), 260lb (118kg)
Longevity: Up to 40 years
Typical depth: 3–656ft (1–200m)
Behavior: Sandbar sharks, also known as brown sharks, are one of the largest coastal shark species. They are often found over sand and mud habitat and in low-salinity environments such as estuaries and mangroves. They are sometimes mistaken for bull sharks, but are nowhere near as aggressive. Sandbar sharks are opportunistic bottom-feeders that primarily hunt small fish, molluscs and crustaceans, mostly during the night.
Predators: Larger shark species, such as tiger and great white sharks

WARNING: The severity of shark bites often depends on the species that bites. Attacks on humans by sandbar sharks are very rare – they are not generally considered to be a threat. Warning signs of a shark attack include head swings, exaggerated swimming, back arching and lowered pectoral fins. Attacks usually result in biting or raking with the teeth, which can cause deep lacerations.

TREATMENT: Exit the water as soon as possible. Rinse the bite with soap and water, and apply pressure to control bleeding. Shark attacks often result in shock, so keep the patient warm, calm and shaded. Elevate the feet unless that may cause additional injury. Do not provide anything to eat or drink. Seek medical attention as soon as possible, since even minor bites require cleaning and suturing.

BULL SHARK
CARCHARHINUS LEUCAS

Maximum size: 13ft (4m), 697lbs (316kg)
Longevity: Up to 32 years or more
Typical depth: 3–150ft (1–46m)
Behavior: Bull sharks are aggressive and typically inhabit shallow, coastal waters. They are fairly common and considered one of the most dangerous sharks in the world. They tend to feed on bony fish, rays, other sharks, carrion and even garbage.
Predators: Larger bull sharks and large crocodiles

WARNING: Along with Great Whites and tiger sharks, bull sharks are considered the most likely sharks to attack humans. While unprovoked attacks are not common, they do happen. Bull sharks do not respond well to being disturbed. Warning signs of an attack include head swings, exaggerated swimming, back arching and lowered pectoral fins. Attacks usually result in bites that can cause deep, sometimes life-threatening lacerations, often around the legs.

TREATMENT: Exit the water as soon as possible. Rinse the bite with soap and water, and apply pressure to control bleeding. Shark attacks often result in shock, so keep the patient warm, calm and shaded. Elevate the feet unless that may cause additional injury. Do not provide anything to eat or drink. Seek medical attention as soon as possible, since even minor bites require cleaning and suturing.

SOUTHERN STINGRAY
DASYATIS AMERICANA

Maximum size: 7ft (2m) disk diameter, 300lbs (136kg)
Longevity: Unknown, but probably over 10 years
Typical depth: 0–170ft (0–53m)
Behavior: Stingrays are most active at night when they hunt for hard-shelled prey such as snails, crabs, lobsters and occasionally fish. During the day, they are often found buried up to their eyes in sand.
Predators: Sharks and large grouper

WARNING: Stingrays have a serrated venomous spine at the base of their tail that they use for defense. The area around a puncture wound from this spine may become red and swollen, and you may experience muscle cramps, nausea, fever and chills.

TREATMENT: If you are stung, exit the water immediately. Apply pressure above the wound to reduce bleeding, clean the wound and soak the area with hot water, ideally around 113°F (45°C), to reduce the pain. Apply a dressing and seek medical attention. Antibiotics may be needed to reduce the risk of infection. Stingray injuries can be very painful, often reaching a peak around one hour after the injury and lasting up to two days. But they are rarely fatal unless the injury is to the head, neck or abdomen.

GREAT BARRACUDA
SPHYRAENA BARRACUDA

Maximum size: 6ft (2m), 110lbs (50kg)
Longevity: Around 20 years
Typical depth: 3–330ft (1–100m)
Behavior: Barracuda are most active during the day, feeding on jacks, grunts, grouper, snapper, squid and even other barracuda. They are often solitary in nature, but occasionally school in large numbers. They have even been documented "herding" fish they plan on consuming. Barracuda use their keen eyesight to hunt for food. They are one of the fastest fish in the ocean, capable of bursts of speed up to 30mph (48kph). Along with their two sets of razor sharp teeth, there are few prey capable of escaping a barracuda once it decides to attack.
Predators: Sharks, tuna and large grouper

WARNING: Barracuda do not usually attack divers or snorkelers unless provoked. However, evidence suggests they are attracted to objects that glint or shine, such as necklaces, watches or regulators, which they may mistake for prey. The bite of the barracuda is not toxic, but their teeth can produce a severe laceration or deep puncture wound.

TREATMENT: Exit the water as soon as possible and apply pressure to reduce bleeding. The wound should be cleaned and dressed. Medical attention may be necessary for severe bites, including sutures to close the wound and antibiotics to reduce the risk of infection.

SPOTTED SCORPIONFISH
SCORPAENA PLUMIERI

Maximum size: 18in (45cm)
Longevity: Around 15 years
Typical depth: 3–197ft (1–60m)
Behavior: Spotted scorpionfish spend much of their time lying motionless on the seabed, using camouflage to ambush fish and crustaceans. They have a large, expandable mouth capable of creating a vacuum to suck in prey, which they swallow whole.
Predators: Large snapper, sharks, rays and moray eels

WARNING: Scorpionfish have a dozen venomous dorsal spines for self-defense. The spines can penetrate skin (most commonly when stepped on), injecting a toxin that causes severe pain that can last from several hours to several days. The area around the injury may also swell and become red.

TREATMENT: Exit the water quickly and rinse the affected area with seawater. Remove any spines and use pressure to control any bleeding. Apply the hottest water you can stand to reduce pain, ideally around 113°F (45°C). Let the wound heal uncovered, but antibiotics may be required to avoid infection. The toxin can be painful, but it is not usually fatal. However, seek medical attention if concerned or if symptoms are worse than described.

RED LIONFISH
PTEROIS VOLITANS

Maximum size: 15in (38cm)
Longevity: Around 10 years
Typical depth: 7–180ft (2–55m)
Behavior: Red lionfish are originally from the Indo-West Pacific, and are considered an invasive species in the Western Atlantic. They are most active at dusk and during the night when they hunt for fish, shrimp, crabs and other reef creatures. Lionfish can live without food for up to three months.
Predators: Occasional predation by certain sharks and grouper

WARNING: Lionfish have up to 16 venomous dorsal and anal spines that can deliver a powerful neurotoxin when they puncture skin. Lionfish do not generally attack divers and snorkelers, but may sting in self-defense if you get too close. Divers and snorkelers may feel intense pain after being stung, followed by swelling and redness around the wound.

TREATMENT: Exit the water as soon as possible and remove any pieces of the spines that may remain in the wound. Use pressure to control the bleeding and apply the hottest water you can stand, ideally around 113°F (45°C), to reduce the pain. Some people experience shortness of breath, dizziness and nausea. There have been no known fatalities from a lionfish sting, but there is always a risk of complications for vulnerable individuals, including congestive heart failure. Seeking medical attention is advised. The pain may last anywhere from several hours to several days.

JELLYFISH & SIPHONOPHORES
HYDROIDOMEDUSAE
& SIPHONOPHORAE

Maximum size: 7ft (2m) with tentacles extending much farther
Longevity: From a few hours to several years
Typical depth: 0–66ft (0–20m)
Behavior: Jellyfish and siphonophores are both types of cnidaria. Jellyfish are individual animals, while siphonophores are colonies of specialized cells called zooids, such as the Portuguese man o' war. They both drift in the water and use stinging cells called nematocysts to capture and paralyze prey, including plankton and small fish.
Predators: Salmon, tuna and some sharks and sea turtle species

WARNING: Jellyfish and siphonophores have stinging cells called nematocysts located on their tentacles that can inject a toxin when brushed against bare skin. Depending on the species, jellyfish toxin can cause mild tingling to intense pain, and can be fatal in some rare cases. The contact site may also become red and blistered. Even dead jellyfish on the beach can sting, so avoid touching them.

TREATMENT: Exit the water as quickly as possible, watching out for other jellyfish. Rinse the affected area with seawater to remove any pieces of tentacle on the skin. Do not rinse with fresh water, which can trigger any remaining nematocysts to sting. The best treatment for jellyfish stings may depend on the species, but most can be treated by rinsing the affected area with vinegar or creating a paste using baking soda and seawater. The papain enzyme found in meat tenderizer and papaya can also help. Consider seeking medical attention.

FRENCH ANGELFISH
POMACANTHUS PARU

1

Maximum size: 24in (60cm)
Longevity: Up to 15 years
Typical depth: 10–330ft (3–100m)
Behavior: French angelfish dine primarily on sponges, but may also feed on gorgonians and algae. Juveniles often act as cleaners, eating the parasites from other reef fish. At dusk, French angelfish find shelter from nocturnal predators in reef cracks and crevices.
Predators: Large grouper and sharks

GREY ANGELFISH
POMACANTHUS ARCUATUS

2

Maximum size: 24in (60cm)
Longevity: Unknown, possibly up to 15 years
Typical depth: 6–100ft (2–30m)
Behavior: Grey angelfish are often seen swimming in pairs as they are known to form long-term, monogamous breeding pairs. They are recognizable by their grey-brown bodies and pale grey-white mouths. They frequent coral reefs, feeding on sponges, tunicates, hydroids, algae and sometimes seagrass.
Predators: Large grouper and sharks

BLUE ANGELFISH
HOLACANTHUS BERMUDENSIS

3

Maximum size: 18in (45cm)
Longevity: Unknown, possibly up to 15 years
Typical depth: 6–300ft (2–91m)
Behavior: Blue angelfish are often mistaken for Queen angelfish, but they lack the distinct forehead crown and are paler in color. Like most angelfish, they are often seen swimming in pairs, foraging on sponges and small benthic invertebrates. At night, they sleep hidden away in the reef, safe from predators.
Predators: Large grouper and sharks

QUEEN ANGELFISH
HOLACANTHUS CILIARIS

4

Maximum size: 18in (45cm)
Longevity: Up to 15 years
Typical depth: 3–230ft (1–70m)
Behavior: Queen angelfish are often found swimming gracefully between sea fans, sea whips and corals, alone or in pairs. They feed almost exclusively on sponges, but have been known to snack on algae and tunicates as well. Young Queen angelfish also clean parasites off larger fish.
Predators: Large grouper and sharks

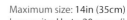

ROCK BEAUTY
HOLACANTHUS TRICOLOR

5

Maximum size: 14in (35cm)
Longevity: Up to 20 years (in captivity)
Typical depth: 10–115ft (3–35m)
Behavior: Adult rock beauties are often found on rock jetties, rocky reefs and rich coral areas, while juveniles tend to be found near fire corals. These angelfish are not picky eaters and will feed on tunicates, sponges, zoantharians and algae.
Predators: Grouper, snapper and sharks

BLUE TANG
ACANTHURUS COERULEUS

6

Maximum size: 16in (40cm)
Longevity: Around 20 years
Typical depth: 3–130ft (1–40m)
Behavior: Blue tangs are often found grazing on algae during the day, either individually or as part of large schools that may also contain surgeonfish, doctorfish, goatfish and parrotfish. At dusk, they settle into a reef crack or crevice to hide for the night.
Predators: Grouper, snapper, jacks and barracuda

OCEAN SURGEONFISH
ACANTHURUS BAHIANUS

7

Maximum size: 15in (38cm)
Longevity: Up to 32 years
Typical depth: 6–130ft (2–40m)
Behavior: Adult surgeonfish often form large schools to graze on benthic algae and seagrasses in shallow coral reefs and inshore rocky areas. Juveniles rarely school, sheltering instead in the back reef. Researchers have observed spawning aggregations of up to 20,000 individuals in the winter months off of Puerto Rico.
Predators: Sharks, grouper, barracuda and snapper

DOCTORFISH
ACANTHURUS CHIRUGUS

8

Maximum size: 15.5in (39cm)
Longevity: Up to 30 years
Typical depth: 6–213ft (2–65m)
Behavior: Doctorfish can be found in shallow, inshore reef habitats and rocky areas. They forage on benthic algae, including the thin algal mat covering sandy bottoms. They generally swim together in loose schools, often with ocean surgeonfish and blue tangs. They have sharp spines near their tail fin that they can use in defense against predators.
Predators: Large carnivorous fish, including tuna

BANDED BUTTERFLYFISH
CHAETODON STRIATUS

9

Maximum size: 6in (16cm)
Longevity: Unknown, but probably around 10 years
Typical depth: 10–60ft (3–20m)
Behavior: Banded butterflyfish are most active during the day when they search the reef for food, which includes polychaete worms, zoanthids, anemones and fish eggs. Banded butterflyfish are often found in monogamous pairs and they defend a joint territory together with their mate.
Predators: Moray eels and large carnivorous fish

FOUREYE BUTTERFLYFISH
CHAETODON CAPISTRATUS

10

Maximum size: 6in (15cm)
Longevity: Around 8 years
Typical depth: 6–65ft (2–20m)
Behavior: Foureye butterflyfish are active during the day when they feed on small invertebrates. Their pointed mouth allows them to pull prey from small crevices. They are often found in pairs, and males and females bond early in life and form long-lasting monogamous pairs.
Predators: Barracuda, grouper, snapper and moray eels

REEF BUTTERFLYFISH
CHAETODON SEDENTARIUS

11

Maximum size: 6in (15cm)
Longevity: Unknown, but probably around 10 years
Typical depth: 16–302ft (5–92m)
Behavior: This species is one of the deepest dwelling Caribbean butterflyfish. Like many members of this family, their color and pattern disguise the head in an attempt to confuse potential predators. Reef butterflyfish are most active during the day when they feed on polychaete worms and small crustaceans. They particularly like to eat the eggs of sergeant majors.
Predators: Barracuda, grouper, snapper and moray eels

SPOTFIN BUTTERFLYFISH
CHAETODON OCELLATUS

12

Maximum size: 8in (20cm)
Longevity: Unknown, but probably around 10 years
Typical depth: 3–98ft (1–30m)
Behavior: The spotfin butterflyfish can be identified by the small spot on the rear end of the dorsal fin. This species is found over an incredibly large geographical area, extending from southern Brazil to as far north as Nova Scotia, Canada. Spotfin butterflyfish are most active during the day when they search for food, which includes polychaete worms, zoanthids, anemones and fish eggs.
Predators: Barracuda, grouper, snapper and moray eels

BLUE CHROMIS
CHROMIS CYANEA

13

Maximum size: 5in (12cm)
Longevity: Unknown, possibly 5 years
Typical depth: 10–70ft (3–20m)
Behavior: Blue chromis gather in schools above the reef to feed on small plankton and jellyfish during the day. They hide in reef crevices at night. Territorial males defend egg nests in the spring and summer.
Predators: Trumpetfish, grouper and snapper

BROWN CHROMIS
CHROMIS MULTILINEATA

14

Maximum size: 8in (20cm)
Longevity: Unknown, possibly 5 years
Typical depth: 3–300ft (1–91m)
Behavior: Brown chromis forage in medium-sized schools above the coral reef, feasting on plankton, mainly copepods. They are frequently seen schooling with blue chromis during the day, although their more territorial congeneric tends to chase them out from hiding places in the reef at night.
Predators: Trumpetfish, grouper and snapper

PURPLE REEFFISH
CHROMIS SCOTTI

15

Maximum Size: 4in (10cm)
Longevity: Up to 10 years
Typical depth: 49–381ft (15–116m)
Behavior: Purple reeffish are members of the damselfish family and closely related to brown and blue chromis. They are occasionally referred to as purple chromis. Typically a blue/purple color, they can also appear brown or tan. They feed mainly on crustaceans and plankton.
Predators: Grouper, snapper and eels

YELLOWTAIL REEFFISH
CHROMIS ENCHRYSURA

16

Maximum Size: 4in (10cm)
Longevity: Up to 10 years
Typical depth: 16–479ft (5–146m)
Behavior: Yellowtail reeffish are another species of damselfish found along Florida's Gulf Coast. They feed mainly on crustaceans and plankton and are found slightly deeper than most other chromis – usually greater than 100 feet (30.5 meters). This species has an extensive distribution that extends to the eastern Atlantic, as well as South Africa and the Indian Ocean.
Predators: Grouper, snapper and eels

REGAL DEMOISELLE
NEOPOMACENTRUS CYANOMOS

17

Maximum Size: 4in (10cm)
Longevity: Up to 10 years
Typical depth: 16–98ft (5–30m)
Behavior: Regal demoiselles are native to the Indo-West Pacific and the Red Sea. They were first spotted in the Western Atlantic off the coast of Mexico in 2013, and have since spread slowly along the northern Gulf of Mexico from Louisiana to Florida. The species feeds mainly on crustaceans and plankton and is occasionally spotted in small schools in the water column or above reefs.
Predators: Grouper, snapper and eels

SERGEANT MAJOR
ABUDEFDUF SAXATILIS

18

Maximum size: 9in (23cm)
Longevity: Unknown, possibly 5 years
Typical depth: 3–33ft (1–10m)
Behavior: Sergeant majors get their name from their telltale black bars that resemble military stripes. They are usually found in shallow water, typically along the tops of reefs, and often form large feeding schools of up to a few hundred individuals.
Predators: Grouper and jacks

COCOA DAMSELFISH
STEGASTES VARIABILIS

19

Maximum size: 5in (12.5cm)
Longevity: Up to 15 years
Typical depth: 3–100ft (1–30m)
Behavior: Like numerous other species of damselfish, cocoa damselfish tend small gardens of algae. Males use their garden to attract a mate, who will lay her eggs in the male's territory. He will defend them aggressively until they hatch. This species is found throughout the Caribbean, from Brazil to northern Florida. They feed on algae, sponges and anemones.
Predators: Grouper and jacks

BICOLOR DAMSELFISH
STEGASTES PARTITUS

20

Maximum size: 4in (10cm)
Longevity: Around 15 years
Typical depth: 3–328ft (1–100m)
Behavior: Bicolor damselfish defend small algae territories in the same way as other damselfish species. While they generally live alone, this species occasionally forms small groups of up to 20 individuals, usually led by a dominant male. Bicolor damselfish feed on benthic algae, but also consume plankton.
Predators: Grouper and jacks

BLUEHEAD WRASSE
THALASSOMA BIFASCIATUM

21

Maximum size: 10in (25cm)
Longevity: 3 years
Typical depth: 0–131ft (0–40m)
Behavior: Bluehead wrasses can be found on reefs, near inshore bays and over seagrass beds feeding on zooplankton, small benthic animals and even parasites on other fish. They start life as female but eventually become males, gaining an unmistakable bright blue head in their terminal phase.
Predators: Grouper, trumpetfish and soapfish

YELLOWHEAD WRASSE
HALICHOERES GARNOTI

22

Maximum size: 7in (19cm)
Longevity: Unknown, possibly between 3 and 5 years
Typical depth: 3–100ft (1–30m)
Behavior: Yellowhead wrasses are mainly found near coral reefs and rocky ledges. Adults feed on invertebrates while juveniles sometimes clean parasites off larger fish. Yellowhead wrasses are protogynous hermaphrodites, meaning they start life as female but become males at around 3in (7cm) in size.
Predators: Mackerel, grouper and snapper

SPANISH HOGFISH
BODIANUS RUFUS

23

Maximum size: 16in (40cm)
Longevity: Unknown
Typical depth: 10–230ft (3–70m)
Behavior: Adult Spanish hogfish feed on bottom-dwelling invertebrates, such as brittlestars, crustaceans and sea urchins. Juveniles set up cleaning stations to pick parasites off larger fish. Male hogfish (who start out life as a female) typically manage a harem of three to 12 smaller females.
Predators: Sharks, mackerel and snapper

HOGFISH
LACHNOLAIMUS MAXIMUS

24

Maximum size: 36in (91cm)
Longevity: Up to16 years
Typical depth: 10–100ft (3–30m)
Behavior: Hogfish live in small groups with a dominant male and several smaller females – a common pattern in wrasses. Their name comes from how they root around in the sand with their snout looking for crustaceans and molluscs. Larger individuals frequent the main reef, while smaller individuals are often on patch reefs.
Predators: Sharks and large grouper

EMERALD PARROTFISH
NICHOLSINA USTA

25

Maximum Size: 12in (30cm)
Longevity: 7 years
Typical depth: 0–246ft (0–75m)
Behavior: While emerald parrotfish can be found in deep water, they are predominantly found in shallow seagrass habitat less than 3 feet (1 meter) deep. They are active during the day when they are often seen feeding in small groups on seagrass and small invertebrates.
Predators: Grouper, eels and snapper

PEARLY RAZORFISH
XYRICHTYS NOVACULA

26

Maximum size: 15in (38cm)
Longevity: Around 3 years
Typical depth: 3–492ft (1–150m)
Behavior: Pearly razorfish, sometimes referred to as cleaver wrasses, are common throughout the Caribbean and the Mediterranean. They favor sand and mud habitat and often dive into the sediment when threatened. This species is active during the day, feeding on small invertebrates, such as crabs, shrimp and worms.
Predators: Grouper, snapper, barracuda and greater amberjack

STRIPED BURRFISH
CHILOMYCTERUS SCHOEPFI

27

Maximum Size: 10in (25cm)
Longevity: Unknown
Typical depth: 3–295ft (1–90m)
Behavior: Striped burrfish are members of the puffer family. Their spines are always erect rather than lying flat until inflated like with porcupinefish and balloonfish. They feed mainly at night on invertebrates, such as hermit crabs, shrimp, barnacles and snails. They use their powerful parrotfish-like beak to crush their prey. They can also consume algae.
Predators: Sharks

SAUCEREYE PORGY
CALAMUS CALAMUS

28

Maximum size: 22in (56cm); 3.3lbs (1.5kg)
Longevity: Unknown, possibly around 15 years
Typical Depth: 1–75ft (0.3–23m)
Behavior: Adult saucereye porgies are common on coral reefs, but juveniles favor seagrass habitat. They have a varied diet consisting of molluscs, worms, brittle stars, crabs and sea urchins. Globally, there are 13 species of porgy, also sometimes called bream. Only one of these, the Australasian snapper, occurs in the Pacific Ocean.
Predators: Sharks and barracuda

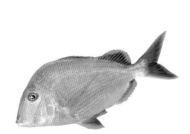

SHEEPSHEAD
ARCHOSARGUS PROBATOCEPHALUS 29

Maximum size: 36in (91cm)
Longevity: Around 20 years
Typical depth: 3–49ft (1–15m)
Behavior: Sheepshead are an important species for the recreational fishing industry in Florida. Also called convict fish due to their striped appearance, they are found in many habitats, including rocky reefs and seagrass beds, as well as around jetties and piers. They are omnivorous, feeding on algae and invertebrates.
Predators: Sharks, grouper and other large carnivorous fish

PINFISH
OLAGODON RHOMBOIDES 30

Maximum size: 4.5in (11.5cm)
Longevity: About 5 years
Typical depth: 30–50ft (9–15m)
Behavior: Pinfish are the only members of the genus Lagodon. They are closely related to breams and porgies and found mainly in the Gulf of Mexico and the U.S. coastline as far north as Massachusetts. Young pinfish feed on crustaceans, fish eggs, worms and insects, but as they age, their diet shifts increasing toward plants and algae. As adults, pinfish are almost entirely herbivorous.
Predators: Grouper and cobia

BLUESTRIPED GRUNT
HAEMULON SCIURUS 31

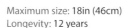

Maximum size: 18in (46cm)
Longevity: 12 years
Typical depth: 3–98ft (1–30m)
Behavior: One of the largest members of the grunt family, the bluestriped is also one of the most brightly colored, sporting numerous gold and blue stripes. Juveniles begin life in seagrass beds and move to coral reefs as they become adults. This species can form large schools and is often wary of divers.
Predators: Grouper, snapper, barracuda and sharks

WHITE GRUNT
HAEMULON PLUMIERII 32

Maximum size: 21in (53cm)
Longevity: Unknown, could be up to 12 years
Typical depth: 10–131ft (3–40m)
Behavior: White grunts tend to look more silver/white than other grunts, hence the name. They can form large schools around rocky reefs and wrecks. They are nocturnal, and typically feed on small crustaceans, polychaete worms and molluscs. Floridians often cook them in a traditional dish known as "Grits and Grunts."
Predators: Sharks, grouper, snapper and barracuda

TOMTATE
HAEMULON AUROLINEATUM
33

Maximum size: 10in (25cm)
Longevity: Unknown, but probably around 10 years
Typical depth: 3–98ft (1–30m)
Behavior: The tomtate is by far the most common member of the grunt family in Florida. This species is found in large schools on coral reefs, but forms pairs for breeding. They have a varied diet consisting of small crustaceans, mollusks, polychaetes, plankton and algae.
Predators: Grouper, snapper, trumpetfish and scorpionfish

PIGFISH
ORTHOPRISTIS CHRYSOPTERA
34

Maximum size: 18in (46cm)
Longevity: Up to 5 years
Typical depth: 16–65ft (5–20m)
Behavior: Pigfish are a species of grunt found throughout the Caribbean, but they are most common in the Gulf of Mexico and the U.S. coastline as far north as Massachusetts. Pigfish can be found on coral reefs, but they favor firm sandy habitat where they hunt for crustaceans and small fish, mostly during the night. This species undergoes seasonal migration, which appears to be related to changes in water temperature.
Predators: Sharks, grouper, eels, snapper and snook

LANE SNAPPER
LUTJANUS SYNAGRIS
35

Maximum size: 24in (60cm), 7.7lb (3.5kg)
Longevity: Around 10 years
Typical depth: 33–1312ft (10–400m)
Behavior: These relatively small, bottom-feeding snapper hunt crustaceans, molluscs, and smaller fish during the night. They are a popular species with fishers, who often use hook and line to catch them. Lane snapper form large schools during spawning season, which usually takes place between May and August. They are found from North Carolina to southern Brazil.
Predators: Sharks, grouper, eels and barracuda

MUTTON SNAPPER
LUTJANUS ANALIS
36

Maximum size: 37in (94cm), 34lb (15.6kg)
Longevity: 29 years
Typical depth: 82–311ft (25–95m)
Behavior: Mutton snapper can be identified by the small black spot located on their upper back. Many individuals also have one or two blue stripes that run across the cheek and around the eye. Mutton snapper feed both day and night on a mix of fish, crustaceans and gastropods. They are very popular fish with anglers and spearfishers and though size and bag limits exist, the species is still listed as "near threatened" by the IUCN Red List.
Predators: Sharks, large grouper, moray eels and barracuda

CUBERA SNAPPER
LUTJANUS CYANOPTERUS

37

Maximum size: 5ft (1.6m); 126lbs (57kg)
Longevity: 20 years, but possibly up to 50 years
Typical depth: 3–280ft (1–85m)
Behavior: Cubera snapper are the biggest of the Atlantic snapper species. Adults are often seen alone on deeper reefs and wrecks, while juveniles are generally in shallower water near vegetation, including estuaries. Cubera snapper feed on fish as well as crustaceans, such as shrimp, crabs and lobster. Large individuals are rarely removed from the water when caught on fishing lines, due to concerns about ciguatera poisoning.
Predators: Sharks, large grouper, barracuda and mackerel

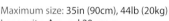

MANGROVE SNAPPER
RHOMBOPLITES AURORUBENS

38

Maximum size: 35in (90cm), 44lb (20kg)
Longevity: Around 20 years
Typical depth: 16–590ft (5–180m)
Behavior: Mangrove snapper (also called grey snapper) are often found schooling, sometimes in large numbers. They feed mainly at night on a range of organisms, including shrimp, crabs, worms and small fishes, rarely moving far to feed.
Predators: Moray eels, sharks, large grouper and barracuda

VERMILION SNAPPER
LUTJANUS APODUS

39

Maximum size: 24in (60cm), 7.1lb (3.2kg)
Longevity: Around 10 years
Typical depth: 90–980ft (27.5–300m)
Behavior: These relatively small, reddish-gold-colored snapper are often confused with the larger red snapper. Both species live in deep water and feed on fish, squid, shrimp, crabs, worms, and other bottom-dwelling invertebrates. The main differences between the two species are that vermilion snapper have forked tails and are generally smaller, both in mouth size and overall body size, than red snapper.
Predators: Sharks, grouper, eels and barracuda

RED SNAPPER
RHOMBOPLITES AURORUBENS

40

Maximum size: 3ft (1m), 50.4lb (22.8kg)
Longevity: At least 57 years, but possibly more
Typical depth: 33–623ft (10–190m)
Behavior: Red snapper are large, deep-bodied, red fish found around much of the coast of Florida, Mexico, the Caribbean and north to Massachusetts. They are often referred to as the northern red snapper, to differentiate them from a similar species, known as the Caribbean red snapper, which is absent in the waters around Florida. They feed mainly on fish, shrimp, crabs and worms. Red snapper are highly sought after as a food fish.
Predators: Sharks, grouper, eels and barracuda

SHORT BIGEYE
PRISTIGENYS ALTA

41

Maximum size: 12in (30cm)
Longevity: Unknown
Typical depth: 6.5–656ft (2–200m)
Behavior: As their name suggests, short bigeyes have a horizontally compressed body with large eyes. This bright red, nocturnal species is generally solitary and may occasionally defend a shelter against other fish. During the day they are often found hiding beneath overhangs and within wreck structures, while at night they hunt for small fish.
Predators: Grouper, snapper and eels

BLACKBAR SOLDIERFISH
MYRIPRISTIS JACOBUS

42

Maximum size: 10in (25cm)
Longevity: Unknown
Typical depth: 7–115ft (2–35m)
Behavior: Blackbar soldierfish are nocturnal, often hiding in caves and crevices during the day. They congregate around coral and rocky reefs at night to feed on plankton and invertebrates. They most commonly occur on shallow inshore reefs, but can be found at depths of 330ft (100m).
Predators: Snapper, grouper, jacks and trumpetfish

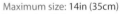

LONGSPINE SQUIRRELFISH
HOLOCENTRUS RUFUS

43

Maximum size: 14in (35cm)
Longevity: Unknown, but potentially up to 14 years
Typical depth: 0–105ft (0–32m)
Behavior: Longspine squirrelfish often form schools of 8 to 10 individuals at night when they forage for benthic organisms, such as crabs, shrimp, gastropods and brittlestars. During the day, these big-eyed fish seek shelter in holes and crevices in the reef, defending them from other squirrelfish.
Predators: Sharks, grouper, snapper and trumpetfish

YELLOWHEAD JAWFISH
OPISTOGNATHUS AURIFRONS

44

Maximum size: 4in (10cm)
Longevity: Unknown, possibly up to 5 years
Typical depth: 10–131ft (3–40m)
Behavior: Jawfish live in burrows in the sediment that they line with stones and bits of crushed shell and coral. Active during the day, they often hover over their burrow and feed on zooplankton. They rarely move far from their burrow and often retreat tail-first when threatened.
Predators: Snapper, grouper and lionfish

REDLIP BLENNY
OPHIOBLENNIUS ATLANTICUS

45

Maximum size: 7in (19cm)
Longevity: Around 2 years
Typical depth: 0–27ft (0–8m)
Behavior: Redlip blennies are common in shallow reef areas with relatively high wave action. Their body shape and modified fins let them "hold on" to the reef. They are herbivorous and territorial, defending a patch of algae during the day and hiding in the reef at night.
Predators: Grouper, snapper and trumpetfish

FEATHER BLENNY
HYPSOBLENNIUS HENTZ

46

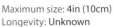

Maximum size: 4in (10cm)
Longevity: Unknown
Typical depth: 0–33ft (0–10m)
Behavior: The feather blenny is found only in the northern Caribbean, Gulf of Mexico, and the southern and Atlantic coasts of the U.S. Individuals have been found as far north as Nova Scotia, Canada. Feather blennies get their name from the feathery cirri located on the top of their head that help them sense movement in their environment. They mainly eat small molluscs and crustaceans. Males aggressively guard eggs, which are laid on the substrate.
Predators: Grouper, snapper, eels and tripletail

SPOTTED GOATFISH
PSEUDUPENEUS MACULATUS

47

Maximum size: 12in (30cm)
Longevity: At least 7 years
Typical depth: 0–115ft (0–35m)
Behavior: Spotted goatfish are most often encountered in shallow water over rocky or sandy habitat near reefs. They feed on bottom-dwelling crabs, shrimp and small fish. Spotted goatfish are easily recognizable by the three dark blotches along their back and the telltale barbels they use to stir up the sand when they hunt.
Predators: Sharks, snapper and jacks

YELLOW GOATFISH
MULLOIDICHTHYS MARTINICUS

48

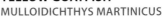

Maximum size: 15in (39cm)
Longevity: Unknown
Typical depth: 0–115ft (0–35m)
Behavior: Yellow goatfish are commonly found swimming in large schools over sandy bottoms. They use their long, sensitive barbels to locate polychaete worms, clams, isopods, amphipods and other crustaceans in the sand. When not feeding, they are often found in groups, sheltering in the reef.
Predators: Sharks, tuna, mahi mahi, grouper and jacks

SPOTTED DRUM
EQUETUS PUNCTATUS

49

Maximum size: 11in (27cm)
Longevity: Unknown, but probably around 10 years
Typical depth: 10–98ft (3–30m)
Behavior: Spotted drums are found under ledges, jetties and near small caves during the day. They are solitary and mostly active at night, when they hunt for crabs, shrimp and worms. Drums can emit a drumming sound when they feel threatened, which is the origin of their name.
Predators: Moray eels, grouper and barracuda

JACK-KNIFEFISH
EQUETUS LANCEOLATUS

50

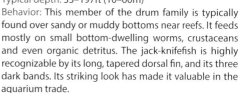

Maximum size: 10in (25cm)
Longevity: Unknown, but possibly as little as 5 years
Typical depth: 33–197ft (10–60m)
Behavior: This member of the drum family is typically found over sandy or muddy bottoms near reefs. It feeds mostly on small bottom-dwelling worms, crustaceans and even organic detritus. The jack-knifefish is highly recognizable by its long, tapered dorsal fin, and its three dark bands. Its striking look has made it valuable in the aquarium trade.
Predators: Sharks, eagle rays and large carnivorous fish

HIGHHAT
PAREQUES ACUMINATUS

51

Maximum size: 9in (23cm)
Longevity: Unknown
Typical depth: 15–195ft (5m–60m)
Behavior: Highhats are more typically found in shallower coastal areas but can also be found at greater depths. They often shelter beneath ledges alongside the similar looking cubbyu. Highhats have the elongated dorsal fins typical of drums, but not as exaggerated as in other drum species. They generally feed at night, preying on amphipods, shrimp and other crustaceans.
Predators: Sharks, rays and grouper

CUBBYU
PAREQUES UMBROSUS

52

Maximum size: 10in (25cm)
Longevity: Unknown
Typical depth: 15–300ft (5m–91m)
Behavior: Cubbyu are often found together with highhats – their lookalike congenerics in the drum family. Cubbyu prefer to shelter under ledges, and they typically feed at night on crustaceans and brittlestars. Like other members of the drum family, their elongated dorsal fin becomes less pronounced as individuals age
.
Predators: Sharks, rays and grouper

SCRAWLED FILEFISH
ALUTERUS SCRIPTUS

53

Maximum size: 43in (110cm), 5.5lbs (2.5kg)
Longevity: Unknown
Typical depth: 10–394ft (3–120m)
Behavior: Scrawled filefish are commonly found on offshore reefs. They are active during the day, feeding on algae, seagrass, hydrozoans, soft corals and anemones. Juveniles sometimes drift with sargassum mats, which explains how this species is found throughout the tropics, and on many non-tropical reefs.
Predators: Barracuda, mahi mahi and large tuna

GREY TRIGGERFISH
BALISTES CAPRISCUS

54

Maximum size: 23.5in (60cm), 13lbs (6kg)
Longevity: Up to 16 years
Typical depth: 0–328ft (0–100m)
Behavior: Male grey triggerfish establish territories in sandy areas from the spring through the summer, where females lay close to 800,000 eggs. The eggs hatch within 24 to 48 hours, and a male may defend as many as three nests at once. Young triggerfish can spend more than six months as plankton, which has extended their range far beyond the tropics – even to Northern Scotland. Grey triggerfish feed mainly on crustaceans, urchins and molluscs.
Predators: Amberjack, grouper, sharks and some pelagic species

QUEEN TRIGGERFISH
BALISTES VETULA

55

Maximum size: 60cm (24in)
Longevity: At least 7 years, possibly up to 13 years
Typical depth: 7–900ft (2–275m)
Behavior: Queen triggerfish are carnivores that specialize in eating hard-shelled prey, such as sea urchins, lobsters and crabs. They are most active during the day and often use specialized feeding techniques on their prey of choice.
Predators: Larger grouper, jacks and sharks

CARIBBEAN SHARPNOSE PUFFER
CANTHIGASTER ROSTRATA

56

Maximum size: 5in (12cm)
Longevity: Unknown, but possibly up to 10 years
Typical depth: 3–130ft (1–40m)
Behavior: Sharpnose puffers prefer reefs where gorgonian corals are common. They are most active during the day as they search for small reef invertebrates such as crabs, shrimp, worms and snails. They are territorial, so if you happen to see two individuals near one another, they may be engaged in defensive displays.
Predators: Grouper, snapper, barracuda and moray eels

HONEYCOMB COWFISH
ACANTHOSTRACION POLYGONIUS **57**

Maximum size: 20in (50cm)
Longevity: Unknown
Typical depth: 7–262ft (2–80m)
Behavior: Honeycomb cowfish are protected by hexagon scales that form a rigid carapace over much of their bodies. They are relatively slow and wary, which makes their external armor an essential defense against potential predators. They usually forage alone, feeding on sponges, tunicates and shrimp.
Predators: Sharks

SCRAWLED COWFISH
ACANTHOSTRACION QUADRICORNIS **58**

Maximum size: 21.5in (55cm)
Longevity: Unknown
Typical depth: 33–100ft (10–30m)
Behavior: Scrawled cowfish are a colorful member of the boxfish family. They are protected by a set of rigid, hexagon-shaped dermal plates and a pair of horns on their heads that look like cow horns. They have matching horns that extend from the back corners of their box-like bodies. These slow-moving fish feed on sponges, tunicates and shrimp.
Predators: Sharks, rays and grouper

SMOOTH TRUNKFISH
LACTOPHRYS TRIQUETER **59**

Maximum size: 18.5in (47cm)
Longevity: Unknown
Typical depth: 0–164ft (0–50m)
Behavior: Smooth trunkfish are easily recognized by their black mouth and white-spotted, triangular, armored shape. They are not fast swimmers, relying instead on their armor and toxins to deter predators. They are easily approached and can often be seen hunting bottom invertebrates by jetting water from their mouth to disturb the sand and locate their prey.
Predators: Mahi mahi, cobia and large carnivorous fish

ROCK HIND
EPINEPHELUS ADSCENSIONIS **60**

Maximum size: 26in (65cm)
Longevity: Up to 12 years
Typical depth: 2–100ft (0.5–30m)
Behavior: Rock hinds are solitary fish that inhabit rocky reefs. They are found along much of the Western Atlantic coastline from New England, in the U.S. to southern Brazil. They primarily hunt crabs and shrimp, but also small fish, including blennies. They are a popular food fish, hunted across much of their range.
Predators: Shark, grouper and mackerel

BLACK GROUPER
MYCTEROPERCA BONACI

61

Maximum size: 5ft (1.5m), 220lbs (100kg)
Longevity: More than 30 years
Typical depth: 19–246ft (6–75m)
Behavior: Black grouper are rarely seen and tend to shy away from swimmers. Commercially fished in many places, their populations are generally declining as a result. They are solitary except when they congregate to spawn. Adults feed on smaller reef fish such as grunts and snapper.
Predators: Sharks

SCAMP GROUPER
MYCTEROPERCA PHENAX

62

Maximum size: 3.5ft (1.1m), 31lbs (14.2kg)
Longevity: Up to 31 years
Typical depth: 75–300ft (23–91m)
Behavior: Scamp prefer low-profile bottom and are most often seen at depth. However, they occasionally venture up into shallower water and many congregate around wrecks and artificial reefs. They are excellent ambush predators, preying on any fish small enough to fit in their mouths, along with crabs and shrimp. Scamp are a popular food fish, and are particularly sought out by spearfishers.
Predators: Shark, greater amberjacks and other large grouper

GAG GROUPER
MYCTEROPERCA MICROLEPIS

63

Maximum size: 4.75ft (1.5m), 80.5lbs (36.5kg)
Longevity: Up to 31 years
Typical depth: 75–300ft (23–91m)
Behavior: Gag grouper are the most common grouper in the Eastern Gulf of Mexico. They typically inhabit deep, offshore ledges and reefs, although juveniles may forage for crabs in shallow coastal seagrass beds. Adult gag grouper prefer to eat fish, crustaceans and shrimp, and can be seen alone or in groups.
Predators: Shark, greater amberjacks and other large grouper

GOLIATH GROUPER
EPINEPHELUS ITAJARA

64

Maximum size: 8ft (2.5m), 1,000lbs (455kg)
Longevity: Nearly 40 years
Typical depth: 0–330ft (0–100m)
Behavior: Goliath grouper are the largest grouper species in Northwest Florida. This massive, solitary fish does not have a large home range, but will defend its territory aggressively against intruders by making loud "barking" noises with its swim bladder. They have even been known to charge divers, so beware. Goliath grouper feed on lobsters, fish and even turtles and stingrays.
Predators: Sharks

BANK SEA BASS
CENTROPRISTIS OCYURUS

65

Maximum size: 12in (30m)
Longevity: 7 years
Typical depth: 36–330ft (11–100m)
Behavior: Sea bass are small predatory fish that are closely related to grouper. The bank sea bass prefers hard-bottomed habitat and rubble seabeds in offshore waters. They feed primarily on crabs, crustaceans, squid and small fish.
Predators: Grouper and snapper

BLACK SEA BASS
CENTROPRISTIS STRIATA

66

Maximum size: 26in (66cm), 9.5lbs (4.3kg)
Longevity: Up to 20 years
Typical depth: 3–100ft (1–30.5m)
Behavior: Black sea bass are found along much of the U.S. Atlantic coast, from Maine to Florida and into the Gulf of Mexico. Juveniles are brown in color, and prefer shallow, coastal waters, while adults are dark black and prefer structured habitats, such as jetties, piers, reefs and ledges. This species hunts crabs, shrimp, worms and small fish.
Predators: Shark, mackerel, swordfish and flounder

BELTED SANDFISH
SERRANUS SUBLIGARIUS

67

Maximum size: 4in (10cm)
Longevity: Unknown
Typical depth: 0–60ft (0–18m)
Behavior: Belted sandfish, also known as dwarf sea bass, are members of the grouper family. They are not generally associated with coral reefs and are rarely seen as far south as the Florida Keys, but may be present on artificial reefs and rocky ledges. Their range extends from the Gulf of Mexico north to the Carolinas. They generally eat small fish and crustaceans in the crepuscular hours of dawn and dusk.
Predators: Grouper, snapper and eels

SAND PERCH
DIPLECTRUM FORMOSUM

68

Maximum size: 12in (30cm)
Longevity: Likely 6 to 7 years
Typical depth: 2–25ft (0.5–7.5m)
Behavior: Sand perch are typically found in shallow, coastal waters next to seagrass beds and on sand or rubble bottoms. They build burrows and retreat into their shelters when scared. They primarily hunt shrimp, crabs and small fish.
Predators: Grouper, snapper, drums and sea bass

WHITESPOTTED SOAPFISH
RYPTICUS MACULATUS

Maximum size: 8in (20cm)
Longevity: Up to 5 years
Typical depth: 15–130ft (4.5–39.5m)
Behavior: Whitespotted soapfish typically rest on the bottom during the day. They are common on artificial reefs and near coral heads and ledges. They are more active at night, feeding on shrimp, crabs and smaller demersal fish, particularly cardinalfish. Like other soapfish species, they secrete a frothy mucus when stressed.
Predators: Sharks and eagle rays

FLYING GURNARD
DACTYLOPTERUS VOLITANS

70

Maximum size: 21in (50cm)
Longevity: Unknown, but likely more than 5 years
Typical depth: 3–262ft (1–80m)
Behavior: Flying gurnards are often found along sand-bottomed areas near the reef, foraging for benthic crustaceans, crabs, clams and small fish. They get their name from their fan-like pectoral fins that make it look like they are flying when they swim.
Predators: Sharks, tuna, mahi mahi, grouper and bigeye

POLKA-DOT BATFISH
OGCOCEPHALUS CUBIFRONS

71

Maximum size: 15in (38cm)
Longevity: Around 10 years
Typical depth: 3–230ft (1–70m)
Behavior: These odd-looking fish tend to live on sandy bottoms or among coral rubble. Their flattened bodies are often held up by stout pectoral fins that can be used to "walk" along the seabed. They are easily confused with other batfish species in the region, specifically the similar shortnose batfish. Polka-dot batfish typically feed on juvenile fish, small crustaceans and molluscs.
Predators: Unknown

TOADFISH
SANOPUS AND OPSANUS SPP

72

Maximum size: 12–15in (30–38cm)
Longevity: 8 to 12 years
Typical depth: 3–160ft (1–49m)
Behavior: Multiple species of toadfish are found in the Gulf of Mexico that can be difficult to differentiate. Some, such as the gulf toadfish, are typically found in shallower water and on sandy or rubble bottoms, while others are found at greater depths. Toadfish have flat heads with small, fleshy tabs along their jaw line. Relatively camouflaged when at rest, they are often easy to approach. There are a number of toadfish species in the Gulf of Mexico.
Predators: Dolphins, barracuda, snapper and octopus

OCELLATED FROGFISH
FOWLERICHTHYS OCELLATUS

73

Maximum size: 15in (37cm)
Longevity: Possibly up to 20 years
Typical depth: 10–70ft (3–21.5m)
Behavior: Experts at camouflage, frogfish are highly sought out as subjects by underwater macro-photographers. Ocellated frogfish are one of the largest frogfish species in the western Atlantic. They use their pectoral fins to "walk" along the seafloor and their short lure to hunt most fish and crustacean species that will fit in their large mouths.
Predators: Moray eels and other frogfish

GULF FLOUNDER
PARALICHTHYS ALBIGUTTA

74

Maximum size: 28in (71cm)
Longevity: About 3 years
Typical depth: 1–200ft (0–61m)
Behavior: Gulf flounders tend to prefer sandy bottoms, although they can also be found in seagrass beds and on rubble bottoms. They are well-camouflaged and usually lie flat and motionless on the bottom, often partly buried in the sediment. They are ambush predators that hunt schooling fish, such as grunts, pigfish, pinfish and shrimp.
Predators: Dolphins and sharks

SPOTTED MORAY EEL
GYMNOTHORAX MORINGA

75

Maximum size: 3.3ft (1m), 6lbs (2.5kg)
Longevity: Around 10 years, but possibly up to 30 years
Typical depth: 0–656ft (0–200m)
Behavior: Spotted moray eels are most active at night, when they hunt for a wide variety of prey, including parrotfish, grunts, trumpetfish, crustaceans and molluscs. During the day, they are often seen with their head sticking out of a reef hole or crevice.
Predators: Dog snapper and Nassau grouper

LINED SEAHORSE
HIPPOCAMPUS ERECTUS

76

Maximum size: 7.5in (19cm) with tail outstretched
Longevity: 1 year, likely longer
Typical depth: 1–40ft (0.3m–12m)
Behavior: Lined seahorses are relatively rare and can be incredibly hard to spot because of their excellent camouflage. They are often found holding on to the branches of gorgonians or seagrasses with their prehensile tail. They feed on small crustaceans and other small organisms such as amphipods and copepods, sucking them up through their tube-like mouths. Some lined seahorses develop flesh-like appendages when they live in clumps of sargassum.
Predators: Rays, mahi mahi and tuna

BERMUDA CHUB
KYPHOSUS SECTATRIX

77

Maximum size: 30in (76cm), 13lbs (6kg)
Longevity: Unknown
Typical depth: 3–330ft (1–10m)
Behavior: Bermuda chub are a schooling fish found in shallow waters above sandy areas and seagrass beds, and near coral reefs. They feed on benthic algae, but also on small crabs and molluscs. Juveniles often associate with floating sargassum mats, letting them disperse across great distances.
Predators: Sharks, barracuda, snapper, moray eels and scorpionfish

BAR JACK
CARANX RUBER

78

Maximum size: 23in (59cm)
Longevity: Unknown, possibly up to 30 years
Typical depth: 3–330ft (1–100m)
Behavior: Bar jacks sometimes swim alone, but are usually found schooling in shallow, clear water near coral reefs. They feed on fish, shrimp and other invertebrates. They are the most abundant species of jack in the Caribbean, and are easily approached by divers.
Predators: Grouper, mackerel, mahi mahi and large jacks

ALMACO JACK
SERIOLA RIVOLIANA

79

Maximum size: 3ft (96cm), 58lbs (28kg)
Longevity: Possibly 12 to 15 years
Typical depth: 50–80ft (15-24m)
Behavior: Almaco jacks are found all around the world, particularly in offshore waters. They closely resemble the larger greater amberjack and can be differentiated by their longer dorsal fin. Almacos are often curious, checking out divers' bubbles. They eat crabs, squid and a variety of fish, including flounder and mullet. They tend to reach a larger size in the Pacific than they do in the Atlantic.
Predators: Sharks and large pelagic fish

GREATER AMBERJACK
SERIOLA DUMERILI

80

Maximum size: 6ft (1.9m), 180lbs (81kg)
Longevity: 15 years, possibly more
Typical depth: 60–240ft (18–72m)
Behavior: Greater amberjacks are an important species to the recreational fishery in Florida. They are found in oceans around the world, typically spotted on the seaward, outer side of reefs and over deep drop-offs; they also like hanging out around wrecks. They are often found in small groups or alone, and forage on fish and invertebrates.
Predators: Sharks, barracuda and tuna

RAINBOW RUNNER
ELAGATIS BIPINNULATA

81

Maximum size: 6ft (1.8m), 102lbs (56kg)
Longevity: Up to 6 years
Typical depth: 6–33ft (2–10m)
Behavior: Rainbow runners are one of the larger members of the jack family, and they are found near the surface of the water over reefs . Though they can get quite large, individuals measuring 2–3ft (60–90cm) are more common. Rainbow runners can form large schools, where they feed on invertebrates and small fish.
Predators: Sharks and tuna

BLUE RUNNER
CARANX CRYSOS

82

Maximum size: 27.5in (70cm)
Longevity: Up to 11 years
Typical depth: 0–330ft (0–100m)
Behavior: Blue runners are a pelagic species that tend to form schools near shore. They are often associated with sargassum mats as juveniles, using the habitat for both protection and to forage on invertebrates. Adults forage on other fish, along with shrimp and invertebrates, and are not generally associated with reefs.
Predators: Mahi mahi, sailfish, tuna, marlin and barracuda

LITTLE TUNNY
EUTHYNNUS ALLETTERATUS

83

Maximum size: 4ft (1.2m), 36.5lbs (16.5kg)
Longevity: 8 to 10 years
Typical depth: 20–200ft (6–61m)
Behavior: Little tunny spend most of their time in open water but are often found close to shore and in areas with stronger currents. They opportunistically feed on anything they can find, including fish, crustaceans and squid, sometimes creating a frenzy at the surface as they hunt a bait ball of herring or anchovies.
Predators: Sharks, mackerel and other large, pelagic fish

LOOKDOWN
SELENE VOMER

84

Maximum size: 19in (48cm)
Longevity: Up to 20 years in captivity
Typical depth: 2–30ft (0.5–9m)
Behavior: Lookdowns frequent shallow coastal waters, including estuaries, from Maine to Brazil. They prey on small crabs, shrimp and fish. Their sloped, blunt forehead makes it easier to forage along the bottom, and makes it appear as if they are "looking down" as they hunt, hence the name.
Predators: Mackerel and other large fish

SPANISH MACKEREL
SCOMBEROMORUS MACULATUS

85

Maximum size: 3ft (91cm), 13lbs (6kg)
Longevity: 5 years
Typical depth: 33–115ft (10–35m)
Behavior: Spanish mackerel form large schools as they migrate throughout most of the Western Atlantic and Gulf of Mexico. A popular sportfish and commercial fishery, they spend most of their time in open water, but are often found above coral reefs and wrecks. They prey on small fish, such as sardines and herring, and often corner large bait balls of prey near the surface.
Predators: Pelagic sharks, other mackerel and cobia

KING MACKEREL
SCOMBEROMORUS CAVALLA

86

Maximum size: 6ft (184cm), 100lbs (45kg)
Longevity: 14 years
Typical depth: 50–150ft (15–46m)
Behavior: King mackerel are a popular sportfish found throughout the Western Atlantic and the Caribbean. They spend most of their time in open water but are often found above coral reefs and wrecks. They are usually solitary, and typically seen by divers during safety stops as they can become curious and draw close.
Predators: Pelagic sharks, little tunny and dolphins.

COBIA
RACHYCENTRON CANADUM

87

Maximum size: 6.5ft (2m), 150lbs (68kg)
Longevity: 15 years
Typical depth: 1–60ft (0–18.5m)
Behavior: Cobia are found worldwide in temperate and tropical waters. Their habitat includes shallow estuaries and inshore reefs, as well as the offshore pelagic zone of the ocean, typically around drifting or stationary objects such as a vessel or oil rig. They are a popular gamefish, often caught using handlines or by trolling. They eat small grouper and other fish, as well as crabs and squid.
Predators: Sharks and mahi-mahi

ATLANTIC SPADEFISH
CHAETODIPTERUS FABER

88

Maximum size: 35in (90cm)
Longevity: Up to 20 years
Typical depth: 10–115ft (3–35m)
Behavior: Atlantic spadefish are often found in schools of up to 500 individuals, swimming above reefs and shipwrecks. They feed during the day on plankton and benthic invertebrates, such as worms, crustaceans and molluscs. To hide from predators, juveniles often drift on their side to mimic debris.
Predators: Grouper and sharks

CARIBBEAN REEF OCTOPUS
OCTOPUS BRIAREUS
89

Maximum size: 39in (1m) with arms spread, 3 (lbs (1.5kg)
Longevity: Less than 2 years
Typical depth: 13–82ft (4–25m)
Behavior: Caribbean reef octopuses like to hide in reef caves and crevices during the day. They are masters of camouflage and incredibly hard to spot, since they can change their color, texture and shape. They are most active at night, hunting for crustaceans, clams, snails and small fish.
Predators: Grouper, snapper, nurse sharks and moray eels

SLIPPER LOBSTER
SCYLLARIDAE SPECIES
90

Maximum size: Up to 20 in (50cm)
Longevity: Possibly 10 years
Typical depth: 3–440ft (1–135m)
Behavior: Slipper lobsters include around 90 species in total that are found in warm waters throughout the world. They are not true lobsters, as they lack claws. They are closely related to spiny lobsters, but have flat plate-like antennae in the place of the long, thick spiny antennae of their cousins. Slipper lobsters tend to be slow-moving and nocturnal, feeding primarily on small crustaceans, detritus and carrion.
Predators: Grouper, triggerfish and other predatory fish

NURSE SHARK
GINGLYMOSTOMA CIRRATUM
91

Maximum size: 14ft (4.3m), 242lbs (110kg)
Longevity: Up to 25 years
Typical depth: 0–430ft (0–130 m)
Behavior: Nurse sharks are large nocturnal reef predators. At night, they search for hard-shelled prey, such as lobsters, crabs and conch, which they consume with their specially designed jaws. During the day, they are often found resting in caves or beneath coral overhangs.
Predators: Larger shark species

SPOTTED EAGLE RAY
AETOBATUS NARINARI
92

Maximum size: 10ft (3m) disc width, 500lb (230kg)
Longevity: Up to 20 years
Typical depth: 3–260ft (1–80m)
Behavior: Spotted eagle rays are carnivores that specialize in eating hard-shelled prey such as conch, clams, crabs and lobsters. They sometimes eat octopuses and fish as well, and are often found over sand habitat. They have electro-receptors in their snout to help search for buried prey.
Predators: Tiger, bull, lemon and hammerhead sharks

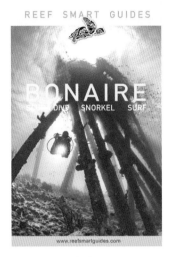

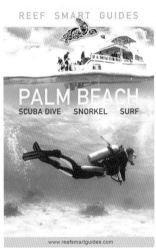

Stay tuned for new titles coming soon, including guidebooks for the **Florida Keys** and for the **Cayman Islands: Cayman Brac and Little Cayman.**

Index of sites

Courtesy of UMA ©   Super reef modules are ready to be deployed in the waters off Northwest Florida.

ABOUT THE AUTHORS

Ian POPPLE
ian@reefsmartguides.com

Born and raised in the U.K., Ian earned his undergraduate degree in Oceanography from the University of Plymouth in 1994. He worked for five years at Bellairs Research Institute in Barbados, supporting research projects across the region, before completing his Master's in marine biology at McGill University in 2004. He co-founded a marine biology education company, Beautiful Oceans, before founding Reef Smart in 2015, to raise awareness and encourage people to explore the underwater world. Ian has published in both the scientific and mainstream media, including National Geographic, Scuba Diver Magazine and the Globe and Mail. He is a PADI Dive Instructor with over 3,000 dives in 30 years of diving experience.

Otto WAGNER
otto@reefsmartguides.com

Born and raised in Romania, Otto graduated from the University of Art and Design in Cluj, Romania in 1991. He moved to Canada in 1999 where he studied Film Animation at Concordia University in Montreal. In 2006, Otto turned to underwater cartography and pioneered new techniques in 3D visual mapping. He co-founded Art to Media and began mapping underwater habitats around the world. Throughout his 25-year career, Otto has received numerous awards and international recognition for his work, including the Prize of Excellence in Design from the Salon International du Design de Montréal. He has also illustrated twelve books. Otto is a PADI Advanced Diver with over 500 dives in more than 15 years of diving experience.

Peter McDOUGALL
peter@reefsmartguides.com

Born and raised in Canada, Peter received his undergraduate and Master's degrees from McGill University. His focus on behavioral ecology and coral reef ecology led him to two field seasons at Bellairs Research Institute in Barbados, in 1999 and again in 2002. After graduating in 2003, Peter moved to the United States and began a career in science communication and writing, publishing in both peer-reviewed academic journals and the popular press. He has written on a variety of coastal ecosystem issues, including extensive work surrounding the science of ocean acidification. He is a PADI Rescue Diver with over 300 dives in 20 years of experience.